be happy

ALSO BY ROBERT HOLDEN, PHD

● ● ● ● ●

books

*Success Intelligence** \
*Happiness NOW!** \
Balancing Work & Life (with Ben Renshaw) \
Shift Happens! \
Every Day is a Gift (with Marika Borg (Burton))

● ● ● ● ●

cd programs

*Be Happy** \
*Happiness NOW!** \
*Success Intelligence**

● ● ● ● ●

flip calendar

*Happiness NOW!** \
*Success NOW!** \
(available August 2009)

*Available from Hay House

158-1

be happy

release the power of happiness
in YOU

Robert Holden, PhD

HAY HOUSE

Australia • Canada • Hong Kong • India
South Africa • United Kingdom • United States

First published and distributed in the United Kingdom by:
Hay House UK Ltd, 292B Kensal Rd, London W10 5BE.
Tel.: (44) 20 8962 1230; Fax:(44) 20 8962 1239. www.hayhouse.co.uk

Published and distributed in the United States of America by:
Hay House, Inc., PO Box 5100, Carlsbad, CA 92018-5100.
Tel.: (1) 760 431 7695 or(800) 654 5126; Fax: (1) 760 431 6948 or (800) 650 5115.
www.hayhouse.com

Published and distributed in Australia by:
Hay House Australia Ltd, 18/36 Ralph St, Alexandria NSW 2015.
Tel.: (61) 2 9669 4299;Fax: (61) 2 9669 4144. www.hayhouse.com.au

Published and distributed in the Republic of South Africa by:
Hay House SA (Pty), Ltd, PO Box 990, Witkoppen 2068.
Tel./Fax: (27) 11 467 8904. www.hayhouse.co.za

Published and distributed in India by:
Hay House Publishers India, Muskaan Complex, Plot No.3, B-2, Vasant Kunj, New Delhi
– 110 070. Tel.: (91) 11 4176 1620; Fax: (91) 11 4176 1630. www.hayhouse.co.in

Distributed in Canada by:
Raincoast, 9050 Shaughnessy St, Vancouver, BC V6P 6E5.
Tel.: (1) 604 323 7100; Fax: (1) 604 323 2600

Design: Jenny Richards
Indexer: Richard Comfort

© Robert Holden, 2009

A catalogue record for this book is available from the British Library.

ISBN 978-1-8485-0105-8

Printed in the UK by CPI William Clowes Beccles NR34 7TL

to
Bo
Love
Holden

contents

PART VI: FINDING THE PRESENT

foreword

It is said that when the student is ready, the teacher appears. We are all students, and life always has another lesson to teach us. When Robert Holden asked me to write a foreword for this book, I said, "Sure." I expected to fly through the book and write something quickly. Little did I know that I would become so immersed in the course that it took me several days to read the book and do the exercises.

It was an eye-opening experience to read this book, as I was encouraged to go deeply into myself to discover and begin to release the unnoticed pockets of resistance I had to being happy (truly happy).

Wow! What a powerful book this is. You have a big treat in store for you. And the pay-off is joy. Joy and happiness for each of you. Do yourself a favour and make sure you do all the exercises. You will learn things about yourself that you were not aware of. Good things, freeing things. At the end of this course you will like yourself so much more, even love and adore yourself. That would make anyone happy.

I thought I was a happy person and I was. Now after completing the course, I am happier on a deeper, quieter level. I also notice that I am happiest when I am being grateful. Thank you, Robert. This student was definitely ready for you, my latest teacher. I love learning. I know that the week I leave the planet I will be enrolled in a new course learning something new.

Dear reader, read on. You have an amazing experience ahead of you. Just think how wonderful it would be if everyone on the planet would experience their own happiness. No more wars. No more greed. No more getting even. Life would be filled with laughter, kindness, and love.

I am so proud to welcome Robert Holden to our Hay House family.

I am ready to enjoy my life today.

Louise L. Hay
Founder of Hay House

prologue

I have written this book to give you an experience of what it is like to attend my eight-week happiness course, which is the signature event of my work with The Happiness Project. My deepest wish is that this book will assist you in your inquiry into happiness and bring a greater sense of joy and love to every area of your life. My invitation to you is, therefore, that you don't just read the book, but *take the course*.

The first eight-week happiness course happened in the summer of 1992, which was three years before I founded The Happiness Project. I posted a dozen flyers on bulletin boards in local hospitals and health centres advertising a course on happiness that I described as *a support group for people who want to be happy*. The invitation was to meet for three hours a week, over eight weeks, to explore the psychology of happiness. Together we would create a space to examine what happiness is, what happiness is for, what blocks happiness, and how we can be happier.

In the first week, we had a group of 20 people that was made up of three doctors, four psychologists, five nurses, six journalists and just two members of the public. My idea had certainly created some interest. Within weeks, we had a waiting list of over 500 people. The response of the health authority's chief administrator to this popularity was to close the course. "It has got too big," she said. Fortunately, her boss, the Director for Public Health, was very supportive. She was convinced of the positive power of happiness, and she was eager to see if people really could learn to be happy.

Not everyone liked the idea of the happiness course. Some psychologists and doctors were particularly vocal in their objections. Early on, two damning articles appeared in the local press. One article was written by a psychologist who argued emphatically that happiness couldn't be taught. His main argument was that there is no evidence to be found that proves happiness is teachable. In my reply, I asked him for any evidence to the contrary – any references to courses that had tried to teach happiness and failed. He couldn't find any. Neither of us knew of anyone who had run a happiness course before.

The other article quoted a Christian doctor who accused the health authority and me of practising "devil medicine". Why? Because the happiness course syllabus featured meditation exercises. The headline for the article read, "Satanic Worship on the NHS". I feared my experiment to teach happiness would now be stopped. Fortunately, the Director for Public Health came to my support again. Curiously, attendance at the happiness course doubled at the next session. "Are you here to learn how to be happy, or are you searching for some new spells?" I asked.

The happiness course represented a significant shift in direction for me in my work. For three years previously, I had been the director of a National Health Service stress clinic called Stress Busters. In that time, I had worked with people with stress-related illnesses such as anxiety, depression, phobias, hypertension and cancer. My work was problem-oriented. The emphasis was on diagnosing problems, removing obstacles and healing conflict. Stress Busters enjoyed an excellent reputation for helping people to be less stressed and less unhappy, but I am not sure if I actually helped people to be happy. At best I helped them to be semi-happy.

Not suffering is not the same thing as being happy. Over time, I saw that most of the so-called illnesses I was treating were really symptoms of something else. Something deeper. My hypothesis was simple – *maybe we get stressed and depressed because we forget how to be happy.* Also, *perhaps the most effective remedy for any disease is, ultimately, to remember how to be happy.* More and more I was convinced that learning to be happy can help you to heal your life and also to live your best life. In other words, happiness is a healer and happiness is a teacher.

The BBC Documentary

In October 1995, Brian Edwards, director of True Vision, an Emmy Award-winning TV production company, approached me with his idea to conduct a scientific test to see if it is possible to teach people to be happy. His idea had been accepted by the BBC's *QED* science editor, Lorraine Heggessey, who had agreed to commission a 40-minute TV documentary. Brian wanted my eight-week happiness course to be the test case for the most public experiment on happiness ever conducted. The synopsis for the scientific test read:

> Modern science has endowed the human race with just about every gadget under the sun to improve the human lot, but it has cast little light so far on what is of prime importance to us all – how to be happy. Millions of man-hours have been invested in the treatment of depression, yet people remain depressed. We want to conduct an experiment to make people happy.[1]

The True Vision production team selected three volunteers to take my happiness course. They were Dawn, a 30-something-year-old working mother who experienced high levels of stress and anxiety; Caroline, in her 50s, who was a full-time carer for her elderly mother and who experienced chronic depression; and Keith, in his early 40s, who described himself as successful and unsatisfied. I played no part in the selection of these volunteers. In fact, I did not meet them until the first day of the happiness course.

True Vision also assembled a panel of independent psychologists and scientists to measure, both subjectively and objectively, the progress of Dawn, Caroline and Keith in the happiness course. For a subjective measurement, Professor Michael Argyle, of Oxford University, used two well-validated psychology questionnaires, the Oxford Happiness Inventory (OHI) and the University of Otago Affectometer (developed at one of New Zealand's top research universities).[2] The volunteers were asked to complete both questionnaires two weeks before the course began, then weekly during the course. The results would show how happy each volunteer felt and would also plot a graph to measure their true progress.

For an objective measurement, Professor Richard Davidson, of the University of Wisconsin-Madison, agreed to monitor the brain wave function, or "laterality," of one volunteer, Caroline, during the course. Professor Davidson has built up an extensive database of electroencephalograph readings of hundreds of subjects that reveals a marked difference in laterality (which means the difference in activity between the left and right parts of the front of the brain in a resting state) between people who report themselves to be depressed and people who report themselves to be happy. Caroline's scores would be compared with this unique database and would give us the scientific proof of whether the happiness course really worked or not.

At no time was I allowed to see the results of either the subjective or the objective measures, and so I was as eager as anyone to see how Dawn, Caroline and Keith had fared. One week after the happiness course finished, I was shown the results. The subjective measure, which used the OHI and Affectometer questionnaires, showed that each volunteer had made positive progress. Here is a summary of the scientific report:

By the end of the eight-week course, all three volunteers were showing a dramatic improvement in their happiness, with Caroline especially almost going off the scale. The OHI measures happiness in a positive scale from 0 to 90 and the Affectometer measures negative or positive "affect" from -80 to +80. Two weeks before the course began, Keith's combined score was +30, Dawn's combined score was -21 and Caroline's combined score was -34. At the end of the course, Keith's score had risen to +76, Dawn's score had risen to +55 and Caroline's score had risen to +115. (See Graph A.)[3]

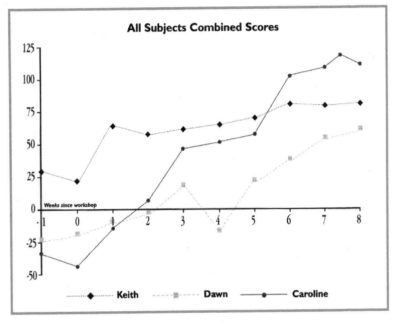

GRAPH A

For the objective measure, Professor Davidson tested Caroline again at the end of the course. In the first test, taken two weeks before the course began, Caroline's laterality score was measured at about +0.1, which is well below the average and is consistent with people who have a history of depression. In the second test, Caroline had made a wonderful improvement, as can be seen in Graphs B and C. In these graphs, the grey curve represents the differences in EEG laterality of 175 random people. The scientific report read:

In the second test, Caroline's brain function turned out to have shifted so much it was beyond the capabilities of the Madison University computer to plot her on the standard graph. In fact, she had a brain asymmetry reading of -0.22 and the furthest the graph had ever been drawn before was -0.2. In other words, there was a very dramatic shift in Caroline's underlying level of happiness or, as Professor Davidson put it: "What these results show is that the happiness training has not only changed the way you feel; it has actually changed the way your brain functions."[4]

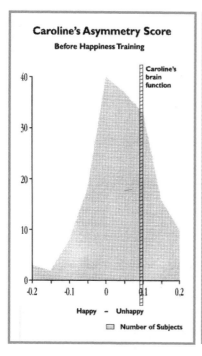

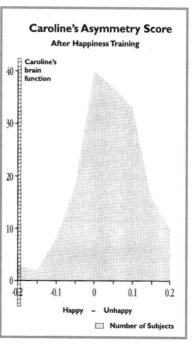

GRAPH B   GRAPH C

When Lorraine Heggessey, the BBC science editor, saw the results of the happiness course, she decided to delay the transmission of the TV documentary by six months. The reason for this was that she wanted to test how long the positive effects of the course would last. So, exactly 24 weeks after the first day of the course, the three volunteers took the OHI and Affectometer tests again. The scientific report read:

In late July, Dawn, Keith and Caroline returned to Oxford to meet up with the production team and Robert Holden once again. The results were impressive. They showed that all the improvements had been maintained and even built upon. All three volunteers had fundamentally changed their happiness levels. (See Graph D below.)[5]

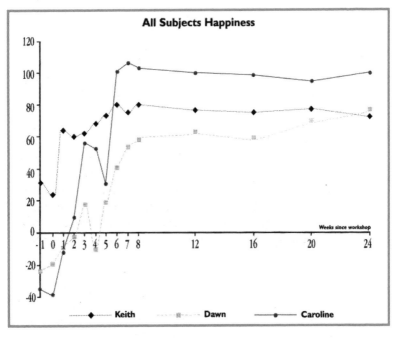

GRAPH D

The most public experiment ever conducted proved most conclusively that people really can learn to be happier. This landmark research inspired a new generation of scientists and psychologists to conduct further studies, which have also since concluded that it is possible to learn how to be happier.[6]

The Happiness Course

On August 28, 1996, at 9.25 PM, five million television viewers tuned in to watch the BBC *QED* documentary called "How to be Happy"[7]. The response to the TV show was exceptional. In the first week, the Happiness Project office received approximately three thousand letters and phone calls. Over the next few months, the documentary was shown around the world to over 30 million viewers. Each new broadcast brought a fresh flurry of interest and opportunity for the Happiness Project team.

Since 1996, a team of presenters at The Happiness Project has run hundreds of conference keynotes, public workshops and other happiness events worldwide. We have worked closely with psychologists and doctors, theologians and philosophers and also politicians and economists. We have also worked in-house with organisations like The Body Shop, Dove and Virgin – each well known for its commitment to spreading joy through its success. Over the years, the jewel in our crown has always been the eight-week happiness course.

The happiness course continues to grow and evolve. No two courses are the same. I would like to think that the happiness course today is even better than the ones that have been tested before. We have certainly learned a lot over the years. There are essentially two basic forms of the happiness course. One form is a weekly three-hour class over eight continuous weeks. This is ideal for people who live locally. The other form is a series of four weekend workshops, held over eight weeks. This suits people who live out of town. Both forms are supplemented with daily e-mails, home-learning modules and other activities that you will learn about in this book.

In writing *Be Happy*, I have had the opportunity to review 16 years of course transcripts, notes, correspondence and research. This book is filled with stories of people who have attended the happiness course. Many of the quotes I have used are exactly word for word because of the detailed records we keep. Names of the people mentioned have been changed where requested, in keeping with the confidentiality agreement we make at the start of each course. Writing this book has been an enormous task, but one that has undoubtedly helped me to deepen my own inquiry into happiness. For that alone, I am truly grateful.

Now, it's your turn to read the book and to take the course. To assist you, I recommend that you keep a "Happiness Journal" (see page 160) so that you can participate fully in the exercises I outline. As you read this book, please keep this one thought in mind:

**Your happiness and your healing are your gift
to the world.**

Robert Holden
London
September 2008

PART I

hello happiness

CHAPTER 1

the
happiness
genie

One week before you begin my happiness course, you are sent in the mail a document called "The Happiness Interview". The idea is that you set aside one hour to interview yourself on happiness. You are the interviewer – although there is nothing to stop you from pretending that Oprah or another talk-show host is interviewing you. You may wish to do "The Happiness Interview" alone or with a friend, a partner, or anyone else you are close to. All I ask is that you take a full 60 minutes (or more), that you answer the questions as honestly as possible and that you hand in a copy to me on the morning of our first class.

"The Happiness Interview" is a friendly primer that helps you to prepare for your happiness journey over the next eight weeks.* It is designed to help you start thinking more consciously and more deeply about the true nature of happiness. The interview includes questions like "What is your definition of happiness? And are you living it?" And "Who is the happiest person you know? And what have they taught you about true happiness?" I find that few people have ever given a full hour of their lives to this important subject. And yet, everyone who does this interview gains some valuable insight and knowledge.

---

* Go to Appendix A on page 279 to see an example of "The Happiness Interview"

"The Happiness Interview" asks you why you want to take the happiness course (or, indeed, why you want to read this book). "What are your primary intentions and motivations?" Clarity of intention helps you, I believe, to be more receptive and to engage more fully in whatever you give yourself to. The interview also asks you to name any hopes or fears you have about the course. This helps me to tailor a program that meets the specific needs of the individuals and the group.

The main reason for "The Happiness Interview" is that I want you to reflect on where happiness ranks in your life. "How important is happiness to you? And why?" For instance, is happiness a primary life goal for you? Do you ever make happiness a conscious intention at the start of your day? Do you consider happiness to be part of your life's purpose? Right now, is your priority to be happier or to make more money? Do you want to be truly happy, or do you prefer to play it safe? The more you acknowledge the importance of happiness in your life, the more deeply you will want to dive into your happiness inquiry. And

> **the deeper you inquire into the nature of true happiness,**
> **the more fully true happiness will reveal itself to you**.

To prepare for writing this book, I reread several hundred Happiness Interviews handed in over the last 16 years. I could fill this entire book with marvellous excerpts, but, instead, I offer just one – written by Jo, a medical doctor in her 40s, who attended the course in 1998. Here is what she wrote:

> I don't think I have ever let myself admit just how important happiness is to me. I've always wanted to be happy. I guess I just "hoped" happiness would bump into me one day. Just like a happy accident. Maybe I'm scared of committing to happiness – and failing. Imagine attending a happiness course and getting a failing grade at the end. What could be worse?! Or maybe I've become too cynical for my own good. I feel like a part of me has given up on happiness. These days, I just try to look cool.
>
> I really want to commit to happiness now – not just for my sake, but for my husband's sake and for my children's sake. I know I will be a better wife, mother AND FRIEND to them if I am happier. I don't just want to play safe – and get through life "unhurt". I want to get to the TRUTH of what life is really about – and I think this happiness course can help. I don't want to look cool; I want to be REAL. And I want to participate WHOLEHEARTEDLY in my life – starting from now. So, I sign up. And I commit 100% to this course. Now, Robert, let's get started!

Indeed! Your happiness course has already begun. And from now on I invite you to imagine you are sitting in the class with me as you continue to read this book.

Wishing for Happiness

Imagine you were granted one personal wish for your life. What would you wish for? Remember, it's a personal wish of which you are the sole recipient. So really, it's your chance to give yourself a gift. One good answer is, "I'd wish for a lot more wishes." But let's imagine this is a one-shot deal. What do you most wish for yourself? Think carefully. Now, *name* your wish. *Visualise* your wish. *Feel* your wish. And wish that your wish come true.

On the first morning of the happiness course, I introduce the participants to an exercise called "The Happiness Genie".* The purpose of this exercise is to test even further how important happiness is to you. I set the scene by asking you to imagine you have just met your own personal happiness genie. I invite people to describe what their genies look like and what they are wearing. Typical answers include "Brad Pitt" and "Not much". I try to help the group stay focused, but sometimes it's difficult. Eventually, after a few more explicit fantasies, reality kicks in again.

Next, I explain that your happiness genie is going to grant you a set of 10 "either/or" wishes. I reveal the wishes one by one and I collect the votes as we go. I have played "The Happiness Genie" with many groups over the years and the results are always very similar and also very revealing. They teach us a lot about how important happiness is to us and they also reveal something about *why* happiness is so important.

Wish #1: Wealth or Happiness. A no-brainer, surely? By choosing "wealth" you have no more money worries ever. You need never cut up another credit card. There will be no more "transaction declined" moments at cash registers. And, just for the fun of it, you can visit an ATM, punch in your PIN and enjoy the beautiful scenery of your huge bank balance. And the rest of your life will be a paradisiacal and leisurely shopping spree in which you can purchase happily ever after. *Score: on average, 90 people out of 100 choose happiness.*

---

* Go to Appendix B on page 281 to see an example of "The Happiness Genie."

Wish #2: Success or Happiness. The personal happiness genie offers you the chance to enjoy unlimited, guaranteed success in whichever field you choose. *Score: on average, 92 people out of 100 choose happiness.* David, a very wealthy former CEO of a global information technology company, attended the course in 2001. Like many other people, he chose happiness. "I've experienced success without happiness before," he said, "and what I've learned is that happiness is the one life goal that makes all other life goals meaningful."

Wish #3: Fame or Happiness. Today's society worships the "celebrity culture". Who doesn't want to be famous? Growing up, all I ever wanted was to be a guitarist in a world-famous rock band. I was so committed to this goal that I practised signing my autograph for hours a day. I even got detention for practising my autograph during a maths test. Who needs maths when you're going to be famous? *Score: on average, 94 people out of 100 choose happiness.*

Wish #4: Status or Happiness. Status, recognition, power and the need to be "above average" are primary ego drivers. We compare ourselves incessantly, both upwards and downwards, with anyone who gets close to us. *Score: on average, 98 people out of 100 choose happiness.* Sally, a former model, who had worked for over 20 years in the highly competitive world of fashion, also chose happiness. She said, "One of the beautiful effects of true happiness is that I stop comparing myself so neurotically and tragically with others."

Wish #5: Attractiveness or Happiness. Humans love to look good and to feel good. But which do we like the most? In social research surveys, some men and the majority of women say they would like to look more attractive. *Score: on average, 90 people out of 100 choose happiness.* "Happiness is attractive," said Debbie, a fashion designer. "I often forget this, but I really do look my best when I feel happy. Happiness outperforms mascara every time." Research confirms that people who score high on happiness are attractive to others.[1]

Wish #6: Sex or Happiness. This wish always gets everyone's full attention. Clare, a shiatsu practitioner, attended the course in 2002. She was particularly vocal in her opinions. "Last week I massaged Russell Crowe at the clinic. And let me tell you, if my happiness genie had given me the choice of great sex or lifelong happiness, I would have kissed happiness bye-bye." Aside from these momentary lapses . . . *Score: on average, 82 people out of 100 choose happiness.*

Wish #7: Health or Happiness. The world's great thinkers have described health as "the first of all liberties", as "real wealth", and as "life's greatest blessing".[2] And, for the first time in "The Happiness Genie", the scores are much closer. Health is undoubtedly very important to everyone. That said, the general thinking is that happiness creates health, maintains health and even restores health. Happiness *is* healthy and there is no true health without happiness. *Score: on average, 65 people out of 100 choose happiness.*

Wish #8: Enlightenment or Happiness. Now the stakes are really high. Would you turn down enlightenment for happiness? You are being offered the chance to know the secrets of the universe. You will never have to Google anything ever again. From now on, you can enjoy a sweet mystical sundae of truth, beauty and oneness, dripping with lots of metaphysical toppings. Or you can choose happiness. The scores are close. On two occasions I have had to organise recounts. *Score: on average, 60 people out of 100 choose happiness.*

Let's pause for a moment. Your personal happiness genie still has two more "either/or" wishes for you, which I will leave for now, but promise to return to at the end of this chapter. What I will tell you now is that in these final two wishes most people do *not* choose happiness. What can be more important than happiness? Can you guess? Is it obvious?

A good question to ask me at this point is, "Robert, how representative are the people who take your happiness course?" This is a nice way of saying, "Are these people in their right mind?" In recent years, a new wave of researchers, positive psychologists, have carried out many studies investigating the importance of happiness in people's lives. And their results are very similar to the scores of "The Happiness Genie". In some cases, I think the results from these studies are even more startling.

Professor Ed Diener, of the University of Illinois, is one of the world's leading happiness researchers. In 2003, Ed and his colleague Shigehiro Oishi conducted a survey that rated the importance of happiness against other values such as health, wealth and attractiveness. They interviewed 9,000 people in 47 nations. Happiness came first over and over again. They even asked people to rate the importance of happiness compared with "going to heaven". The score was based on a scale of 1 (not at all important) to 9 (extremely important). Happiness scored an average of 8.0 and "going to heaven" scored an average of 6.7.[3] Happiness outscored heaven!

The Power of Happiness

Happiness is evidently very important to people all over the world. It is truly a universal goal that each one of us – regardless of creed, nationality, race, gender, age and class – shares in common. We are united in our wish for happiness. So, the next big question must be – *why is happiness so important?* What is it about happiness that makes us want to choose it over wealth, success, fame, health, enlightenment and even getting to heaven? Keep reading. I'm about to give you the answer – in the very first chapter! Isn't that refreshing!

"The Happiness Genie" is a fantasy game that is based on having to make an "either/or" choice. Herein lie the tension and drama. But what if in reality you don't have to make a choice? Maybe the choice is a false choice. In other words, you don't have to choose between happiness and wealth, or between happiness and success, for instance. On the contrary, *all you have to do is choose happiness*. Why? Because when you choose happiness you make everything else more possible too. In other words,

happiness makes your wishes come true.

Could this be why happiness is so important? Is happiness really this powerful? Or is this just wishful thinking?

Classically, the thing to do now is for the author (i.e. me) to quote Pythagoras or the Buddha or Lao-tzu or some other great scholar – for they will all tell you that happiness has the power to transform your life and help you enjoy more of everything you truly wish for. Even more convincing, perhaps, are the findings and conclusions of some hard-nosed research scientists who care only for concrete evidence and measurable results. Increasingly, the ancient philosophers and the modern psychologists are seeing eye to eye.

Professor Sonja Lyubomirsky, at the University of California-Riverside, has devoted the majority of her research career to studying the causes and effects of human happiness. Like many of her colleagues, she adopts a suitably cautious approach to her work. And yet, the evidence she presents (particularly the longitudinal studies) strongly suggests that happiness precedes fantastic outcomes for a truly flourishing life. Sonja writes:

> A recent review of all the available literature has revealed that happiness does indeed have numerous positive by-products . . . The benefits of happiness include higher income and superior work outcomes (e.g. greater

productivity and higher quality of work), larger social rewards (e.g. more satisfying and longer marriages, more friends, stronger social support and richer social interactions), more activity, energy and flow, and better physical health (e.g. a bolstered immune system, lowered stress levels and less pain), and even longer life.[4]

In other words, *happiness attracts greater success in your life, your work and your relationships*. Professor Barbara Fredrickson, from the University of North Carolina, is a pioneer in the beneficial effects of positive emotions. She describes happiness as having an "active ingredient" that helps you to a) broaden your capacity to engage more creatively and more fully with life and b) build and grow your potential for increased success on all levels – physical, intellectual, social and spiritual.[5]

But wait, it gets even better. These scientists concur, as do I, that the power of happiness has the potential not only to transform individual lives, but whole organisations and communities too. They refer, in particular, to the "morality of happiness", which inspires people who are happy to want to serve and benefit others. In other words, when we feel good, we do good. Barbara Fredrickson concludes that happiness and other positive emotions may have the power to "change your life and your community, but also the world and in time create a heaven on earth".[6]

Two Divine Clues

People wish to be happy. We consider happiness to be even more important than many major life goals like wealth, health and success. And one big reason why happiness is so important is that it actually helps us to attract these other goals and to make them feel enjoyable and meaningful. The next question is, *When we are wishing for happiness, what are we really wishing for?* Do you have any idea? What is happiness?

I will return you now to "The Happiness Genie", as promised and to your final two "either/or" wishes. Remember, I told you that most people *do not* choose happiness in these two wishes – and I think this may reveal two divine clues as to the true nature of happiness. So, here goes:

Wish #9: Authenticity or Happiness. The scores are close, but authenticity just takes it. *Score: on average, 60 people out of 100 choose authenticity.* When I ask a group for reasons why, the responses are often thick with indignation and incredulity. For example, "I would never sell myself for happiness," and

"I won't betray myself for happiness," and "I would rather be dead than inauthentic."

We are loath to compromise ourselves for happiness or indeed for anything else. And the good news is, you don't have to. In fact, as I will expand on later, being authentic is the key to happiness. The truer you are to yourself, the more you improve your chances of happiness. "I have learned that happiness increases when I dare to be more real," says Sue, an advertising executive, who attended the course last year. I will also add one simple truth to Sue's statement, which is: *You cannot be inauthentic and feel happy.*

Wish #10: Love or Happiness. I don't play "The Happiness Genie" only with people who attend the course; I have also used it in my executive work with law firms, media groups, global companies and political organisations. And, every time, without exception, when people are asked to choose between love and happiness, the majority choose love. Yes, even the lawyers, and even the politicians, and some psychologists too. *Score: on average, 70 people out of 100 choose love.*

Bill, a professional poet, attended in 1997. He wrote something in his "Happiness Interview" that I think is very apt here. He wrote, "If scientists could dissect a lump of pure happiness they would surely discover in every single cell a double helix of joy and love, joy and love, joy and love." Happiness is love and love is happiness. And anyone who has ever experienced either one – if only for a single moment – knows this is true.

So, to close this first chapter, I will leave you with one thought to contemplate, which is,

**when you wish for happiness you are
really wishing to be the most loving
person you can be.**

● ● ● ● ●

CHAPTER 2

talking
about
happiness

When I run the happiness course in London, I normally take a black cab from my home through Hyde Park to the venue, which is near Notting Hill. On one occasion, my driver was Harold – a big, friendly 50-something-year-old man, hailing from the East End of London. We both remarked on what a beautiful morning it was, and then Harold asked me what I was doing today.

"I'm off to teach a course," I said.

"On what?" he asked.

"Happiness."

"Blimey, that's different."

Harold paused, and then he asked, "How do you do that, then?"

"Well, we normally start by talking about happiness," I replied.

"Is that it?" he quizzed.

"Well, it's a start," I said.

"And what exactly is your role?"

"I mostly listen," I said.

"Like me, then," he quipped.

"How's that?" I asked.

"Well, I'm a professional listener," said Harold.

Harold told me how he listened to people all day long, six days a week, while ferrying them around in his black cab. He said he learns as much about people from listening to *how* they talk as he does from *what* they talk about. His theory is that all psychology students would be much better qualified if they spent at least one term driving people around in a taxi.

"Most people want to talk," he said.

"What about?" I asked.

"Well, for one thing," said Harold, "they never talk about happiness."

"Well, that's what I do," I said.

We continued to chat about happiness. And it turned out that Harold was quite a philosopher – as, indeed, most cab drivers are. "We get the time to think," said Harold. Eventually, I asked Harold what his definition of happiness was. Harold didn't answer right away. A minute or two passed and then he said, "Everyone wants to be happy, but hardly anyone recognises it."

"So what is happiness?" I asked.

I don't think I will ever forget Harold's answer. Especially now that I have put it in this book, I suppose! Harold began by asking me an odd question. "You sound to me like a proper gentleman, sir. Is that true?"

Cautiously, I responded with something like, "Yes, I think so."

"Well then, if I tell you my definition of happiness, you will have to excuse my language," Harold said.

"You are excused," I said, in readiness.

"Well then," said Harold, "happiness is fucking breathing."

I founded The Happiness Project in 1995.[1] My co-director Ben Renshaw[2] and I talked at length about what our mission statement should be. One suggestion was, "The Happiness Project exists to help Robert Holden *finally* discover true happiness." Fair enough! After all, I am a firm believer that we teach what we want to learn. Finally, after much discussion, we published our first mission statement. It was somewhat brief, but to the point. It read: *Talk happiness.*

Our aim was to create spaces for people to dive deep into conversations that really matter, like conversations on happiness, on love, on spirituality and on forgiveness. The space could take any form, e.g. talks, workshops, retreats, one-on-one sessions, website chat rooms. The important thing was to make sure people felt safe and respected. Our belief is that if people are encouraged *to talk* about happiness it helps them *to think* about happiness and thereby, ultimately, helps them *to be* happier.

Our *talk happiness* approach was in direct contrast to my years of training in psychology and philosophy, during which happiness and love were barely ever mentioned. The syllabus was packed with many fascinating lectures and symposiums on central themes like neurosis and psychosis, defence mechanisms and the shadow. We also explored many of the lesser-known disorders, such as *hyperphrasia* ("n. excessive volubility, talkativeness and compunction to natter on about anything and everything"). Even so, there was still no time for talking about happiness.

My first major project after graduation was to set up a government-backed Stress Busters Clinic.[3] The clinic offered a free service to local residents, which included a variety of workshops and talks on mental health and wellbeing. Each month, I presented a very popular programme of events that included stress inoculation, beating the blues, anxiety management and facing your fears. Finally, after running Stress Busters for two years, I had an epiphany – to run a class on happiness. And in that moment, the idea of The Happiness Project was born.

Word soon got around that The Happiness Project was open for business. Almost instantly, Ben Renshaw and I were invited to give talks on happiness. The invitations soon started arriving from all over the world. We visited schools, universities, hospitals, prisons and hospices. We presented keynotes at mental health conferences. We facilitated workshops in-house at major organisations. I was also offered a regular talk show on BBC radio. Wherever we went, our hosts told us, "This is the first time we have had a talk about happiness."

The Happiness Monologue

I describe the happiness course as a big conversation about happiness that lasts for eight weeks. In truth, your conversation about happiness began the moment you were created, and I doubt if the conversation ever really ends. What I am certain of, however, is that the quality of your conversation about happiness influences directly, tangibly and irrefutably the quality of your life.

Our life evolves through the conversations we are willing to have with each other. Through conversation you have an opportunity to explore, to articulate, to test, and to clarify your thinking. Talking about happiness helps you to think about happiness. And the clearer you are about what true happiness is and is not, the happier you will be. I put this philosophy to the test throughout the happiness course by introducing a number of "talking exercises", which always have a profound effect on those who really participate.

"The Happiness Monologue" is a good example of a *talking exercise.* It's very simple. And very powerful. First, I ask the group to break into pairs, to sit facing each other, with a hint of knees touching (but not quite), and to choose a person A and a person B. Once decided, I explain that person B will go first. The reason for this is that I believe secretly, deep down inside, person B really wanted to go first. I have no scientific evidence for this. It's based purely on intuition. Or mischief, perhaps.

The instructions for this exercise are very brief. I usually say something like, "This exercise is called 'The Happiness Monologue.' Person B will speak for 10 minutes. Person A will listen. And your time starts now." The instructions are brief because I don't want person B to rehearse his monologue, or even to think about it; I want him to free associate. The only other instruction I will sometimes offer is to encourage the speaker not to try to impress the listener. This is not a performance. The goal is not to look good or to sound smart – it is to speak honestly.

I strongly encourage you to do a variation of "The Happiness Monologue" before reading on. One way you can do this is to speak into a voice recorder for 10 minutes. Or, if you like, you can simply put the book down now and just start speaking. I should warn you, however, that if you are on public transportation right now you run the risk of getting diagnosed by the mental health professional sitting behind you. Of course, you could just tell her you are speaking to an invisible friend. But she may have an invisible friend too. And then it gets complicated.

After person B has completed the 10-minute monologue, it is the turn of person A. And after that, we make time for feedback. I usually begin by asking an open-ended question like "How did that feel?" Common responses include, "At first, my mind went blank," and "It felt like an hour," and "I felt very self-conscious." Indeed, the point of the exercise is to get you to be self-conscious. I want you to pay attention to your conversation about happiness – the one you are having right now that is determining the quality of your life.

As part of the feedback process, I ask three more direct questions. The first question is, "What is the main lesson you learned about yourself and your relationship to happiness by doing 'The Happiness Monologue'?" Some people describe how scattered their minds are; others report how the exercise helped them to crystallise their thinking. The second question is, "What was the most truthful thing you said?" One of the goals of this talking exercise – and indeed of the whole happiness course – is to help people to speak their truth. The third question is, "Is there anything else you wish you had said?" Once people start talking, they really discover their voices – and new insights and revelations sound forth.

Over the next eight weeks in the happiness course you are given specific *talk happiness* assignments, such as having a conversation about happiness with members of the family you grew up in, e.g. parents, grandparents and siblings (more about this later in Chapter 17), and also, if relevant, with the family you are creating now, e.g. husband/wife, partner, children, mother-in-law, brother-in-law, etc. You are also encouraged to talk about happiness with best friends, work colleagues and anyone else who is important to you.

Most of all, I encourage you to get clear on the conversation about happiness you are having with yourself. I want you to get conscious about how much happiness you tell yourself is possible. Also, I want you to get conscious about how you talk yourself out of being even happier. *It's all in the conversation.* Below is an excerpt from feedback e-mailed to me by Andy, a high-school drama teacher, who attended the course last year.

> That exercise ["The Happiness Monologue"] was so difficult, but I am glad I did it because I am reaping the benefits now. What rocked me was how unconscious and unmindful I am about what I think about happiness. Worse still, I realised I have no idea what my partner thinks about happiness. Or, for that matter, what anyone in my family thinks about happiness. AND, I tell everyone we are a close-knit family. What an oversight!
>
> This week at school, I set my kids an assignment to talk about happiness for 10 minutes. Sound familiar? It was such fun. The whole class was totally energised by it. I watched the kids grow in confidence before my eyes. The headmistress heard about it and she's now asked me to do it at the next staff team meeting. And, yesterday, I phoned my dad and booked him for dinner next Monday. "Let's talk," I said. I'll keep you posted.

The Happiness Paradigms

Like Harold the cab driver, I consider myself to be a professional listener. I have trained myself, over the years, to listen to what people say and how they say it. Samuel Johnson, the 18th-century scholar, best known for writing the *Dictionary of the English Language,* once observed, "Language is the dress of thought." And I agree. The language you use, and the words you choose to express yourself with, reveal so much about what you think, how you see yourself and the reality you create.

When I listen to people speak about happiness I am listening for what they really think about happiness – and, above all, what they really think about themselves. More specifically, I am listening for primary ideas, concepts and beliefs that shape your thinking about happiness. Your language both *reveals* and *shapes* what you think. I am listening for the voice of hope, the voice of cynicism, the voice of fear and the voice of truth. I want to know if what you think about happiness is your truth or simply some regurgitated nonsense.

My real goal is to help you to listen to yourself. Why? Because the more conscious you become about what you think and what you say, the greater clarity you will achieve about what you think happiness is, how you block happiness, and how you can allow yourself to be happier. Clarity is the goal. This is central to my work. Why? Because despite the burgeoning number of people in our society today who are officially diagnosed with mental disorders, I honestly believe that the people I meet are not fundamentally damaged or in need of fixing. Simply put, my creed is,

**most people do not really need therapy;
they need clarity.**

In the course I often talk about the paradigms of happiness. A paradigm is a pattern of thinking based on concepts, values and beliefs. Your happiness paradigm, that is, *the way you think about happiness,* is reflected in your speech and it arranges the shape of what you experience. Hence, your paradigm either opens you up or closes you off from a greater experience of happiness *right now.*

I will show you what I am listening for when I listen to people talk about happiness. I will do this by sharing with you six popular happiness paradigms. The first four paradigms are commonly expressed by people who believe that happiness exists *outside* them; the fifth paradigm is commonly expressed by people who believe that happiness exists *inside* them; and the sixth paradigm is adopted by people who experience happiness as beyond the duality of inner or outer. These people experience happiness as a quality of their essential self.

For each paradigm, I have included a "Red Flag" that highlights a possible block to happiness and also a "Joy Mantra" that is designed to help you be more open to a greater experience of happiness now.

Paradigm #1: The Achievement Paradigm. This paradigm is driven by a belief that happiness is a by-product of effort, action and doing. Apparently, happiness does not exist naturally; it is something you must accomplish. A magazine article with a title like "10 Ways to Achieve More Happiness" appeals to people who adopt this paradigm. The ticket to life is in achievement, in the work ethic and in "making things happen". *Red Flag:* this paradigm overlooks the happiness that is effortless and that exists before you set about ticking off your to-do list. *Joy Mantra:* joy is the organic state of your soul; it is not something you achieve; it is something you accept.

Paradigm #2: The Possession Paradigm. A journalist e-mailed me yesterday asking me to contribute to an article on happiness. One of her questions was, "What advice would you give to someone who wants to get more joy out of life?" Key words to listen for in this possessing paradigm are words like "having", "manifesting", and "attracting". Happiness is related to as an external object, as an "it" or a "thing" that you can find and keep. *Red Flag:* to borrow from the great psychologist Erich Fromm, this paradigm encourages a "having mode" rather than a "being mode". *Joy* Mantra: joy is not in things; it is *who* you are.

Paradigm #3: The Reward Paradigm. According to this paradigm, happiness is not natural; it has to be earned and deserved. Apparently, it is a medal you win for being good enough, for being responsible and for succeeding at something. Happiness is a cosmic Oscar bestowed on the worthy. But bestowed by whom or what? Some say by God; I say by your superego, which is the little voice inside your head that drives you on and on and on. *Red Flag:* you deny yourself any feeling of happiness until you earn a lifetime recognition award – hopefully not posthumous. *Joy Mantra:* joy is a recognition, not a reward.

Paradigm #4: The Destination Paradigm. Another name for this paradigm is "The Searching Paradigm". This paradigm is about "looking for love", and hoping to "find my purpose", and a belief in the "pursuit of happiness". The focus is on the future and the language is about "becoming happy" rather than "being happy". Apparently, happiness is a finishing line you will cross someday. It's all about "getting there". *Red Flag:* the more you strive and search for happiness, the more you overlook the possibility that it is here already. *Joy Mantra:* the way to get to happiness is to be there already.

Paradigm #5: The Choice Paradigm. People who adopt this paradigm relate to happiness as a state of mind. Happiness is cognitive and affective. They talk about "inner peace", they experience "joy within", they believe that you can "choose your life", and they advocate that "happiness is an inside job". *Red Flag:* What happens to joy when you have a toothache or a period pain? Is the joy still there, or does it only exist because you choose it? *Joy Mantra:* joy is a way of being, not just a state of mind.

Paradigm #6: The Identity Paradigm. People who experience happiness as a "way of being", as "a simple harmony", and as "our true nature" favour this paradigm. They relate to happiness as an impersonal potential, shared by all, that infuses the whole of creation – on both the inside and the outside of a person. Wordsworth put it well when he said, "I saw one life and felt that it was joy."[4] In this paradigm happiness is sometimes referred to as a "frequency", an "energy", or a "harmonic". *Red Flag:* this idea is too big for your ego "to get"; in fact, it has nothing to do with your ego. *Joy Mantra:* the soul is JOY.

· · ● ● ●

CHAPTER 3

defining
true
happiness

I was 21 years old, and it was the summer of '86, when I first visited New York City. I had been offered a short contract with Bear Stearns, the investment bank, courtesy of my cousin Juliet and her banker husband, Christopher. Only twice before had I travelled outside England, once to stay in a small tent in France and once to visit the little island of Madeira. And now I was living in the Big Apple. What an education. So many life lessons.

I was so English. New York was so American. I was so young. New York was so awesome. When I say "awesome", I don't mean like, "Wow, this hamburger is so awesome," or "What an awesome Hershey bar," or "Isn't this root beer awesome?" I mean more like, "Wow, this city, this architecture, the energy, Manhattan, the theatre, Greenwich Village, the museums, the whole shebang, is so *awe-some*." I was so excited – and intimidated.

Day one at Bear Stearns: I was shown to "my desk", which I shared with 20 other people, who were busily looking into a bank of computer screens and shouting into telephones. We shared our office with at least 200 more people. A sea of cashmere suits. Suspenders and cigars. Shouts of "Sell!" No one talked. Everyone yelled. It was the only way you could make yourself heard. "The guys" gave me a friendly welcome. "We'll do lunch, Bob," they said. I had never been called Bob before.

My induction for my new job was short. "Here, do this," the man said. My first assignment was to check a spreadsheet and to make sure the decimal point was in the right place in a long row of zeroes. The deadline was "thirty minutes ago". I had to work quickly. I decided to use a pencil, not a pen. Just in case I made a mistake. "I mustn't make a mistake," I told myself. And so, I made a mistake.

I needed to correct my mistake, so I looked around for a rubber. I couldn't find a rubber. So I asked the guy next to me if he had a spare rubber. "A what?" he asked. "Can I borrow your rubber?" I asked. "I don't bring rubbers to work with me," he said. I asked him if Bear Stearns supplied rubbers. "A corporate rubber, with a logo on," I explained. He said, "No." I was on a deadline, time was tight, and so I stood up and yelled at the top of my voice, "I need a rubber. Has anyone got a rubber?"

I never expected to get such an enthusiastic response. People started cheering, and clapping, and whooping, and yelling "Way to go" and "Fast work, Bob" and "Who are you taking out to lunch?" I was quickly informed that the word *rubber* has a different meaning in America than in England. I didn't mean "condom". I meant "eraser". It wasn't my fault. The cause of my embarrassment lies solely in the changeable nature of language and the different meanings we give to words.

Different words mean different things to different people. That's the challenge with words like "rubber", and also with words like "happiness", and "satisfaction", and "contentment", and "joy", and "ecstasy", and "bliss".

The Meaning of Happiness

If I were to ask you what the word *happiness* means to you, what would you say? When I encounter a question like this in a book I am reading, I am often tempted to read on without considering what I really think. I invite you, right now, to pause for a moment and to reflect on the meaning of happiness *for you*. What does the word *happiness* mean to you?

The next page in this book is blank. As you can see, all it has is the heading "My Definition of Happiness". This page is potentially the most important page in this book. It is for you to write, scribble, doodle and draw what happiness really means to you. Your mission, should you choose to accept it, is to arrive at a definition of happiness you are happy to live by. The final deadline for this mission is 10 minutes after you have finished reading this book.

my definition of happiness

● ● ● ● ●

The course is an eight-week meditation on the question "What is happiness?" Early on, I invite the students in the course to share their personal definitions of happiness with the rest of the group. The interesting thing is, most people don't have a conscious definition of what happiness is. It seems that everyone is into the *goal of happiness* and everyone wants more tips, techniques and tools for the *how of happiness,* but very few people have ever stopped to think about the *meaning of happiness.*

A primary aim of the course is to help you better understand your own definition of happiness. Every assignment in the course is designed, directly or indirectly, to help you clarify your thinking and to discern what true happiness is and is not. I notice that many of my students, when faced with the question "What is happiness?" want to arrive at an answer as fast as possible. This is usually because they are compensating for self-doubt, for a lack of clarity and for feeling uncomfortable about not "having" an immediate answer.

Meditating on the question "What is happiness?" is one of the most important things you can do with your life. Why? Well, for one reason,

your definition of happiness influences every other significant decision in your life.

How you define happiness influences your entire relationship to yourself and to life. Specifically, it influences your attitude, the pace you live at, the way you relate to people, your career choices, what you call a priority, your relationship to money and how you greet each new day. The aim, therefore, is not to answer this question *fast;* it is to answer it *well.* And for that reason, I encourage my students to *live the question* for the full eight weeks of the course before they give me their answer. Likewise, I encourage you to take your time with your meditation on "What is happiness?" This meditation is not a race; it's a journey.

The Happiness Circle

So, what is happiness? The literal answer to this question is, *Happiness is a word.* This might not seem like a very helpful answer, but I encourage you to stay with me. "Happiness" is a verbal symbol, a sticky label, that we use to name an experience we are having (linguists refer to this "naming" as *nominalisation*). Of course, this is how language works. And this is what makes language so helpful and so problematic.

Just because I say the word "happiness" to you, it does not mean you know what I mean by happiness. And therefore, just as with "rubber", what I mean by "happiness" might be different from what you mean by it. Similarly, when I say "God" you might think I am referring to a bearded bloke in the sky, just like in a Cecil B. DeMille movie, when what I actually mean by "God" is *a universal intelligence, an unconditional love, that creates and sustains all life.*

The purpose, then, of meditating on the question "What is happiness?" is to get past the word *happiness*. It is to go beyond your learned ideas and concepts so as to enjoy a direct experience – with your whole being – of what the word *happiness* means. It's like "happiness" is the sign on the door and your goal is to actually walk through the door and discover for yourself what happiness really is. This is a powerful journey. Sometimes it means honouring everything you have ever learned; other times it means letting go of everything you think you know.

"The Happiness Circle" is a powerful exercise for discovering what you really mean by happiness. It is usually done in a seated circle of four or five people. It is a "sentence completion" exercise, which means that I give people the start of the sentence and then they have to complete the sentence. Once the first person completes the sentence, the person to his left goes next and then the next person, and so on. The sentence is passed around the circle several times, until a bell sounds, signalling that it is time to stop.

There are three distinct parts to "The Happiness Circle". In part one, the sentence to be completed begins with "Happiness is . . ." For instance, "Happiness is a herbal mud wrap." This part lasts about seven minutes. I then ask for a minute's silence before I introduce part two. The sentence for part two begins, "True happiness is . . ." This part also lasts about seven minutes. After another minute's silence, I introduce part three. The sentence this time begins, "My favourite definition of happiness is . . ." Each person in the happiness circle completes this sentence once only.

This exercise takes only 20 minutes in total and yet at the end of that time most people tell me that they have significantly advanced their understanding of what true happiness is. In part one, for "Happiness is", most people skim across the surface of their awareness. In part two, for "True happiness is", there is a greater honesty, intimacy and sharing. And in part three, people experience greater clarity, inner wisdom and a profound revelation that is *beyond words*.

In years of listening to people talk about happiness, I have noticed that the happiness they describe falls into three main categories. An awareness and appreciation for these three "types" of happiness is very helpful for understanding the nature of true, lasting happiness. In the remainder of this chapter, I will introduce you to a short description of each type of happiness.

Pleasure: Sensory Happiness

"Pleasure" is the name we give to the happiness we experience through our physical senses. It is the idol of hedonism. It is what makes for a good time.

Healthy pleasures are natural, innocent and life-affirming. The positive enjoyment of pleasure is as beneficial as the denial of pleasure is harmful. In short, the benefits can be summed up with three words: 1) **Aliveness:** through pleasure you get a taste of life, you enjoy your physicality and you digest and metabolise your experience of the world. *We come to life through our senses.* 2) **Connection:** you join with others through your senses; you are touched by life; and you also come home to yourself. In deep pleasure, you discover at-one-ment and you enjoy a temporary cessation of physical separateness.

And, 3) **Presence:** the enjoyment of simple pleasures helps you to enter into everyday experiences with greater awareness and appreciation. For example, I love to drink a cup of coffee each morning. For me, coffee is more than just a hot drink; it is a spiritual experience. I actually believe that coffee is a physical delivery device for the Holy Spirit. I savour the whole experience: the bean, the roast, the aroma, the body and the taste. If I know the coffee farm owners, which I often do, I will take a moment to thank them for the gift I am about to receive. Coffee is spiritual, I tell you.

A wonderful way to spend an hour of your life is to compose a list of your most life-enhancing pleasures. Then make sure you really let yourself enjoy these pleasures. Sitting here at my desk, I notice as I type these words that my senses are delighting in the smell of my jasmine oil candle, the sight of my beautiful orchid collection, the taste of my Kona coffee and the sound of Robert Norton's beautiful songs from his album *Embracing the Moment*.[1] My senses are happy and I enjoy the calming effect this has on my mind and my heart.

Pleasure (a.k.a. sensory happiness) also has some serious shortfalls. Firstly, it is wholly reliant on a "stimulus and response" action. No stimulus; no response. It appears and disappears. It comes and goes. Secondly, it is a transient experience that vanishes once the effects of dopamine and other pleasure chemicals wear off. Thirdly, it is a personal experience, not a universal one; we don't all receive sensory impressions the same way, as evidenced in the condition known as synesthesia, in which people *see* the colours of numbers and letters, for example.[2] Also, my pleasure might be your poison. For example, I was once told that there are some people on this planet who don't like coffee.

Fourthly, pleasure exists in duality with a twin called pain. Actually, pain is more than just a twin. In some cases, both pleasure and pain can be the "split personality" of the same experience. For instance, I drink only one cup of coffee a day; occasionally two; and never three. Why? Because a third cup of coffee would take me to the dark side – physical tension, emotional irritability, mental tiredness and a devilish thought that tries to convince me the Holy Spirit has deserted me.

Satisfaction: Circumstantial Happiness

"Satisfaction" is the name given to the type of happiness that is most commonly studied by positive psychologists. It also fits with what some philosophers call "desire theories", which focus on the happiness that comes from "getting what you want".[3] Other words used to describe this happiness include "contentment", "fulfilment", and also the scientific term "subjective wellbeing".[4]

Satisfaction arises when you enjoy circumstances and conditions that are deemed favourable. For example, "I like my life" (life satisfaction) and "I enjoy my work" (job satisfaction). Satisfaction is the result of the thought *I am happy because . . .* For example, *I am happy because my shares have increased in value, my new shoes look so sexy and I have just been given chocolate.* That said, satisfaction is derived not just from "getting things", but also from finding meaning in certain activities, in having a purpose, in loving relationships and in values and ethics.

Above all, satisfaction comes from the sense that our ego is learning and growing. This is particularly gratifying and meaningful to many of us. Also, one positive effect of satisfaction is that it activates an upward spiral of increased gratitude, heightened receptivity and further satisfaction. Another wonderful way to spend an hour of your life, then, is to create a list of all of the most meaningful moments, events and relationships in your life. I guarantee you will feel like your whole life just got better if you do this.

Like pleasure, satisfaction also has some shortfalls. Firstly, it is the by-product of a "cause and effect" dance. No cause, no effect. No bell, no drool. This type of happiness cannot exist except in reaction to something. Secondly, the effects of satisfaction are notoriously short-lived. Satisfaction usually has a short half-life because you adapt so quickly to favourable circumstances. For example, gratitude for your raise at work is fast eaten up by more business-as-usual and more career planning.[5]

Thirdly, satisfaction exists in duality with dissatisfaction. Things that used to satisfy you in the past may no longer satisfy you now. For instance, no one should have to put up with an iPod that has only enough memory for 40,000 songs and 200 hours of video. Satisfaction is all too often bullied into submission by dissatisfaction and its two friends, called "expectations" and "comparison". It's very hard to feel happy when these three fellows have just barged into your mind.

Fourthly, and finally, the problem with satisfaction is that it is wholly dependent on your mind and on the world – neither of which is a particularly safe place to live. When you are not in your right mind, for instance, you may overlook everything that you could appreciate. Not all millionaires smile a lot. Also, when your life doesn't look the way you want and when not all the boxes are checked, your satisfaction may nosedive and you may try to convince yourself that you are a victim of the world.

Joy: Unreasonable Happiness

Joy is the soul of happiness. Like pleasure, it can express itself through the body, but it is not of the body. Like satisfaction, it can be felt emotionally and appreciated mentally, but it is so much more than just an emotion or a state of mind. Other words used to describe this type of happiness include "bliss" and "felicity", and also "ecstasy", which, translated from the ancient Greek *ek-stasis,* means "to stand outside oneself". Joy is bigger than your ego. It exists before the thought of "I".

Joy is impossible to define, but it can be described. The most inspirational people to have walked this earth have tried to express what joy means to them. For example, Helen Keller described joy as "the holy fire that keeps our purpose warm and our intelligence aglow". Mother Teresa wrote, "Joy is prayer. Joy is strength. Joy is love. Joy is a net of love by which you can catch souls." And C. S. Lewis referred to joy as "the serious business of Heaven".[6]

Describing joy is very difficult *and* very worthwhile. The more you tune in to joy and let yourself feel it, the more you learn about what true happiness is. I encourage my students to describe joy by meditating on joy, by painting joy, by singing joy, by dancing joy, by crafting a poem on joy, or by finding a symbol, in nature, for instance, that represents joy. What emerge are commonly felt qualities of joy, five of which I will share with you now.

1. Constancy. When people tune in to the feeling of joy, what often emerges is an awareness that this joy is somehow always with us. Joy is quietly, invisibly ever-present. It is not "out there", and it is not "in here;" rather, it is simply everywhere we are. Joy feels somehow beyond space and time. *Joy does not come and go; what comes and goes is our awareness of joy.* Ironically, we often feel the presence of joy the most when we stop chasing pleasure and we stop trying to satisfy our ego.

2. Creativity. Upon discovering this joy, many people experience a greater sense of creativity that rushes through them. Your ego may get the byline, but really joy is the author. Joy is the doer. Joy is the thinker. Joy is the creative principle. In one of my favourite Upanishads, classic sacred texts of Indian literature, it is written: "From joy springs all creation, / By joy it is sustained. / Towards joy it proceeds, / and to joy it returns."[7] No wonder so many artists take the course.

3. Unreasonable. I like to describe joy as "unreasonable happiness" because it doesn't seem to need a reason. It is a happiness that is based on nothing. In other words, it doesn't need a cause or an effect in order to exist. Certainly good things, favourable circumstances and a happy state of mind can make you more receptive to joy; but joy still exists even when you are not receptive to it. *Joy needs no reason.* And this is why we can be *surprised by joy* even in the most ordinary moments.

4. Untroubled. Unlike pleasure and satisfaction, joy does not have an opposite. It does not swing up and down, as our moods do. And it does not wrestle with positives and negatives, as our mind does. Joy does, however, have a twin. If pleasure's twin is pain and satisfaction's twin is dissatisfaction, then joy's twin is love. When people describe joy to me they always mention love – even the lawyers, the politicians and the psychologists. Like love, joy is fearless and untroubled by the world. It is as if nothing in the world can tarnish or diminish the essence of joy. As such, it is free.

5. Enough. Many people describe a sense of emptiness and a "fall from grace" that follows an encounter with great pleasure and satisfaction. This is not the case with joy, however. One of the most beautiful qualities of joy is the abiding sense of "enoughness". Unlike the ephemeral states of pleasure and satisfaction, *joy does not induce a craving for more, because joy is enough.* If ever we feel joy is missing, it is because we are absent-minded – caught up, probably, in some grief over a passing pleasure or preoccupied with a new object of desire.

Of the three types of happiness – pleasure, satisfaction and joy – only one is true, and that is the one that lasts forever. Hence, from now on when I refer to "true happiness" you know that I am talking about joy. However, I would like to make two points of clarification. First, I am not saying that pleasure or satisfaction is "bad" and that only joy is "good". I advocate wholeheartedly the benefits of healthy pleasure and positive satisfaction. Second, I am not saying you have to choose between pleasure, satisfaction and joy. What I have found, however, is that

> **unless you cultivate an awareness of joy, no amount of**
> **pleasure or satisfaction can make you happy.**

If you continue to overlook the joy of your soul (which exists whether or not your ego experiences pleasure and your mind is satisfied) you will crave more and more pleasure and satisfaction. The danger then is that you will look for extreme pleasures, for bigger hits that come from, for instance, compulsive shopping, a workaholic lifestyle, a bottle of wine each night, a line of cocaine or a gambling addiction. BUT, but, but, by contrast, the more you tune in to joy, the more you will expand your capacity to enjoy healthy pleasure and worldly satisfaction. And for that reason, I am saying that joy comes first.

· · ● ● ● ● ●

CHAPTER 4

a new learning curve

The happiness course affords people the opportunity to give an uncommon level of attention to life's most cherished and elusive goal. So far, I have described the course as a journey (in Chapter 1), a conversation (in Chapter 2) and a meditation (in Chapter 3). Another way to describe the happiness course is to call it *an inquiry*. This is perhaps the most accurate description because so many of the exercises we do together are inquiry exercises.

The word *inquiry* means "a search for knowledge" and "a request for truth". For eight weeks, we inquire deeply into four main sources of wisdom. First, we look to the universal spiritual principles and to what I call the "spiritual rumours", that are found in 5,000 years' worth of Christian Psalms, Buddhist sutras, Islamic poetry, Hindu Upanishads, Zen koans, Taoist philosophy and Greek scriptures. These spiritual rumours include radical propositions like "Happiness is within," "Happiness is free," and "You are already happy." Together these rumours create a golden thread of joy that weaves its way through great wisdom traditions.

Second, we inquire into 100 years of Western psychology. Specifically, we look at the empirical research from studies into subjective wellbeing (since the 1960s)[1] and positive psychology (since 2000).[2] We also reference personality models such as the Enneagram, which has become increasingly popular in recent times.[3] Third, we draw on the experience and research accumulated from running The Happiness Project over the last two decades. Fourth, and by far the most significant, *I encourage you to inquire deeply into your own personal wisdom.*

Inquiry, in its purest form, is a system of learning that is guided by the ethos "The one who asks is the one who knows." I believe that *happiness is not taught; it is recognised.* We don't learn happiness as if for the first time; we *remember* happiness, we consciously *reconnect* to happiness and we *remind* ourselves what happiness is. And so I am not really a teacher of happiness; I am a teacher of inquiry. My goal is to help you *recall* what, deep down, you already know. This is the truth and in ancient Greek the word for truth is *aletheia,* which means "not forgetting".

If I were to teach you what I know about happiness, you would not remember much; but if I can teach you what you already know about happiness, you will remember it all. Wisdom, like happiness, is not an object or a "thing" that can be passed around like a ball. And in truth, it is neither acquired nor lost. It exists already and it is either recognised or not. The tuition I offer is very traditional in that it is inspired by the Latin word for *educate,* which is *educere,* derived from the roots *e* and *ducere,* meaning "to draw out from within", as our work draws out the knowledge of happiness you already possess.

Looking back, I think I got my first lesson in the absolute folly of trying to give someone else my answers when I was just 15 years old. It was the beginning of a new year of school. I was in my final year and my younger brother David, who was 11 years old, was starting his first year. On the eve of our first day of term, I took David into my bedroom to give him the greatest gift in the world – a gift so brilliant he would remember it not just for the rest of this life, but for the next few lifetimes too.

At the bottom of my bed there was an old captain's chest, about three feet wide and two feet deep. It was made of a dark mahogany wood, with lighter wood panelling and brass fittings. Pointing to my "treasure chest", I asked David to open it up. He gave me a cautious look, as it was normally out of bounds for him – because it had "my things" in it. When he opened up the chest, he saw a row of books piled right up to the top. "What is it?" he asked.

"David," I said, "here are *all of the answers* for *all of the classes* you will take in the first four years of your new school." David was quiet. It was understandable, really, as it was such an enormous gift. For the previous four years I had saved up all of my notebooks and essays on all the main subjects like mathematics, English, geography, physics and history. In effect, what I had just given David was a complete education – a ticket, if you like, to kick back, enjoy himself and get some good grades along the way.

Once David understood what I had given him, he was suitably grateful. And I was over the moon because I loved David so much and I just wanted to do my best for him. AND, the big AND, is that over the next four years I didn't see David open the treasure chest once! From time to time, I would remind David to look and he always said he would, but he never did. And he still got great grades and he still excelled at the subjects he loved. And what I learned was that his own education was of more interest and value to him than my education. And rightly so.

Living Your Truth

One of the most challenging exercises in the course is when each person is invited to stand up and repeat an affirmation that is just five words long. The affirmation is: "I am a wise person."

The purpose of this simple exercise is to begin to explore your relationship to your wisdom and to your inner voice of truth. Many people find this exercise so difficult that they notice strong physical reactions as they say, "I am a wise person." These physical reactions include difficulty breathing, weak knees, trembling hands and sweaty palms. "I felt faint, like I was about to have an out-of-body experience," said Tim, a police officer. "Yeah, like I was going to die," said Laura, a university lecturer.

These physical reactions are caused by a person's mental response, that is, what it feels like to say, "I am a wise person." Many people tell me they feel as if they are being arrogant. I point out that I did not ask them to say, "I am *the wisest* person here." As it turns out, most people have no problem believing that everyone can be wise; the difficulty is in believing that "I am a wise person." Many people also report a sense of grief: "It's like I know I can be wise," said Sandra, a stay-at-home mother to her two kids, "but I rarely listen to myself, and I forget to live my truth."

The real problem is one of *identification*. It is the inability to identify with the idea of *being a wise person* that causes a person to doubt himself or herself. Growing up, many of us lacked the necessary encouragement from our parents and teachers to explore our own wisdom. This is probably because they lacked encouragement also. This lack of attention to our wisdom has to end, though, if we are to be happier. Being willing to listen to and trust in your own wisdom is one of the most important keys to lasting happiness.

As a teacher of inquiry, I ask my students a lot of questions. Big questions like "What is happiness?" and "What is success?" and "What is the purpose of your life?" And many times, people will say, "I don't know." And in the beginning I used to believe that they were telling me the truth. But I don't any more. From years of experience, I now know that there is no such thing as "I don't know." Just because you may feel like you don't know, it doesn't mean you don't really have the answer. Properly translated, "I don't know" means "I don't know that I know."

Nothing really blocks your wisdom other than the self-made beliefs and perceptions that you identify with. These self-made beliefs include ideas like: to be wise you have to be *Greek and dead,* or *not blonde,* or *old and arthritic,* or *fluent in Sanskrit,* or have proof of *an immaculate conception,* or be *a white Caucasian male,* or better still, be *a psychic medium* who is in touch with the good people from the Pleiades.

A teacher of inquiry knows that everyone is wise. We each have equal access to wisdom. Some of us are simply more receptive. I once met an eminent medical doctor who described his inner wisdom as the *heebie-jeebies.* I am good friends with a leading psychologist who gets *goose bumps* when he hears someone get to the truth of a subject. And Louise Hay, founder of Hay House, the publisher of this book, often talks about the "inner ding" that guides and inspires her. These people cannot define exactly what wisdom is, but they have learned to be open to it, to trust it and to be guided by it.

Here is the miracle of inquiry: When a student sits with a teacher of inquiry, the student "discovers" his/her wisdom – and then both the student and the teacher start taking notes. We may cover our ears, or stuff them full of poor education, but the wisdom never leaves us. Your wisdom never stops speaking to you, even if you are not listening. The grace of wisdom is that *the moment you make yourself available to wisdom, wisdom makes itself available to you.* Another way of saying this is that your wisdom is as loud as your willingness to hear it.

Learning About Happiness

Happiness is a learning curve.

There are plenty of learning curves to choose from. Traditionally, many of us have used pain and suffering and sacrifice and failure as our chief learning curves. If this is true for you, you have probably attended the school of hard knocks and you have employed grief and heartache as your teachers. It is well to remember, however, that you can also choose from a range of more pleasant learning curves, such as love as a learning curve, authenticity as a learning curve and success as a learning curve.

You choose your learning curve. No one or nothing else makes this choice for you.

"Happiness Life Lessons" is an inquiry exercise based on the idea that we can all be students of happiness and that happiness can be our learning curve of choice. To introduce this exercise I work with a "focus person" at the front of the room. The way I pick my "volunteer" is great fun – for me! I have a big top hat, like a magician's hat, which holds the names of the students on individual bits of paper. I simply put my hand into the hat and out comes the name of the "volunteer". *Ta-da!* Amazingly, all the volunteers tell me *they just knew* they were going to be picked.

My volunteer comes to the front of the room and stands before three pieces of legal-size paper. Each piece of paper has one word written on it and the word represents a particular focus for the exercise. I begin by inviting my volunteer to close his or her eyes, take a few deep breaths, and then start to tune in to feelings of true happiness. I encourage the volunteer to feel and sense happiness in the mind, in the heart and in the cells of the body, in order to "listen" rather than "think", and thereby participate with his or her whole being.

I now invite my volunteer to step forward and stand on the first piece of paper, which has the word "PAST" written on it in large capital letters. I say, "As you step onto 'The Past', take a few moments to reflect on the story of your life and on your relationship to happiness." The key question for this part of the inquiry is, *What has your life taught you about happiness so far?* Again, I emphasise listening, not thinking. What ensues is a rich conversation full of valuable insights about past events, relationships, successes, wounds, lessons and joys.

I encourage you, dear reader, to reflect on this great question. Here is a wonderful opportunity to honour your major life lessons on happiness. One way to do this is to make a list of the top five lessons of happiness your life has taught you so far. Write down each lesson, specifically. Recall when you learned the lesson. Name the names of anyone else involved. And assess as honestly as you can a) how learning this lesson has influenced your life and b) how well you have learned this lesson (so that it doesn't have to be repeated!).

Next, my volunteer steps forward onto the second piece of paper, which has the word "NOW" written on it in large capital letters. Here I say, "Reflect on what is happening currently in your life, in your relationships and in your work. Notice any major themes. Be aware of any conflict. Take into account any feelings of great joy." The key question for this part of the inquiry is, *What is your life asking you to learn about happiness now?* Again, I invite you to reflect on what your life wants you to learn about happiness right now.

Last, my volunteer steps forward onto the third piece of paper, which has the word "FUTURE" written on it. My instruction here is, "Imagine you have now stepped into your future. Take a few moments to review all your wishes for the future. Then see if you can identity any major life lessons on happiness you still have to learn." When people are honest with themselves, they can identify the lessons they still need to learn about happiness. Sometimes it's an old lesson, or a current lesson, or a new lesson they haven't paid attention to until now.

A variation on this exercise is to imagine for a moment that you have visited planet Earth in order to learn one major life lesson about happiness. I call this your "ULTIMATE" happiness lesson. This lesson is so important because it underpins the overall purpose of your life. If you were to learn this lesson really well, it would radically improve your relationships, your work, your health and everything else about your life. I encourage you to take some time now, or very soon, to identify this ultimate lesson and to benefit from your happiness learning curve.

Thinking about Happiness

Happiness is the new darling of the social sciences. Every day sees the publication of new findings from intriguing studies on "happiness and money", "happiness and culture", "gross national happiness", "happiness and the brain", "happiness and work", "happiness and marriage", and "happiness and spirituality". This collective inquiry into happiness has gained the attention of us all, including politicians, economists, schoolteachers, health professionals, church leaders and business leaders.

In the spring of 2006, the BBC science department marked the 10th anniversary of the BBC TV *QED* documentary called "How to Be Happy" (based on my happiness course) by broadcasting a new six-part series called *The Happiness Formula*.[4] Series producer Mike Rudin and writer-presenter Mark Easton did an excellent job in presenting a most comprehensive mix of happiness surveys, experiments and opinion polls – many of which challenge us to rethink our most basic assumptions about life and how to be happy.

The Happiness Formula's inquiry confirmed the existing evidence of a worldwide decline in happiness levels in recent decades. "The proportion of people saying they are 'very happy' has fallen from 52 per cent in 1957 to just 36 per cent today," reported Mark Easton. Worse still, the number of adults diagnosed with depression or other serious mental illnesses has increased tenfold. Also, a worldwide report by UNICEF on the "critically low levels" of wellbeing among our children has called for an honest appraisal by government and society of how we live.[5]

An inquiry into happiness is an opportunity to rethink your life. As you deepen your happiness inquiry you get to test the truth of all of your assumptions and beliefs. Sometimes your inquiry will confirm what you already know to be true and other times it will ask you to let go of ideas that you may have identified strongly with until now. Thinking about happiness takes great personal honesty and courage, but the rewards are also great. Below are five examples of how thinking about happiness can help you to get clearer about everything else that truly matters.

Rethink #1: Happiness and Money. When people are asked what they need to enjoy "the good life", the most common answer is, "Show me the money!" This is the right answer, at least to begin with, if you are either a) one of the three billion people living in the Third World who earn just $2 a day or b) a First World citizen who is living below or close to the poverty line. "Once the gross national product exceeds $8,000 per person, however, the correlation [between purchasing power and happiness] disappears and added wealth brings no further life satisfaction," reports Professor Martin Seligman.[6]

The majority of people's big game plan for increased happiness is to earn more money. The fact is, however, that while money helps to take care of life's basic needs, after that it doesn't do much for us. Even the very wealthy, such as Forbes 100 Club members, who earn millions a year just in interest from their savings, are only slightly happier than the average person – and in some cases they are less happy. Seligman concludes most forcibly:

> The change in purchasing power over the last half-century in the wealthy nations carries the same message: real purchasing power has more than doubled in the United States, France and Japan, but life satisfaction has changed not a whit.[7]

Rethink #2: Happiness and Circumstances. Almost everyone agrees with the idea that *if my life circumstances improve, my levels of happiness will increase*. This is the basis for almost every political and economic strategy the world over. And yet the scientific inquiry into happiness dismisses this theory out of hand. One leading researcher, Richard Kammann, of New

Zealand, reports, "Objective life circumstances have a negligible role to play in a theory of happiness."[8] Even a big improvement in circumstances, like winning the lottery, has been found to give people only a temporary uplift. Most researchers agree that over the long term, life circumstances influence happiness levels by 10 per cent at most.

Rethink #3: Happiness and Education. A popular theory in society today is that a better education will create more happiness for our children. This has resulted in more tests for pre-school children, more focus on regular exams and more money spent on private education. Surely a better education increases happiness, doesn't it? "Sorry, Mum and Dad, neither education nor, for that matter, a high IQ paves the road to happiness," states Claudia Wallis, who compiled a report called "The New Science of Happiness" for *TIME* magazine.[9] Clearly, the scientific inquiry into happiness is challenging us to rethink what a "better education" really is.

Rethink #4: Happiness and the Future. So, at least we can expect to be happier in the future, right? Wrong! Longitudinal happiness studies that record the happiness levels of subjects over the course of 20 years suggest that the best predictor for how happy you will be in the future is *how happy you choose to be now*. The fact is, the future won't make you happy. Why? *Because nothing is going to make you happy.* That's right, not even shopping. Let me clarify what I mean by sharing one of my conclusions from my first book on happiness, called *Happiness NOW!* The conclusion is:

> **Nothing in the world can *make* you happy,**
> **but everything in the world can *encourage***
> **you to be happy.**[10]

Interestingly, what the happiness research has taught the researchers is that their initial inquiry into happiness is based on a limited line of questions like "What determines happiness?" and "What makes you happy?" What the researchers need to do now in order to advance their inquiry is to ask new questions, like "What does happiness mean to you?" and "What have you learned about happiness?" and "How do you choose happiness?"

Rethink #5: Happiness and You. The modern scientific inquiry into happiness recognises that *everyone can be happy*. Happiness does not discriminate. It is an equal-opportunity provider. Leading researchers David

Myers and Ed Diener conclude, in their article entitled "Who Is Happy?": "Happiness and life-satisfaction are similarly available to the young and the old, women and men, blacks and whites, the rich and the working-class." Happiness research teaches us that the "enduring characteristics of the individual" are more important to happiness than external life circumstances.[11]

Happiness researchers have recently begun to study the "very happy" people for more lessons on happiness. This inquiry is also challenging us to rethink major life issues. For instance, researchers have found a correlation between high happiness scores and marriage. It is too simplistic, however, to say that *marriage makes you happy*. If that is the case, why are divorce rates soaring? Clearly, we need to deepen the inquiry into happiness and marriage and explore the influence of, for instance, love, forgiveness, intimacy, shared purpose, communication and kindness.

Researchers who study the "very happy" have also found a strong link between religion and happiness. Again, however, it is not enough to say that *religion makes you happy*. If that is the case, why are fewer people attending church these days? The inquiry into religion and happiness has to examine more deeply, for instance, the influence of a living faith, the need for meaning and purpose, a belief in a loving God, a sense of oneness and a spirituality that is bigger than any one religious book.

I firmly believe that the more we learn about the nature of true happiness, the better we will learn to live. I will close this chapter now with the concluding remarks of Mark Easton, the writer-presenter of the BBC series *The Happiness Formula*. He said:

> The logic of the new science [of happiness] is breathtaking. If it is right it requires us to rethink some of our most basic assumptions about how we work, how we live and what we are trying to achieve. In short, the science of happiness may provide us with a new definition of what we mean by human progress.[12]

● ● ● ● ●

PART II

your
spiritual
dna

CHAPTER 5

a
spiritual
path

It happens every time: I am always struck by how everyone on the happiness course feels so totally familiar to me. This familiarity is instant. It's there at the start of the course. Before the first word has been spoken. Could it possibly be that we made a prior arrangement, in another time and place, for us all to meet up now? Or perhaps we feel familiar to each other because we share a similar intention and purpose, which is to remember the truth about who we are, what happiness is and what our life is really for.

The first session on day one of the happiness course is devoted to personal introductions. Each person is invited to tell the "short story" about why he or she has chosen to attend this course. I am always keen to know what specifically moved them to be here. Why happiness? And why now? People's personal stories are often very moving. In the last course, a woman stood up and said, "My mother and my father both committed suicide when I was a teenager and last year my husband also committed suicide. These days, I often feel like I want to die. But I am here because *I also want to live.*"

One by one, everyone tells their stories. And the stories often feature the death of loved ones, diagnoses like AIDS and cancer and the trauma of broken relationships. There are also stories about new beginnings, finding a purpose, expressing creativity and wanting to enjoy life more. And then there are the fun stories of synchronicity and destiny. "I was helping my friend set up his new computer," said Tom, "and I noticed an e-mail in his in-box about this course. Most irrationally, I knew right then that I HAD to be here today."

There are so many great stories I could tell you about what really moves people to attend the course. I will share one more story with you now – a story that, I believe, contains an essential element in all the stories ever told. Avril Carson, a former actress with the Royal Shakespeare Company, attended in Oxford in 1997. This is the story she told:

> One Sunday afternoon I went to do an audition with four casting directors. For my audition, I chose to play three character parts. I had always been attracted to playing characters who were eccentric, interesting and completely unlike me. My hope was to impress the casting directors with my broad and creative repertoire. But afterwards they seemed distinctly unmoved. They then said something to me that was a total shock to my system. "Come back for another audition and play someone who is more like you," they said.
>
> Well, I just freaked! The problem with playing someone more like myself was I didn't know who I was. After a lot of soul-searching over the next week, I gave an audition in which I played a person of a similar age to me, with a similar background and who lived in the same city I grew up in. It was very real and I didn't try to dramatise it in any way. When I finished I noticed that three of the casting directors had been moved to tears. Until that moment, I had no idea that being authentic could pack such a powerful punch.
>
> In my desire to impress others, I had overlooked the fact that the most impressive thing is to be myself. I got the job! However, the most significant outcome was that I became interested in knowing more about who I really am. More than anything, I want to learn about the essence of who I am and who we all are. Who is the real me? And what am I made of? This is the purpose of my work now, and this is my spiritual path, and this is why I am here.

After Avril completed the course, she attended a certification training programme called Coaching Happiness run by The Happiness Project.[1] For the last 10 years, Avril has been a regular presenter for us. Avril opens many of our sessions with her passionate, delightful recitals of prose and poetry by William Shakespeare and also by William Wordsworth, Walt Whitman, Mary Oliver, Emily Dickinson, Rumi and Hafiz. She is adept at helping people to meet themselves and to be more like who they really are.[2]

The Purpose of Happiness

Have you ever asked yourself, "What is happiness for?" One reason why psychologists did not traditionally study happiness is because they were unclear as to what the purpose and value of happiness were. They commonly regarded happiness as little more than a pleasurable emotion with no evolutionary value. A few conceded that, at best, happiness offered a temporary escape – a short emotional vacation from the routine pain of human existence. However, there was also a strong lobby that viewed happiness as a thoroughly irrational and inappropriate response to life.

This "irrational" view of happiness is well illustrated by a research paper entitled "A Proposal to Classify Happiness as a Psychiatric Disorder", which appeared in the *Journal of Medical Ethics* in 1992. The author is Richard Bentall and his abstract for the paper reads:

> It is proposed that happiness be classified as a psychiatric disorder and be included in future editions of the major diagnostic manuals under the new name: major affective disorder, pleasant type. In a review of the relevant literature, it is shown that happiness is statistically abnormal, consists of a discrete cluster of symptoms, is associated with a range of cognitive abnormalities and probably reflects the abnormal functioning of the central nervous system. One possible objection to this proposal remains – that happiness is not negatively valued. However, this objection is dismissed as scientifically irrelevant.[3]

When I ask my students in the course, "What is the purpose of happiness?" I often encounter strong support for the idea that *happiness exists for its own sake*. In other words, *happiness just is* – and this should not in any way diminish its value. That said, many people also testify not only that happiness has a purpose, but also that the purpose of our life is *to know what happiness is* and *to be happy*. In other words, we evolve, ultimately, in the direction of happiness – and through happiness we learn to be all that we really can be.

One big clue to the real purpose and value of happiness is found in "The Happiness Genie", featured in Chapter 1 of this book. If you remember, when people are asked to choose between a wish for happiness and a wish for authenticity, the majority choose *authenticity*. When asked to give a reason, the most common response is that a person cannot be inauthentic and happy and also, when people are authentic, *they are happy!* Thus, when you learn to be truly happy, you learn to be your true self. Happiness helps you to be who you really are.

I am convinced that the real purpose of happiness is to help you retrace your steps back to your original nature. Happiness helps you to abide in the true nature of your self – that is, your "Unconditioned Self", which is usually obscured by the "Learned Self", which has had to work hard to adapt to a world with many different cultures and strange politics. To put it another way,

> **happiness is a spiritual path. The more you learn about**
> **true happiness, the more you discover the truth of who you are,**
> **what is important and what your life is really for.**

By walking back to happiness – the happiness that exists within you right now – you reacquaint yourself with your true identity, with your true values and with your true purpose. This inherent happiness holds the key to enlightenment and greater understanding of who you are. In other words, *true happiness is Self-realisation.*

The Cause of Suffering

When you forget who you are, you forget what happiness is. And when you forget what happiness is, you suffer.

Who taught you who you are? Who is the person reading this book right now? I mean, *the real you.* Imagine that you are in my course and that I have just picked your name out of my "volunteer hat". This is your cue to join me at the front of the class. Picture yourself sitting with me and imagine I ask you to answer just one question: "Who are you?" Would you know what to say? Do you have an answer already? Do you know who you really are?

I find that most people are absolutely flummoxed, baffled and bamboozled by the seemingly simple question, "Who am I?" Most of us know something about life. For example, you may be able to locate every major organ in your body; you may have memorised the important dates of your country's history; you may also know how to fill out a map of the world; and you may even be able to recite all of the words to all of the songs of The Beatles. But still the greatest party trick ever – the greatest knowledge of all – is to know something that is true about you.

My favourite book is called *A Course in Miracles.*[4] I have been a student of *A Course in Miracles* for as long as I have taught the happiness course. I study this book daily. If I could take only one book with me to a desert island for the rest of my life, it would be *A Course in Miracles*. I mention this book now because I want to share one line from it that has influenced my entire work on happiness. The line is:

> **"There is no conflict that does not entail the**
> **single, simple question, 'What am I?' "**[5]

This is a great truth that has been expressed in similar ways by many great sages, both ancient and modern. The primary cause of all suffering is forgetting the true nature of your Unconditioned Self. Think about it: If you are not clear on who you really are, how can you know what is best for you? And how can you know what it is you *really* want as opposed to what you *think* you want, or what other people tell you that you *should* want? Your lack of Self-knowledge plays itself out in countless ways – three of which I will focus on now.

1. The Search. The purpose of the happiness course is to help you identify with the unreasonable happiness (a.k.a. joy) of your true nature. The more you identify with this joy, the more you discover about your true self – the Unconditioned Self that existed before the world began, before the ego-thought of "I am." The more you identify with this joy, the more you will enjoy the world for what it is and the more you will enjoy your life. But *when you forget that you are made of joy, something very strange happens – you begin to search for happiness.*

The search for happiness seems natural enough, but on closer inspection this so-called search is a masquerade in which we dance further and further away from where happiness is *right now*. Our search betrays our confusion: we are not really sure who we are and we have misplaced happiness. All of our pain comes from thinking *happiness is not here* and believing that the source of happiness must be outside ourselves. Truth be told, *the search for happiness is the denial of happiness.* And,

> **for as long as you deny the joy of your being, your ego**
> **and your personality will never be completely**
> **satisfied or pleased with the world.**

The search for happiness is a hoax. You only search for that which you fear you do not have, or for that which you are not yet willing to accept that you have already. The truth is, *you are what you seek.* This means that whatever joy you hope to "get" after you find your true partner, get the dream job, or buy the ideal home is *already with you.* And until you really know this about yourself, the partner, the job and the home will not satisfy you. Why? *Because it is impossible to "find" happiness for as long as you overlook your true nature.*

Only by calling off the search for happiness will you discover just how happy you really can be.

2. Feeling Inadequate. When you forget to identify with the joy of your Unconditioned Self, you literally start to feel *inadequate.* This forgetting of Self turns your mind into a haunted house where mental ghosts and ghouls come out of the dark to taunt you with accusations that you are not good enough, that there is something missing in you and that you will never find what you are looking for.

The secret inadequacy that even the most accomplished people feel is caused by a lack of Self-knowledge. In truth, none of us is really inadequate; it's just that we don't know enough about who we really are. This lack of knowledge causes us to fear that *happiness is somewhere else* – and also that love is somewhere else, heaven is somewhere else and the end of the rainbow is somewhere else. The fear of inadequacy projects the illusion that "something is missing" onto every person, event, job and relationship we encounter.

A lack of Self-knowledge also makes it very difficult for you to believe in yourself. You have so little faith in yourself because you are unwilling to accept that you are made of joy. This causes you to stay away from yourself and to avoid any Self-inquiry, because you fear you cannot trust yourself. At the same time, you start to search outside yourself for the answers, for happiness and for the Holy Grail. But the point is, you were never inadequate. All along you have simply been suffering from the effects of Self-neglect. All that was ever missing was some personal attention. And when you give yourself the gift of your own attention, you rediscover the happiness you thought you had lost.

3. Living in Exile. When you lose your conscious connection with the joy of your true nature, you feel like you also lose your connection with everything else. Thus, you are a stranger to yourself, you are an outsider to the world and you feel like you are a long way from home. In short, you feel lost. It is as if you have personally enacted the fall from grace and you are now living in exile from the joy of your true nature. You feel abandoned by God. You feel overlooked by society. You feel misunderstood by people. No one really gets you. But then again, neither do you.

In happiness, we find ourselves again. And that is why I have run the happiness course for all these years. Happiness is God's way of reminding you who you really are. Happiness is your "forgotten song".[6] Below is an excerpt from an e-mail from Gillian, a senior editor of a women's magazine, who attended in 2001. She writes:

> Robert, this is the most *Gilliany* I have ever felt in my life. For as long as I can remember, I have felt like a misfit who was never entirely at home anywhere, including with myself. I always felt something was missing. And so I went searching. And I searched for a teacher. And I searched for the answers. And I searched for romantic love. And I searched for the great job. And I have searched for happiness. And now, with your help, I realise that what I was really searching for was MYSELF – an honest experience of my true self. As the song goes, "I've been to paradise, but I've never been to me." But now I have been to me. And the search is over.

The Joy of Happiness

Happiness is your original nature – it is what you first experienced before you began to identify with a body, a family role, some school grades, your nationality, your business card, your National Insurance number and other mistaken identities. Hence, *the joy of happiness* is that the more you learn about true happiness, the more you will discover who you really are; and the more you discover about who you really are, the happier you feel.

How often do you feel very happy? Not just mild happy, or okay happy, but *very happy?* One of my favourite Self-inquiry exercises is called "Very Happy". The exercise has three distinct parts to it. In part one, I invite you to complete the following sentence at least 10 times: "I am very happy when . . ." Dear reader, I encourage you to put this book down for a moment and write your list of when you are very happy. Or at least promise to give yourself some time to do this exercise this evening, before you turn the lights out.

Your "Very Happy" list will probably include people, places, moments, books and hobbies. The goal is to identify when you experience real JOY, as opposed to just pleasure and satisfaction. This list is about when you feel a complete sense of wholeness, peace and fulfilment. Next, for part two, I invite you to place next to each entry the date of when you last experienced it. Don't be surprised if it's been a few months, or years even. And finally, for part three, take a few moments to notice what this short exercise has taught you about yourself.

We always follow up a self-inquiry exercise like "Very Happy" with a group feedback session. This is valuable in group work because, by sharing with others what we have learned, we strengthen the learning for ourselves. Also, when we listen to others we may discover some insights that we would have missed if we had only done the exercise alone. Therefore, it can be extra beneficial and most illuminating to do the "Very Happy" inquiry with someone else.

When we focus on part three of the "Very Happy" exercise (What has this inquiry taught you about yourself?), many people say they are often "unconscious" of the moments when they are most happy. For that reason, they experience initial difficulty and resistance even doing the inquiry. Here are some typical comments: "It's like I don't register when life is great," and "I dismiss the good moments," and "I don't let myself fully savour the great moments." People also often comment on how rarely they let themselves enjoy the people, places and activities they associate with being very happy.

Another common feedback theme for the "Very Happy" inquiry is *personal deception*. Alan, a former account executive for a major advertising firm, attended in 2002. He shared with us: "I told myself I was very happy in my job for 10 years *and I almost believed it.* I told myself that every account I worked on was brilliant, and that the product was brilliant, and that the people were brilliant to work with, and that my lifestyle was brilliant, and that I was brilliant. And yet the day I quit my job was the happiest day of my life." Alan had experienced the subtle and yet stark difference between *being positive* and *being happy.*

When you lose touch with your authentic Self, you will start to deceive yourself about what makes you happy. Eventually, you may not even recognise the difference between joy and pain and in fact you are very apt to confuse the two. Hence, people will stay put for years in soulless jobs, try to make abusive relationships work, neglect their creativity, rebel against their higher callings, eat themselves unhappy, do drugs and harm themselves in ways that don't even feel that bad at the time. This is the worst-case scenario; however, most of us are still learning about who we are and when we truly feel very happy.

Many people also report wonderful insights, epiphanies and eurekas during the "Very Happy" inquiry. They learn, for instance, that being *very happy* starts with you, not the world. In other words, being *very happy* has a lot to do with being present in your own life, giving yourself fully and being open to each moment. "When I am authentic and I dare to show up – that's when I feel most happy," said Rachel, a researcher at the BBC. "It's not so much what I am doing, but the way I am doing it," she said, as she continued to follow her own line of inquiry.

For many of us, the *very happy* moments are about connection – connection to ourselves, connection to each other, connection to nature and connection to God. These moments are *being moments* and they have little to do with *doing* or *getting* or *chasing* or *searching*. Also, many people notice that being *very happy* has more to do with the intentions, choices and attitude that you bring to each moment rather than the "things" you hope to find in each moment. Perhaps, then, what happiness ultimately teaches you is,

> you are not here to find happiness; you are here to extend it.
> You are inspiration-packed, wisdom-infused,
> made with love and blessed with joy.
> And so is everyone else.

● ● ● ● ●

CHAPTER 6

a tale of two selves

The happiness course is an invitation to accept that the real you – what I call the Unconditioned Self – is already happy. Clearly, I appreciate that this invitation takes some explaining and that's why I've designed a course that happens over eight weeks. Most people's experience of happiness is of "wanting", "searching", and "pursuit", whereas I invite people to experience *happiness now*. How so? Well, it begins with Self-knowledge and with the realisation that *your Unconditioned Self is constantly happy, but your self-image is constantly giving you too much of a hard time for you to notice.*

Happiness requires the acceptance of but one thought – *you are perfectly made*. The way I see it, there is nothing wrong with you and there is nothing missing in you. Your original Self (the Unconditioned Self) is perfectly whole; but I understand that your self-image may choose not to see it that way. I meet many people who find the idea of a "Self" that is beautifully made to be completely unacceptable. They cannot see their "secret beauty" and this is, I believe, why they are still searching for happiness.

Happiness challenges you *to know yourself* and *to accept yourself*. Just as it is impossible to be happy and inauthentic, it is also impossible to be happy and not like yourself. Self-acceptance is the necessary baptism that allows for the blessing of unconditional happiness. Self-acceptance is all it takes to be happy without condition. And the only thing that is in the way of Self-acceptance is *the fear of Self-acceptance.*

Self-acceptance is *unacceptable* to many people because of the fear of what might happen if they were to accept themselves. I often encounter two fears in particular:

Fear #1: All Hell Will Be Let Loose. This is the fear that Self-acceptance is a guilt-free licence to be anarchic, narcissistic and unrepentant. I challenge my students, and you too, to find any evidence that this fear is true. When you treat yourself with love and respect, how strong is your urge to harm other people, to trash your neighborhood and to loot the world for all it's got? Self-acceptance has a conscience that is based on a consciousness of love – and love does not cause harm to self or other.

Fear #2: The End of Self-Improvement. This is the fear that Self-acceptance leads to complacency, stagnation and no more personal growth. I find that the people who are most afraid of Self-acceptance are the ones who have not tried it yet. As a result, their fears are based on theory, not practice. Self-acceptance is not the same as Self-resignation. On the contrary, when you are willing to accept yourself, you are more likely to want to participate, to socialise, to grow and to express your God-given talents and skills. In this sense, *Self-acceptance is the key to Self-improvement.*

My work with The Happiness Project is based on a philosophy of Self-acceptance. In *Happiness NOW!* I wrote extensively on "The #1 Happiness Formula"[1] and "The Self-Acceptance Formula",[2] which can both be summed up in this way: *until you agree to like yourself, you will not enjoy your life.* Phrased in a more positive fashion: *the more willing you are to like yourself, the more you increase your chances of being happy.* I encourage you to reread the last sentence until you can really *feel physically, emotionally and spiritually* the truth of these words. If you will do this, I believe you will uncover something in yourself – a precious jewel – that I call *the miracle of Self-acceptance.*

Simply stated, the miracle of Self-acceptance is that it literally attracts unconditional happiness into your life. Self-acceptance works in complete harmony with the Law of Attraction. Therefore, as you increase your acceptance of yourself, you let yourself accept more of the happiness, love, peace and abundance that you would like to experience. *Like attracts like.* You will attract to yourself that which you identify with. Thus, when you identify with the inherent happiness of your Unconditioned Self, you will attract experiences that are entirely compatible with how you feel about yourself.

Looking in the Mirror

To know what Self-acceptance is, you have to be willing to try it *at least once* in your life. Self-acceptance is the experience of seeing yourself as you really are, without any criticism or attack and without any demands that you should be something more, better or different. To see yourself, without any judgment or recrimination, is life-changing, because when you do this the self-image that you made disappears and in its place your original, Unconditioned Self returns.

"The Mirror Exercise" is literally the most confronting exercise we do. The exercise is done in pairs: Person A holds up a mirror in front of Person B and then Person A invites Person B to take 10 minutes to describe what he or she sees in the mirror. Logically speaking, you might not think this simple exercise would merit any strong emotional reactions, but it does. Indeed, many people find this exercise so appallingly difficult that they hyperventilate, squint, squirm, retch, cry and look away. Remember, all they've been asked to do is to describe what they see.

Pause for a moment and envision how you would respond if you put yourself in front of a mirror for 10 minutes. Better still, go find a mirror now. In the interest of research, I invite you to stand in front of a mirror and notice what you see when you look at yourself and what it feels like to do this. Notice that the mirror is not doing anything. It is not judging, criticising, mocking or distorting the image you see. It can only reflect; it does not compose. The mirror can only show you what you see.

What "The Mirror Exercise" shows so clearly is that perception is entirely personal and subjective. Hence, when you look in the mirror you may see God's holy work – or just cellulite. You may witness yourself as a divine spark of creation, or you may just see an ageing, overweight body. You could choose to see yourself as the culmination of millions of years of wondrous evolution or as someone who is not good enough. The choice is yours: cosmic pearl or split ends; radiant consciousness or sagging breasts; beautiful person or big love handles; eternal loveliness or desperate, needy single person.

Here is the tale of two selves: one self is the Unconditioned Self, which can only be seen without judgment; the other self is a self-image that is composed of all the personal judgments you make about yourself. Your self-image is your self-portrait – it is how you choose to see yourself. Your self-image is a product of your learning – it is a Learned Self, one that you have made. Your self-image is made up of what you choose to focus on – your body, your faults, your strengths, your concepts, your story, your theories and your point of view. As such, your self-image may have no likeness to or bearing on how the rest of the world sees you. In fact, it often does not.

Your self-image does not exist anywhere except in your mind. And it is changing all the time. It is, to quote Austin Powers, your "Mini-Me". It is the sum total of all your small thoughts about yourself. Even a very positive self-image is nothing compared to the Unconditioned Self that is free of all judgments, ego, personality, labels and other second-hand knowledge. Your self-image is very important, however, because it determines your psychology and therefore it influences what you believe you deserve, what you think is possible.

Your self-image is also the lens through which you see the world. Hence, you create the world in your own image. And the world literally mirrors back to you what you choose to see (or not to see) in yourself. Thus, for as long as you deny that happiness is your true nature, you will have to search for happiness somewhere else – and because you refuse to see it in yourself, you will not find it anywhere else either. You may well experience fleeting pleasures and short-lived satisfaction, but they cannot make up for the joy, the peace and the light that you overlook in yourself.

You sign yourself up for a life of mild misery, or worse, when you try to make your self-image happy instead of seeing that your Unconditioned Self is happy already. Remember, your self-image doesn't even exist anyway, except in your mind. Also, your self-image is made up of judgments, and true joy is only possible when we swap judgment for vision. Vision is what you experience when you stop projecting judgments onto something. Vision is what you experience when you give up the story for the truth and when you give up the past for what is here now.

One of the goals of the course is to help you look in the mirror and see past your self-image. If you were looking into the mirror right now, I would coach you to look at yourself without any judgment or criticism. I would then invite you to look at yourself without making any reference to your past or to the story of your life. After that, I would ask you to look at yourself only with love and appreciation. Then I would encourage you to see yourself through the eyes of love. And then to see yourself as someone who loves you sees you. And then to see yourself as a wholly loving God would see you.

**Happiness is experiencing your Self without judgment
and only with love.**

Making Yourself Unhappy

The happiness course is not a self-improvement regime that promises to magically conjure up a *new you;* it is a self-acceptance course that helps you to recover your *original you.* My work is not about *reinvention;* it is about *restoration.* I happen to think God did a great job when God created you. You are God's beautiful creation. You do not need to be *improved;* you simply need to *realise* who and what you really are.

True Self-acceptance is the realisation that the soul is joy. This joy is your spiritual DNA and it exists whether or not your self-made, self-taught self-image will let you see it. Self-acceptance and happiness correlate perfectly, as many social psychology studies have shown.[3] Conversely, for as long as you resist the idea of Self-acceptance, you will continue to make yourself unhappy. And the unhappy effects of a lack of Self-acceptance will play themselves out in a thousand ways, conscious and unconscious.

In one course, I gave the group an overnight assignment to compile a list of classic symptoms of a lack of Self-acceptance. The next morning, I suggested that we do a quick group discussion on the very worst symptoms. At that point, Michael, a London-based psychiatrist, stood up in dramatic fashion and proclaimed, "We don't need to do that. Someone has already published a list of over 1,000 tragic symptoms of a lack of self-acceptance." And with that he walked over to me and handed me a copy of the *Diagnostic and Statistical Manual of Mental Disorders.*[4] This book, *DSM* for short, is published by the American Psychiatric Association and is used by psychiatrists to diagnose people.

For now, I would like to highlight three major effects of a lack of Self-acceptance:

1. Opposition. Without Self-acceptance you will experience the world as being in opposition to you. Everything will be harder than it needs to be, there will always be struggle and the road ahead will be paved with one stumbling block after another. It will always feel like it's *you against the world.* What you are really experiencing, however, is not an unfriendly *universe,* but rather, your opposition to yourself.

Many of us have tried self-improvement, without success. The problem is that we are trying to improve upon a Self that we will not accept. And for that reason, no life makeover, no self-reinvention, no personal empowerment programme can have any real, lasting effect. *No amount of self-improvement can make up for any lack of Self-acceptance.* The problem is that we are trying too hard to overhaul our self-image instead of attempting to befriend the Unconditioned Self that is our true nature.

2. Comparison. The less you accept yourself, the more you will be tempted to compare yourself unfavourably with the 6 billion other people on the planet. For as long as you refuse to love and accept yourself, you will judge that you are not beautiful enough, successful enough, rich enough, loved enough, lucky enough, or *anything-else enough.* This relentless negative comparison is especially tragic when you also compare your weekend golf game *against* Tiger Woods, your love life *against* Angelina Jolie, your home entertaining skills *against* Martha Stewart and your singing in the shower *against* the heavenly voice of Andrea Bocelli.

It gets even worse when you also negatively compare yourself to people who don't even exist. For example, comparing your lifestyle against that of Monica, Chandler, Rachel, Joey, Phoebe and Ross of *Friends,* or comparing the way you look to the cover photograph of a supermodel who has been cosmetically made up, studio-lit, airbrushed, and digitally enhanced. Even the actress Keira Knightley was not beautiful enough, according to the advertising execs working for Chanel, who decided to graphically enhance her breasts.[5] The same enhancement was done to a picture of 17-year-old actress Emma Watson, who was playing 15-year-old Hermione Granger in *Harry Potter and the Order of the Phoenix.*[6]

Happiness researchers have now amassed a huge amount of empirical evidence that reveals a mostly high correlation between happiness and Self-acceptance. People who can look in the mirror and say, "I love and accept myself" – *and really mean it* – are also more likely to agree with statements such as "I like my life," "I enjoy my work," and "My friends love me."[7] Most interestingly, people who see themselves in a positive light *see others the same way too.* Self-acceptance is not competitive or attacking – it is born of a consciousness of love, not fear.

3. Rejection. You will live in constant fear of rejection for as long as you are unwilling to accept yourself. Why? Because you are already rejecting yourself and the pain of that is bad enough. No one really rejects you, but you will interpret it that way when they don't phone first, when they don't return your e-mail, when they are tired, when they don't smile much, when they are having a bad day and when they don't read your mind. Your lack of Self-acceptance makes everyone's treatment of you seem slightly disappointing in the long run.

Your lack of Self-acceptance is what also causes you to reject too much happiness, too much love and too much of a good thing. Whenever you are very happy, you have to either a) overlook, dismiss or sabotage the happiness or b) change your mind about how much happiness you are really worthy of. Everyone has his or her own "personal allowance" when it comes to happiness and the more willing you are to accept yourself, the more happiness you will let yourself accept.

Limiting Your Happiness

Self-acceptance is about being honest with yourself. It is the ability to hold up a mirror and see the original truth of who you are, as opposed to learned self-judgments. Thus, one gift of Self-acceptance is that it improves your awareness of your true self (the Unconditioned Self), which, in turn, helps you to be more authentic and fully integrated with yourself. Another gift of Self-acceptance is *accountability* – the willingness to accept the part you play in your life and in your happiness.

One of the most revealing assignments we do in the course is called "Limiting Happiness". I invite you to try this exercise now. The objective is to compile a list of five ways you are currently limiting your own happiness. As I introduce this exercise to the group, almost everyone smiles or laughs in that "busted" sort of way, as we do when we know that it's time to stop looking good and start being honest. The unspoken question is, "Okay, how dirty are we allowed to get here?" I encourage them – and you – to let it all hang out.

What's so revealing about this exercise is that no one has any difficulty coming up with at least five ways they limit being happy. In the last course, one person jotted down 22 ways without breaking stride. "I could go on," she said. What the "Limiting Happiness" inquiry reveals is a basic dilemma, that is,

**everyone wants happiness and everyone would like to be happier,
and everyone is aware that they limit their own happiness.**

The "Limiting Happiness" exercise is designed to help you hold a mirror up to yourself and to take full accountability for the part you play in how much (or how little) happiness you are currently experiencing. You can blame the economy, your kids, the calories, the government and God all you like, but *if you are ever tempted to blame anyone for your lack of happiness you would do well to look in the mirror first.* Being accountable for your happiness, or lack of it, is an important step in attracting more happiness.

So what are the ways we limit our happiness? Honestly, if I wrote them all out now this book would end up too heavy for you to lift. So, instead, I will give you the digest version. Below are nine excerpts from different people's "Limiting Happiness" lists. They represent nine popular methods of self-deprivation. Notice if any fit with your own preferred ways.

Self-Criticism. "When I look in the mirror I see a droopy bottom, a spare tyre and Caesarean scars. My two-year-old daughter looks at me and thinks I'm the coolest mum on the planet. I have to believe she is right, but sometimes I just don't let myself see what she sees." – Jane, mother of two

Self-Neglect. "When I look in the mirror I struggle to even see myself. The way I limit my happiness is by trying to make everyone else happy first. Inevitably I end up unhappy and then I usually upset the people I love the most." – Terry, nurse

Self-Deception. "My whole life I have looked to others for a sense of value and okay-ness. *I'm okay if you're okay with me. I'm great if you think I'm great. I'm a shit, if that's what you think.* I often lose myself in my work and in my relationships." – Jo, actor

Self-Centredness. "I'm always looking in the mirror. I need to put the mirror away. I forget that life isn't all about me. I get caught up in so much petty stuff. I'm hypersensitive. I forget to take myself lightly." – Chris, actor

Self-Alienated. "I spend a lot of time *by myself,* but not *with myself.* I lose myself in stuff. I can't always name what I really feel or really think. I don't even feel that real to myself. I guess I should hang out with me more." – Ross, musician

Self-Doubt. "I'm always anxious and I don't handle it well. I even get anxious when I feel happy and that limits my enjoyment of things. I usually don't tell people how anxious I am and that makes it worse." – Angela, journalist

Self-Exhaustion. "I definitely pursue happiness. My schedule is always packed. I always overcommit. I'm always ahead of myself. I forget to stop. I'm always on to the next thing." – Dan, restaurateur

Self-Control. "I build walls around myself. I call them invisible walls, but everyone tells me that they can see them. I'm way too self-controlled. I'm way too independent. I don't like vulnerability." – Tom, entrepreneur

Self-Negating. "When I'm low, it's like I wipe myself out. I edit myself. I make myself invisible. I forget to participate. And it's like I'm not even in my own life." – Mike, accountant

What the "Limiting Happiness" inquiry reveals is the need for each of us to treat ourselves with honesty and compassion. Honesty helps you to connect more consciously with your Unconditioned Self and with your natural joy. Compassion helps you to manage your relationship with your self-image, which is potentially the most difficult relationship in your life. When you treat yourself better, your life gets better.

CHAPTER 7

fear
of
unhappiness

People are often very happy to know that I feel unhappy from time to time. They like to know that I regularly meet up with self-doubt, grief, shyness, anger and other "guests" from the dark side. I try not to take this too personally. I understand where they are coming from. In class, I notice that when I self-disclose about, for instance, my father's death, personal setbacks and my "Basil Fawlty moments", everyone moves to the edge of their seat. Why? Because as much as we want to learn how to be happy, we also want to learn how to heal our unhappiness.

Fact: *happy people are unhappy from time to time.* The term "happy people", commonly used by happiness researchers and the media, is a misleading term if you take it to mean "people who never experience unhappiness". Where are these permanently happy people? Have you ever met a person who has not experienced *any* fear, grief or anger? Happiness researchers acknowledge that "even the happiest people, the top 10 per cent in happiness, have moods that go up and down".[1] The term "happy people" does not mean, then, people who experience no unhappiness.

In interviews, I am often asked if I am a happy person. Indeed, if I had a dollar for every time I had been asked that question, I would have nearly $150 by now. Anyway, I normally give two answers to the question "Are you a happy person?" My first answer is, "My soul (a.k.a. my Unconditioned Self) is always joyful, and my ego (a.k.a. my self-image) is occasionally happy." I understand that this answer is a bit metaphysical, but it is honestly how I feel. My *being* is entirely happy and my personality is mostly neurotic.

My other answer to the question "Are you a happy person?" is not at all metaphysical and is easier to relate to. What I say is that since I began running The Happiness Project, I am clearer on what happiness is and I do *let myself* enjoy more *happiness now,* rather than limit or defer it. Even more importantly, though, I have also learned how to face my unhappiness in a more honest, open and effective way. For me, the greatest gift of my happiness inquiry has been that it has taught me how to heal unhappiness. And, thereby, I am genuinely happier.

The goal of the course is not to help you think only "happy thoughts". I can't offer you an emotional lobotomy; what I do offer is a way to experience greater emotional freedom. And by that, I mean experiencing all the emotions (including happiness and unhappiness) without fear, guilt, judgment or self-harm. Essentially put, I don't think happiness can be defined simply as "the absence of sadness". I think happiness is much more than just the absence of something.

> **Happiness is not the absence of sadness;**
> **happiness is the capacity to face sadness –**
> **and to face it with love, not fear.**

I have a question for you: *If you were offered a pill to take once a day that would make you feel permanently happy – would you take it?* I want a straight "Yes" or "No" from you. No e-mails. No phoning a friend for help. This is not *Who Wants to Be a Millionaire?* Just "Yes" or "No." It's a no-brainer, isn't it? Think about your answer and also your reasons for your answer. Also, before I tell you, take a guess as to what most people's answer is to this "Synthetic Happiness" proposition. Percentagewise, how many people do you think vote "Yes" or vote "No"?

In the most recent course, the results for the "Synthetic Happiness" proposition were: 25 per cent "Yes, I'll take it" and 75 per cent "No, thank you." This is exactly the same result as a national opinion poll conducted on the BBC's *The Happiness Formula* television series in which one thousand members of the public were also offered the "happy pill".[2] It seems that most people don't want the sort of happiness that blocks out the unhappy side of life. But why not? Below is a mix of answers – humorous, paranoid, insightful and revealing – that represent my students' responses:

"All experience has value, including unhappiness. I want to learn from everything I feel."

"Honestly, I'd miss the dark side. I want to accept all of me, not just the shiny, happy bits."

"I would rather be able to *feel* all of my emotions and be *honest* about them."

"I want to learn how to experience everything and be happy."

"The truth is that I know *happiness is a choice* – so maybe I could just look at the pill each day to remind me!"

Facing the Unhappiness

If the happiness course is really going to work for you, you have to bring *all of you* to the course and not just your pleasant parts. For that reason, I encourage every group to set a number of ground rules. These ground rules represent the conscious agreement on and commitment to how we would *like to be* together. They are a way of creating a culture and an environment in which each of us feels welcome, respected and safe.

The ground rules consist of a number of "dos" and "don'ts" – each designed to encourage you to bring your whole self to the course. I won't list them all here, but I will mention three of the "don'ts": 1) Don't look good, be real; 2) Don't be positive, be honest; and 3) Don't be nice, be yourself. Over the eight weeks, you get into many conversations, any one of which has the potential to enrich your life for evermore. It's imperative, therefore, that you feel you can participate fully. Your capacity to be honest is what helps to reveal a deeper truth, about both happiness and unhappiness.

Happiness is a most confronting inquiry because it challenges you to be honest about everything, including unhappiness. The truth is, *you can't be truly happy and be dishonest about your unhappiness.* Everyone who comes to the course has to face unhappiness eventually – even the most positive ones. It happened in dramatic fashion to Dawn, who was one of the three volunteers in the course that was filmed for the BBC *QED* documentary "How to Be Happy."[3]

In an interview for a magazine, Dawn explained how she first encountered the happiness course. She said, "I had what you could call an unhappy childhood, traumatic and brutal. I launched into adulthood in a gung-ho, chaotic way and by the age of 24 I had a failed marriage, two children and no job. I moved 15 times over the next few years in an effort to *find happiness*. One day, one incredible day, while I was working as a private investigator, I saw a BBC advertisement asking for people who wanted to be happy. I applied and to my utter amazement was accepted, along with two other volunteers."

When Dawn first showed up, she was optimistic it would work for her. "I approached the course expecting to meet some guy called Dr Robert Holden who was going to make me happy," said Dawn, in the same article. In week four, Dawn sent a fax to the producers saying she didn't want to continue. "Robert's approach to happiness was to blow my mind completely," said Dawn. "During the filming of the series I rebelled at almost every stage, as I wasn't ready to face my unhappiness and let it go. My unhappiness was all I had – it was my identity."

Dawn, the private investigator, wanted to be happier without investigating any of the unhappiness she had kept so private. I met up with Dawn the day after she had faxed her resignation. At our meeting, I gave Dawn an ultimatum: a choice between *hope* and *fear*. I told her that if she faced her unhappiness she would improve her chances of being truly happy, but that if she continued to mask her unhappiness, she would be on the run from herself for the rest of her life, afraid to feel anything, *even happiness*. Dawn made the courageous choice: She chose hope and she chose to face her unhappiness.

By the end of the course, Dawn had made some huge strides. She summed up her experience for the camera by saying, "When I first began the programme in January, I thought it was just going to be a huge hoot and it became hugely serious. And I wasn't expecting that at all . . . I thought it was just going to be a laugh and it became a life-changer." The seeds were sown and over the next few years Dawn continued her private investigation of her happiness and her unhappiness. A few years later Dawn enrolled to take the course again. Her transformation was obvious to all who know her.

What I like most about Dawn's story is the part I haven't told you yet. Dawn's life began to change for the better the moment she became more honest with herself. She faced her fears, her wounds and her unhappy past, and with the steadfast support of her husband and children, she made many life-affirming changes. One of those changes was to train as a mental health recovery worker. Also, Dawn set up a national campaign to support people who have experienced bullying.[4] I know, as does Dawn, that all the help she is now able to give to others is a result of her willingness to face her unhappiness. *Dawn's healing is, literally, her gift to others.*

So how did Dawn face her unhappiness? Clearly, she did so by her own courage and also with a lot of loving support from her family. For my part, what I coached Dawn to do is no different from what I would coach you to do if you attended. To sum it up, I helped Dawn to face her unhappiness by helping her to undo three basic mistakes – mistakes that make unhappiness more painful and more frightening than need be. The three mistakes are:

Mistake #1: Misidentification. If you were to break your arm, would you introduce yourself to people as "a broken-arm person"? Would you say, "I am a broken arm"? And after your arm had healed, would you refer to yourself as "an ex-broken-arm person"? Would you think of yourself as "an ex-breakage"? Most people wouldn't dream of doing so and yet they wouldn't give a second thought to saying, "*I am* sad" and "*I am* anorexic" and "*I am* an ex-addict" or to describing themselves as "a divorcée" or "a widow".

The problem with unhappiness is not that we experience unhappy feelings; it's that we identify with the feelings. We describe ourselves as an emotional state. Literally, we say, "I am sad" and "I am depressed" and "I am angry." In doing so, we lose our identity *and* we lose our objectivity. Instead of noticing the experience of anger ("I am experiencing anger") and choosing a healthy response, we blast off ("I am angry") and we act out an emotion instead of being who we really are. Emotions are something you experience; they are not who you are.

It is the same with wounds and traumas. Dawn identified so strongly with her unhappy childhood that she started to think of herself as an unhappy person and as a victim. Over time, Dawn's unhappy feelings were so familiar to her that they became a central part of her story about herself. I encouraged Dawn to be honest about her unhappy experiences *and also* to be clear that these events in no way define who she is. They are experiences, not a nametag.

When physicians and psychologists attend my Coaching Happiness certification programme,[5] I encourage them to drop the practice of calling their clients by their diagnoses. For example, "The heart attack in bed number 9" and "The A.D.D. booked for 3 P.M." So much pain is caused by mistaken identity. If you are going to let go of the pain your personality has experienced and truly embrace again the unconditional happiness of your soul, you have to be willing to face your unhappiness and say, "This is what I have experienced, but it is not who I am."

Mistake #2: Judging. Many people who attend the course do not tell their best friends or family members that they are doing the course. Why? Because they feel that they "should" be happy and that they "shouldn't" need any help being happy. If you follow this train of thought further, clearly you should be happy all the time, and you should feel sexy all the time, and be confident all the time, and be enjoying peak experiences all the time. Just like everyone else does, right?

Facing unhappiness is made more difficult by the judgments you keep about unhappiness. When you judge anything, you manufacture copious amounts of shame. Judgment creates shame. And the more you judge unhappiness as wrong, bad and negative, the more ashamed and unhappy you will feel. Childhood messages like "Good girls don't cry" don't help, of course. But that was then and this is now. And no one condemns us more for the unhappiness we feel than we do. Indeed, it is often the case that the worse we feel, the worse we treat ourselves.

Unhappiness is not a sin – it is an opportunity to be truthful and to heal. Shame is a defence against feeling bad that actually makes you feel even worse. You can't be truly happy and be dishonest about unhappiness. Similarly, you can't be free and hold on to secrets. A necessary starting point, then, is to accept the feelings rather than judge them. In other words, you have to accept that *there are no negative emotions*. Pain, suffering, guilt and other forms of unhappiness are not implicitly negative – but they can have negative effects, especially if you handle them in negative (that is, unhealthy) ways.

Mistake #3: Resistance. Have you noticed that unhappiness becomes more painful the more you try to resist it? Resisting unhappiness pushes happiness further away. There are plenty of ways to resist unhappiness: You can discard your "negative friends", switch off the television news, keep yourself permanently busy and chant another abundance mantra. However, you need to know that resisting unhappiness can only, at best, make you feel numb and not truly happy.

Emotions like fear, guilt and anger are "guests" that have visited every person who has ever walked the earth – including Jesus, Buddha and Mohammed. No one has ever lived a life without a visit from these "guests". If your chief strategy for happiness is simply to avoid feeling unhappy, you need to know that the odds of you experiencing "no unhappiness" are roughly the same as your odds of "not dying".

To be truly happy, you have to be willing to face unhappiness. Similarly, to be a truly loving person, you have to be willing to face fear. And, to be truly successful, you have to be willing to face failure. I am not saying that you have to *like* unhappiness; what I am saying is that you have to learn how to be *less afraid* of unhappiness. When you stop resisting unhappiness, you can remove the blocks to happiness. Less resistance equals more happiness.

Interviewing the Emotions

The session on "Interviewing the Emotions" is a powerful turning point for many people. To help prepare you for this session, Avril Carson and one other team member recite a poem. The poem is recited twice so that you can listen to it once with your head and once with your heart. The poem we use most often was written by the Sufi poet Jelaluddin Rumi and translated by Coleman Barks. It is entitled "The Guest House". I am most grateful to Coleman for granting me permission to print the poem in full here. I encourage you to read it now, twice.

The Guest House
This being human is a guest house.
Every morning a new arrival.
A joy, a depression, a meanness,
some momentary awareness comes
as an unexpected visitor.
Welcome and entertain them all!
Even if they are a crowd of sorrows,
who violently sweep your house
empty of its furniture,
still treat each guest honourably.
He may be clearing you out for some new delight.
The dark thought, the shame, the malice,
meet them at the door laughing,
and invite them in.
Be grateful for whoever comes,
because each has been sent
as a guide from beyond.[6]

"The Guest House" represents beautifully the spirit of the "Interviewing the Emotions" inquiry, which is essentially a four-step process for helping you to face unhappiness and choose love, face unhappiness and choose joy, face unhappiness and choose peace. I will introduce you now to the four steps. I also invite you to be mindful of any unhappiness or conflict or challenge you are currently facing as you read on. Bring your whole self to this emotional healing process.

Step #1: Meeting the Feeling. "Every morning a new arrival." How true. In every moment, a new guest arrives and an old guest leaves. Moods come and go and when we mistake joy (our spiritual DNA) for our moods (pleasure and satisfaction), we think that joy comes and goes too. However, true happiness cannot and does not leave its source. I find it interesting, though, that when I wake up in the morning and meet joy, I notice a fear arise that joy will be gone by lunchtime; but when I wake up in the morning and meet depression or sadness, I notice a fear arise that this guest will stay forever!

Your job is to be a "host" to the "guests" you encounter, both mental and emotional. And like any good host, your task is to "welcome and entertain them all". In other words, you have to accept the "guests" as they are, rather than try to change them, reframe them, resist them or lock them out. You wouldn't like it if a host did that to you, and emotions don't like it either. When you resist an emotion, the emotion acts up. It behaves in the way it is treated. The more fear you project onto an emotion, the more it acts out its "bad reputation", and then a drama unfolds.

As a true host, you have the task of meeting each "guest" with an open heart. And as you meet each emotion or thought with an open heart, it will speak its truth and the truth will be revealed. No fight; just communication. But here is the real miracle and I call it a miracle because I can't fully explain it: When you accept and welcome a fear or some pain with an open heart, and without any resistance, it usually leaves without fuss. And if it still stays, you can talk to it, peacefully. And you can interview it and you get to know why it has come to visit you.

Step #2: Naming the Lesson. Have you ever wondered what the purpose of unhappiness is? When an emotion like anger, fear or guilt arrives at your door with a "bad reputation", the last thing you feel like doing is getting to know the feeling. However, in this second step of "Interviewing the Emotions" your goal is to get to know your "guest". And you can only get to know your "guest" if you are willing to let go of the "bad reputation". In other words, you have to get past the story and go for the truth.

"The greatest happiness is to know the source of unhappiness," wrote Fyodor Dostoyevsky, the Russian novelist. The unwillingness to learn what is causing your suffering is what causes you to suffer further. The cycle of suffering, resistance and more suffering can only end when you summon up the courage to meet the feeling and learn why it exists, why it is here and what it really wants to say to you. Here are some examples of why your "guests" may have paid you a visit:

Fear – wants you to know you are being way too independent and not trusting enough in life, God or others to help you.

Anger – is trying to tell you that you keep giving your power away inappropriately in certain situations.

Stress – is an invitation to change something. You are being asked to make better, smarter choices.

Resentment – wants you to see that you are in sacrifice, playing the role of martyr and leaving yourself out of your life.

Guilt – is a sign that that you are out of integrity with yourself and that it's time to be as God created you.

Exhaustion – is a message that there is a better way. It wants you to listen to your wisdom.

Envy – is a siren that says, "For God's sake, when are you going to see how beautiful you are?"

Depression – is a call for love. It wants you to know that you need to love yourself and accept more love from others.

Wounds – are invitations to practise forgiveness so that you can set yourself free again.

Grief – wants you to give yourself the gift of your own attention and to make sure you don't lose sight of what is really true.

Pain – is a reminder to be true to yourself, to remember who you are and to stick to your true purpose.

Anxiety – is a call for help. It is asking you to be open to more help from everyone and everywhere.

Emotions are messengers. They carry information. They are like internal memos. Sometimes the information in the message is accurate and sometimes not. "Be grateful for whoever comes, because each has been sent as a guide from beyond," says Rumi. Other times, the message is not accurate and it can simply be discarded. In other words, not all your fears are true. The key is being open to receiving the message and *then* deciding if it is helpful and true or not.

Step #3: Accepting the Gift. Sometimes the "guests" disrupt what is familiar to you and what you identify with: for example, "my life", "my career", "my relationship". "Even if they are a crowd of sorrows, / who violently sweep your house empty of its furniture, / still treat each guest honourably. / He may be clearing you out for some new delight," says Rumi. But it's a common feeling to want things to get better *while hoping that nothing changes too much.* Better the devil you know.

Sometimes the best gifts in life come badly wrapped. The trick is not to let the wrapping put you off. Some "guests" arrive with a message that says "It's time to let go" and "It's time to move on." When Dawn finally stopped and faced her unhappiness, she *really* moved on with her life. In her interview Dawn said, "I had been so unhappy for so long. So I kept moving. Fifteen times! And each time the unhappiness came back. With Robert's help, I stopped running and I finally understood that what I had to do was not to change my home, but to change my mind about me."

"What is the gift here?" That is a good question to ask yourself when you meet a "guest" like fear, pain, anger or sadness. Asking the question helps you to be less defensive and more receptive to what is before you. And, again, the miracle happens: Either the "guest" leaves, because there is no resistance, or the guest leaves a gift. "Our deepest fears are like dragons guarding our deepest treasures," wrote the poet Rainer Maria Rilke.[7] The gift is in the acceptance. It is in choosing love instead of fear. In essence,

**the gift of facing your unhappiness is
the chance to be happier.**

Step #4: Asking for Help. The fourth and final step in "Interviewing the Emotions" is to be willing to receive ongoing help with being honest and open about any unhappiness you meet. With every big challenge that you face, you may be tempted to think that you are beyond help. This thought of "being beyond help" is very frightening, but it too must be met with absolute openness to see if it is true or if it is just a fear. Remember, when you are honest and open, the truth arrives with all the help you need.

On one level, each unhappiness is a message "to accept extra help". My favourite mantra, which I share in all my seminars, whether I am talking about happiness, success, love or abundance, is, "If you are alive, you need help."[8] There's no real shame in asking for help; only strength and power and the chance for greater happiness. Unhappiness disappears into the truth. And the truth is that you are not meant to do your life on your own. That's what unhappiness is really trying to teach you.

●　●　●　●　●

CHAPTER 8

follow
your
joy

I normally conclude the first workshop of the happiness course with a session called "Follow Your Joy". The centrepiece of this session is our first major meditation, simply entitled "Joy", and it features the soul-stirring music of pianist and composer Robert Norton.[1]

Robert Norton took the course in London in 1997. He has been our resident musician and team member ever since. Robert is an accomplished musician who has performed in world-class arenas like the Royal Albert Hall and supported talented artists such as soul singer Barry White. His ability to improvise and play the keyboards so intuitively and so sensitively brings an extra dimension of grace and reality to all the major meditations we do.

Robert's presence and playing help to make every course a truly creative journey. As well as accompanying the major meditations, Robert also introduces the session after lunch. This intro is known unofficially as "The Robert Norton Experience", and Robert has free rein to energise and entertain the group with creative exercises that use music, percussion, movement, spontaneity and voice. Robert has published several albums over the years that feature his live performances in the course. I am listening to one of those albums now as I write these words, and the album is called *Follow Your Joy*.[2]

The "Joy" meditation lasts approximately 20 minutes and it has three main parts to it. This meditation is essentially an attunement, *not* an invocation. The point is, you are not inviting joy to arrive from someplace else or from some other heaven that is far away from here, but tuning in to ever-present joy, tuning in to your Unconditioned Self and tuning in to the spiritual DNA of your being. So, part one is attuning. It's like finding an "inner smile" in your heart. It is sensing the tingle of aliveness in every cell of your body. It is enjoying the spaces in your mind that are empty of psychology and ego and doubt.

Next, in part two, I invite you to appreciate the essential qualities of joy. Joy is so much more than just an idea, a feeling or a thought. While Robert Norton continues to play his sublime music, I encourage you to move beyond the word *joy* and to let yourself have a direct experience of the full force and power of what joy really is. With each inhalation, you breathe in the aliveness, the sparkle, the creativity and the sense of possibility that exists in joy. The goal is to enjoy the innate intelligence of joy, and also its peacefulness, and its wholeness, and its loveliness.

Finally, in part three, I encourage you to acknowledge when, where and with whom you allow your joy to express itself. Is it at work? Is it at home? Is it with the kids? Is it when you go jogging? Is it when you meditate? Is it when you are in nature? I then encourage you to welcome joy even more into every part of your life and to let joy inspire and guide you, direct and navigate you. Essentially, I am inviting you to commit to joy, to follow your joy and to bring joy with you into your day, your work and your life. Let joy lead the way.

After the "Joy" meditation you receive an official "Certificate of Joy", which has your name printed on it. The words at the top read "Follow My Joy". Underneath, it reads, for example, "I, Robert Holden, do hereby commit to ___." The idea is to make a specific commitment to following your joy for the duration of the course (or, in your case, for the duration of reading this book). At the end of the session, we make a copy of your "Certificate of Joy", and halfway through the course we mail it out to you, as encouragement to keep following your joy.

Before you fill out your "Certificate of Joy", the group explores what "follow your joy" means personally. The words "follow your joy" sound so good. They are lyrical, evocative, hopeful and inspiring. But what would an increased commitment to following your joy actually look like in *your* life, *your* work and *your* relationships? To help you in your inquiry, I devote the rest of this chapter to sharing with you four creative exercises that have helped me and my students to *follow our joy.*

The Spiritual Front Page

Following your joy has a deeply spiritual meaning for many people who interpret the function of joy as *helping you to focus on the essential truth of your life.* Joy is what helps you to discern truth from illusion, busyness from purpose and love from fear. Joy helps you to keep that which is most important to you on the front page of your awareness and on the front page of your life.

When I meet up with friends whom I haven't seen for a while, I ask them to tell me about their "spiritual headlines". In other words, I ask them to share their real news, not just the small talk. I want to hear about what is most important to them in their lives right now. I want to know what is meaningful and current. I want to hear about what is challenging and delightful. Sharing our "spiritual front pages" with each other makes for rich conversation and true intimacy. It helps us to let each other in on our real lives, so that we live and grow together in spite of the distance that appears to exist between us.

"The Spiritual Front Page" is a simple metaphor that can also be used as a daily spiritual practice to help you follow your joy. The idea is that each morning you take some quiet time to create your own page for the day. You can do this as a creative visualisation, or you can do it literally, with a pen and a blank piece of paper. First, you take a deep breath and clear your mind. Next, you tune in to what is most important in your life right now and what (and who) needs your best energy, time and attention. And then you draw (literally or, in your mind's eye) your Spiritual Front Page.

The design of your Spiritual Front Page is entirely your own. It is *your news,* after all. You may find you write a headline like "Slow Down and Enjoy My Day" or "Stay in My Power" or "Commit to the Yoga Class" or "Speak My Truth" or "Make Time to Meditate". Alternatively, you may get a picture of someone whom you absolutely need to connect with. The purpose of "The Spiritual Front Page" is to help you connect with your wisdom. And it only takes five minutes, which is about the same amount of time as it takes to read the headlines in the daily newspaper.

If you really want to go for it, the lead article of your Spiritual Front Page could be a personal interview with God. In other words, you could imagine that you have interviewed God on a big subject like happiness, your love life, the purpose of your life, or weight-loss tips, for instance. Talk to God and write down the main points of your conversation on your Spiritual Front Page. Connect to wisdom, connect to the truth and then go about your day.

Like most spiritual practices, "The Spiritual Front Page" becomes even more valuable the more you do it. I encourage everyone who takes the happiness course to adopt a daily spiritual practice – yoga, prayer, meditation, tai-chi – because spiritual practices help you to discern truth from illusion and they also help you to follow your joy.

The Heart Experiment

To *follow your joy* often conjures up thoughts like *to live with heart,* and *to be more loving,* and *to choose love over fear.*

"The Heart Experiment" is a daily exercise that supports your intention to be more heart-centred in everything you do. The goal is to live with a conscious heart and to bring your heart with you wherever you go – be it the boardroom, the ball game, the nail salon, the bedroom, your mother-in-law's or the local deli. Just imagine for a moment how rich and how wonderful your life could be if you made it your intention to be even more heart-centred – starting now.

"The Heart Experiment" is based on the profound realisation that *the heart is always open.* In truth, the heart is never closed and the heart is always open for business. You have the free will to turn away from your heart, but your heart cannot turn itself away from you. Your ego can desert your heart, but your heart cannot leave you. Thus, the enduring qualities of the heart – such as love, wisdom, courage, strength and hope – are available to you the instant you make yourself available to them.

"The Heart Experiment" encourages you to think with your heart. Your heart is the seat of wisdom; love is intelligent; and joy knows the truth of things. In the wonderful ballad "I Forgot That Love Existed", Van Morrison sings this beautiful lyric: "If my heart could do my thinking / And my head began to feel / I would look upon the world anew / And know what's truly real."[3] The heart can see further than the eyes. It can see the truth behind appearances. It knows what you should do in each and every situation you find yourself in. When you trust your heart, you find your true power.

The goal of "The Heart Experiment" is to connect with the voice of your heart. It is to interview your heart and to ask yourself regularly, *What does my heart say?* The goal is also to make it your conscious intention to *listen with the heart* and to *speak from the heart.* Thus all of your interactions will become more honest, more authentic and naturally more heartfelt. What could be more wonderful, unless you prefer to stay defended, cut off, lonely, safe, strategic and only half alive?

By helping you to live from your heart, "The Heart Experiment" is helping you to *follow your joy.* When I share the guidelines for this exercise I suggest that a great starting point is to meditate on the following words of Dr Matthew Anderson: "There is a prayer that lives at the centre of your heart. If you pray it, it will change your life. How does it begin?"[4] I recommend that you pause now, before reading on and listen to what your heart wants to say to you.

The Vow of Kindness

Many people take the words *follow your joy* to mean being kind, having compassion, treating everyone with respect. Kindness, both to self and to others, is a most beautiful doctrine, but it doesn't really mean anything or benefit anyone until you are willing to put it into practice. When you take a vow of kindness, and really mean it, even if only by half of one per cent, you will experience more love and more joy than your ego knows what to do with.

"The Vow of Kindness" is based on an intention to practise greater kindness, both to yourself and to others, for the duration of the eight-week course. The starting point is to reflect on how kind you are now. For example, is kindness a conscious priority for you? Most of my students agree with the statement "Kindness to self and to others is a vital key to enjoying greater love and happiness." But when I ask them to score how kind they are – based on a scale of "very", "quite", "not very", and "not at all" – most vote "quite" for *kindness to others* and "not very" for *kindness to self.*

The first step for "The Vow of Kindness" is to reflect on self-kindness. For eight weeks, I watch my students closely. I see how they treat themselves and I see how they treat others. There is no difference, really. What I also notice is how unconscious we are about how unkind we are to ourselves. In fact, most of us barely notice how we routinely deprive ourselves of happiness and how mean we are to ourselves. *Life is hard because you are so hard on yourself.* It gets easier, for you and everyone else, when you decide to be kind.

When I introduce "The Vow of Kindness", I share a metaphor about "dropping the knife". I learned about this from Daniel Ladinsky, the translator of poems by the 14th-century Sufi poet Hafiz. Daniel writes: "Once, a young woman asked Hafiz, 'What is the sign of someone knowing God?' Hafiz remained silent for a few moments and looked deep into the young person's eyes, then said, 'Dear, they have dropped the knife. They have dropped the cruel knife most so often use upon their tender self and others.'"[5]

Daniel adds a comment of his own to this story. He says, "One's joy, one's creative potential – is the ability to no longer harm oneself and others physically, mentally, emotionally, spiritually." Kindness to yourself and to others is really the same thing. And the capacity for one determines the capacity for both. To follow your joy, you have to be willing to give up your lack of self-kindness, the habitual self-criticism and the fruitless self-attack.

"The Vow of Kindness" works best when you create a shortlist of one, two or three ways to practise greater kindness. A long list rarely works. Here are some examples of what my students say when they vow to practise greater kindness:

"I will be less self-critical and I will celebrate my successes more."

"I will be more open and accepting of people's offers of love and help."

"I will stop pushing myself so hard and I will go out to play more."

"I will appreciate the real me more and I will smile when I catch myself comparing myself negatively with others."

"I will be more compassionate with myself when I don't feel positive and strong."

"I will be kind to the child in me that sometimes feels frightened by the world."

The Wellbeing Pledge

Following your joy for many people means reclaiming a sense of wholeness and making a greater commitment to personal well-being.

"The Wellbeing Pledge" is an invitation to let your wellbeing flourish and prosper over the eight weeks of the course. It harnesses all of your good intentions, plus the support of the group, in making a personal investment in yourself that will pay great dividends in optimal health and vitality. Eight weeks is just right – not too long, not too short – for making a sustained commitment to a positive change. Also, each time the group meets, we review your progress, celebrate the gains, address any blocks and recommit to *following your joy.*

I always emphasise that "The Wellbeing Pledge" is not about good behaviour and it is not something that you *should, must* or *ought to* do. It is about the joy of doing it and the joy you experience because you have done it. Essentially, it is about self-care and self-love. The goal is to make five positive commitments to your personal wellbeing. The first commitment is to your physical wellbeing, the second is to your emotional wellbeing, the third is to your mental wellbeing and the fourth is to your spiritual wellbeing. And, of course, that leaves just one more commitment.

The fifth commitment is an extra commitment for your "blind spot". In my experience most people neglect one of the four essential dimensions of personal wellbeing. For example, you may be emotionally intelligent, enjoy good mental health and read Sufi poetry, but you neglect your body and your body tries to let you know about this. Or, you may be physically fit, mentally strong and spiritually okay, but your love life is always a mess because you're not sufficiently in touch with your heart.

Wellbeing requires harmony between the parts. Therefore, you can't enjoy maximal wellbeing *and* have a blind spot. A good analogy would be to think of the four dimensions of wellbeing (physical, emotional, mental and spiritual) as four wheels of a car. Even if the car is a Ferrari or a Bentley, it still isn't going to get you very far if one of the tyres is flat. The other three tyres may be in perfect working order, but the car still won't get you to the highway.

You can try to self-diagnose your blind spot, if you like. However, I would recommend that you ask your partner, a friend, a boss or your children to give you *their* assessment. I believe others know us much better than we usually give them credit for. The four essential dimensions of wellbeing are so interlinked that what might look like a physical blindspot may really be symptomatic of an emotional block like, for example, the feeling that *I'm not worth it.*

Think about your own Wellbeing Pledge now. Identify the five commitments you would like to make, starting from now, so as to enjoy increased vitality and wellbeing. Even the "small" commitments can have a "big" effect. To help you make your five commitments, I have picked some examples from literally hundreds of pledges made by my students over the years. Again, I want to reiterate that this exercise is really about *following your joy.* The best mental approach to this exercise, therefore, is to have fun.

Physical Wellbeing. Tune in to your body and notice how it is feeling. What are the messages your body is sending you right now? Look for the internal memos that are trying to point out some tension or tiredness. In your mind, ask your body what it needs from you in order to serve you well. Let your body tell you what one commitment it needs from you to help you feel more grounded, strong and energised. Listen to your body, then act. Here are some examples:

1) Sleep: an extra hour in bed each night. It's hard to be happy, nice, spiritual and sleep-deprived. 2) Breathe: your breath reflects your consciousness. Fast and shallow breathing is the norm in a manic and busy culture. Take deep breaths and insert genuine breathing spaces into your schedule. 3) Eat well: look in your refrigerator and notice what it tells you about how well you are looking after yourself physically. 4) Exercise: sweat your body every day by doing something fun and energising like dance, gardening, running, or yoga. 5) Treats: feed your body with healthy treats like smoothies, massages and healthy amounts of the best organic chocolate.

Emotional Wellbeing. Your heart is the centre of your emotional wellbeing. Put your hand over your heart and really feel all the way into your heart right now. Notice what your heart wants to say to you. Notice any emotions you feel as you listen to your heart. And let your heart tell you what one commitment it needs from you at present in order to help you feel even more centred, free and loving. Again, listen and act. Here are some examples:

1) Me Time: What you think of as emotional resilience may be emotional dishonesty. The goal of your life is not to be tough, it is to be truthful. Make time to be honest with yourself about how you are really feeling. 2) Friend Time: make sure you are not one of those people who has "really great friends" you never see. 3) Fun Time: the work is never really done, so stop waiting to finish absolutely everything before you go out to play. 4) Time Out: make sure your schedule always has an upcoming long weekend, sabbatical or retreat that you can look forward to. 5) Extra Time: for hugs, smiles, laughter, romance, thank-you cards, sending flowers and other things that feel so good to do.

Mental Wellbeing. Name five words that best describe your general state of mind at present. Are you, for instance, "optimistic" or "pessimistic", "grateful" or "tired", "trusting" or "anxious"? Find five words that best describe your attitude toward life right now and notice what this tells you about your current levels of mental wellbeing. Watch your mind and let your mind show you what one commitment it needs from you so as to help you experience greater clarity, vision and hope. Again, listen and act. Here are some examples:

1) Education: What are you learning about right now? Read a great book, take a new class, attend a great lecture, recommit to an old hobby or interest that you love. 2) Growth: How are you growing at present? What really inspires you? Who is your mentor? Visit a life coach. Spend two hours in your local museum. Sign up for the happiness course. 3) Balance: Learn how to switch off and know what switches you on. Exercise more. Have more fun. Meditate more. 4) Inspiration: Listen to Puccini, go to the theatre, read *A Course in Miracles*,[6] or anything else that blows your mind. 5) Laughter: Remember not to take it all so seriously. Watch your favourite feel-good movie. Sing a song that makes you smile. Read the comedian Bill Hicks's memoir *Love All the People*.[7]

Spiritual Wellbeing. This is about letting yourself enjoy the grace and power of your true, Unconditioned Self. All too often, we are so identified with our bodies, our careers, our relationships and our personal dramas that we forget to tune in to our real essence and to listen for the "soul whispers" of our true nature. The spiritual level of your wellbeing differs from the rest because, unlike your body, your emotions and your mind, your spirit is never in need of repair. The goal, therefore, is not to nourish your spirit; it is to let your spirit feed you. Here are some examples:

1) Spiritual Front Page: do "The Spiritual Front Page" or another daily spiritual practice that helps you to tune in to the intelligence of your soul. 2) Spiritual Chiropractic: realign yourself with the beliefs, values and ethics that give you a greater sense of faith, meaning and power. 3) Spiritual Teachers: commit to a spiritual path, spiritual teacher, spiritual bible or spiritual community that truly helps you to follow your joy. 4) Spiritual Purpose: identify what you would like your spiritual purpose to be and commit to it. 5) Spiritual Healing: If you let go of the "optical delusion" of separateness and aloneness, you will find more help than your ego could ever give you. *Following your joy always leads to all manner of inspiration and support.*

● ● ● ● ●

PART III

the
unholy
trinity

CHAPTER 9

choosing happiness

The real reason why happiness means so much to you is that happiness is your true nature. Happiness is who you are and it is what you experience when you accept yourself, when you relax and when you stop neurosing about being a "size zero", about "why he hasn't called", and about "what I should be doing with my life". Happiness isn't "out there". And, when you really think about it, the blocks to happiness aren't "out there" either. Why? Because there is no "out there" out there.

The happiness course shows you how your psychology creates the world you experience and how it can either enhance or block your awareness of true happiness. Happiness *is not* a state of mind; it is your true nature. That said, certain states of mind can either help or hinder your experience of happiness. In other words, happiness is your original nature, but you may well be *suffering from psychology*. Your psychology (that is, your perceptions, your beliefs and your self-talk) is what stands between you and happiness now, success now and love now.

Over the years, my work on happiness has been independently tested by psychologists and neuro-scientists who are able to record the wonderful results that happen when people change their psychology. A new belief, a new perception, can undo your mind and open up a whole new world of possibility. Scientists have shown that when students in my course change their thinking they literally alter the chemistry of their brains, which shifts their experience of the world and also increases their happiness, peacefulness and wellbeing.

I begin the exploration of the psychology of happiness by asking my students to answer the following question with a "Yes" or "No". The question is: "Could you be even happier – even if nothing in the world around you changed?" I give my students a full five minutes to choose their answers so that they can really think the question through. That said, most students tell me that they only need about five seconds. The answer is almost always an emphatic "Yes". Over the years, I would estimate a percentage split of 90 per cent for "Yes" and 10 percent for "No". In the most recent course, the score was 100 per cent for "Yes".

These very high scores appear to confirm the "negligible role" that life circumstances play in happiness. To be truly happy, you have to get your head around the idea that circumstances *don't matter as much as you think they do*. Leading happiness researcher Sonja Lyubomirsky says, "The general conclusion from almost a century of research on the determinants of wellbeing is that objective circumstances, demographic variables and life events are correlated with happiness less strongly than intuition and everyday experience tell us they ought to be."[1]

Happiness research studies reveal that most people who score consistently higher levels of happiness than you *do not* experience markedly better life circumstances. Nor are they happier because they haven't experienced any difficult life circumstances. So, what's happening? One answer is, *they know how to enjoy their life better than you*. On the other hand, people with lower happiness scores than you *do not* necessarily experience markedly worse life circumstances. In fact, they may be much better off than you, in financial terms, for instance. It would appear, therefore, that these people are unhappy not because they are suffering from bad circumstances, but because they are *suffering from psychology*.

Happiness scientists, philosophers, physicists and Indian swamis all agree that your state of mind *literally* creates the world you experience. For example, the 19th-century philosopher Ludwig Wittgenstein wrote, "The world of those who are happy is different from the world of those who are not." This idea is supported by Sonja Lyubomirsky's research into why some people are happier than others. She concludes: "A common thread running through the research is that happy and unhappy individuals appear to experience – indeed, to reside in – different subjective worlds."[2]

When my students respond "Yes" or "No" to the question "Could you be even happier – even if nothing in the world around you changed?" I also ask them to write down the reasons for their answers. I have compiled hundreds of responses over the years and all of the reasons for "Yes" fall into five broad categories, each of which testifies to the power of making positive choices. The first positive choice is "choosing to accept myself more". For example, "I can choose to be less critical of myself and accept myself more and that way I will be happier regardless of what happens in my life."

The second positive choice is "choosing to see things differently". For example, "I can change my perception of things that I think are 'wrong' or 'bad' or 'not good enough' and look for the gift in everything." The third is "choosing to be more grateful". For example, "I can be happier by appreciating all of the gifts that are in my life rather than longing for what I don't have." The fourth is "making better choices". For example, "I can choose to slow down, be more present, reprioritise, connect more and attend even more to what really matters." And fifth is "choosing to be happy". For example, "I can choose to be happy, to be loving, to be kind, to have fun and to appreciate my life. It's my mind and I can choose how I work it!"

Familiar Choices

Imagine a happiness scale from 0 to 10. Zero represents "no pulse", below 5 represents degrees of "unhappiness", 5 is "not unhappy", 6 is "quite happy", 7 is "happy", 8 is "very happy", 9 is "almost completely happy", and 10 is "totally happy." According to this happiness scale, how happy are you normally? What would you say is your average score for happiness? Think carefully on this, as the score you give could well be what scientists call your "set point", or what I call your "familiar point".

The happiness set point is a theory used by scientists to explain a phenomenon known as "hedonic adaptation".[3] It is a similar idea to a person's body-weight set point. The theory is that you have a set point or set range that you return to (for example, between 6.5 and 7.5 out of 10) regardless of what your life circumstances are like. This return to the "set point" has been observed by happiness researchers who have found that most people adapt rapidly to their circumstances, both pleasant and unpleasant. Thus, your levels of happiness are hardly ever permanently affected by life circumstances.

The great hope is that buying a new pair of shoes will help you to live happily ever after. Multiple purchases of products with brand names like Manolo Blahnik, Mouton Rothschild, Mont Blanc and Mercedes should guarantee you everlasting happiness. What really happens, though, is that you visit "happily ever after" for a short vacation and then you use a return ticket to catch a ride back to your original set point. There is, however, an upside. For instance, if you scuff your Manolos, or your Mouton Rothschild wine is corked, you may visit the depths of despair, but only for a short spell, because you will eventually make your way home to your set point again.

Hedonic adaptation – the return to your set point – has been observed in the most extreme life circumstances. The most famously cited research is by Philip Brickman and his colleagues, who compared the happiness levels of 22 lottery winners with a control group of 22 people who lived in the same areas.[4] As you would expect, the lottery winners did experience an increase in happiness levels in the short term. However, this increase lasted only for a few months and after about a year they reverted to their original set points. In other words, they were no happier.

Brickman and his colleagues also studied the effect of the set point on people who suffered severe physical injuries that left them paraplegic. Most people who have not experienced paraplegia cannot imagine how anyone in that position could ever feel genuinely good again about life. Indeed, for the first few months, the subjects' happiness levels were a lot lower than the average. However, within a year or so, their happiness levels had risen and were only slightly lower than the happiness levels of the millionaire lottery winners. In fact, 8 out of 10 described their lives as being better than average. All hail to the set point!

So, what is the set point really? Well, firstly, it is helpful to remember that the set point is not a physical thing that is "real" as such. It is merely a description of your average happiness score over time. It is the score or range that you are most familiar with, and that is one reason why I call it your "familiar point" or "familiar range". But there is also another very significant reason why I like to call it your familiar point and not your set point, and that has to do with what actually determines the "point" in the first place.

Most happiness scientists will tell you that your set point is determined in large part by your genes. They differ as to exactly how much – some say as much as 80 per cent, but most say 50 per cent.[5] The next question, then, must surely be, "What are your genes made of?" or "What determines your genes?" Here there are two schools of thought: One school describes your genes as being made of "physical stuff", permanent and unchanging, that programmes your psychology and behaviour. If this is true, genes are a physical miracle – they are the only physical things in the universe that do not change and evolve.

The other school describes your genes as "bits of code" that are being turned on and off by your perceptions, your beliefs and your self-talk. Thus, your genes change in much the same way the chemistry of your brain changes whenever you change your psychology. This school suggests, therefore, that your genes determine your thinking *and are also influenced by your thinking.* In other words, the thoughts you think most often, that are most familiar to you and that you most identify with are what make your genes determine your happiness "familiar point".[6]

My theory is that your happiness familiar point is set by your sense of identity (that is, your self-image), which, in turn, determines your psychology. From watching people for many years now, I believe that most people think like the people they perceive themselves to be. For example, if you relate to yourself as "a victim", you will think like a victim. Your sense of identity is what is encoded in your genes and this is what programmes your psychology. Therefore, you can only experience a lasting increase in happiness if you can identify with it and not let your old self-image sabotage it.

The reason that you place yourself at 7 out of 10, for instance, on the happiness scale is because this score is familiar to you and your self-image can identify with it. Your familiar point can probably extend to a familiar range, up to 8 out of 10, for instance. But if you were to experience 9 out of 10 on the happiness scale and not return quickly to your familiar point, you would have to be willing to let go of your old self-image and its psychology and intentionally embrace more of your Unconditioned Self.

When I ask my students to stand at 9 out of 10 on the happiness scale, or even 10 out of 10, the first question I ask them is, "Can you picture yourself here?" I want to know if they can visualise being "here" or not. Many times they will say, "I like the idea of it, but it's just not me." This much happiness is too unfamiliar and uncomfortable for their self-image. It is not compatible with the story they are currently telling about themselves. So, now you have to choose between the learned stories of your self-image and the original joy of your Unconditioned Self.

When you change your mind about yourself, you change your brain chemistry, you change your psychology, you change your genes, you change your future and you change your relationship to happiness. The more you truly accept yourself, the more you will automatically let go of an old self-image that is made up of thoughts of lack, unworthiness and fear. The old guilt and struggle that were once so familiar to the old Learned Self no longer fit and now your happiness levels increase as you once again identify with your Unconditioned Self, which is literally made up of happiness.

Preconscious Choices

How much of your life is determined by personal choice and how much by external circumstances? For example, would you say 40 per cent personal choice and 60 per cent external circumstances? Take a moment to think about what percentage split accurately reflects your attitude toward life.

When I give this question to my students I tell them I am not after one right answer, which is just as well, because I always get a wide range of answers. On one end, I get scores as low as 20 per cent personal choice, 80 per cent external circumstances. These scores suggest a philosophy of determinism: for example, my choices are determined by my DNA, by my childhood, by my school grades, by the current economic climate, by my partner's mood, by the sports scores and by whether or not my children have cleaned their rooms.

At the other end, I get scores of 80 per cent personal choice, 20 per cent external circumstances. This reflects a philosophy of adaptation: for example, just because my four-year-old daughter has tried to flush a papaya down the toilet doesn't mean she is trying to ruin my life. Life happens, but I can choose how to respond to life. Some people even score 100 per cent personal choice. This reflects a philosophy of creation: for example, I create my life because I choose my circumstances. This philosophy sees that everything is ultimately a choice, including your future.

When we study the psychology of happiness, I give my students a question to consider that throws a whole new light on how we choose happiness. The question is, "On a scale of 0 to 10, how good will you let this happiness course be?" A similar question for you might be, "On a scale of 0 to 10, how much will you let this book change your life for the better?" The really interesting thing about questions like these is that everyone has an answer. But where does the answer come from? Is the answer just made up, on the spot? Or is the answer pre made? If this is the case, you may well have decided your future already.

Amazingly, you have already decided how happy you are going to be in this lifetime. At least, that is my hypothesis. What do you think? As you read these words, see if you can find the place in your mind where you have already decided how happy you will be today and how much you are going to enjoy yourself today. Also, see if you can find the place in your mind where you have already decided how happy you are going to be this week and for the rest of your life.

The scientific research into "preconscious choice" challenges us to rethink how we create our reality. Baroness Susan Greenfield is a professor of synaptic pharmacology at Lincoln College, Oxford. We have met on many occasions over the years and I always keep up with her research into the brain and consciousness. With regard to preconscious choice, she concludes, "The actions and decisions we take every day which feel like instant conscious choices are actually the result of slowly emerging subconscious processes in the brain."[7]

My hypothesis is that somewhere in your mind you have already decided how much happiness is possible and how much is too good to be true. You have already decided, for instance, if the people you are yet to meet in your life can be trusted or not. Furthermore, you have decided already if you will find love or not, how much success you will enjoy and how abundant your life will be. You have made these choices already and they are programmed into your genes by your thoughts – and right now you are playing out your choices in the world.

One of the first times I became aware of preconscious choice was in a course when I was in dialogue with Elaine. Elaine described herself as being divorced, middle-aged and "stuck in unhappiness". Her divorce had been finalised the week before she started the course. She described the divorce as being entirely her fault. For 20 minutes, I listened to her speak. "Elaine, I agree with your diagnosis: You are stuck in unhappiness," I said. I did not give up on Elaine, however, because one thing I have learned about the "psychology of stuck" is that being "stuck" is, on some level, a choice.

Next, I decided to examine Elaine's prognosis for her "stuckness". "Elaine, how long do you think you will be stuck in unhappiness?" I asked. "Six and a half years," she replied, without any hesitation. Elaine was clearly taken aback by the power of her answer. "Wow," she said, "I have no idea where that answer came from." We talked a bit more and then I asked her, "How long were you married?" Elaine replied, "Four and a half years, plus two years of being engaged." A total of six and a half years. Was this number just a coincidence or a preconscious choice?

Choosing Again

When I ask people the question "Can you choose your thoughts?" I normally get three different answers. The first is, "No," which is rare. The second is, "Yes," which is common. The third is, "No and yes," which is intriguing. When you watch your mind, say for five minutes, it does seem that thoughts arise and subside without any conscious choice. That said, once the thoughts arise, you can choose consciously whether or not to identify with them and whether or not to give them your energy and your power.

"I believe I can choose my thoughts 100 per cent, but I am only able to do it 70 per cent of the time," said Claire, one of my students. I can identify with that. Can you? I encourage everyone who takes the course to practise some form of meditation or self-reflection so as to be more conscious and aware of thinking. The goal is to become the observer of your thoughts. This is so helpful because the more you watch your thoughts, the less reactive you become and the more easily you can discern between the daily nonsense of the ego and the real thoughts of your Unconditioned Self.

Happiness is always possible – the only thing that really holds you back is your mind. You have probably already noticed that the happiest times in your life are when you are not thinking. It's a wonderful thing to stand outside your ego, to surrender to the flow and to participate fully in a hobby, in nature, in meditation, in prayer, in art, in dance, in sport and in the moment. For the rest of the time, your mind is a madding crowd of judgments, fears, guilt and anxiety. I know of no one who would feel entirely comfortable at the prospect of having a transcript of his or her daily thoughts made public. And yet happiness is only ever one thought away at most.

You choose your thoughts and you choose your future. Right now, in this moment, you can choose to think differently and you can choose to create a different future. The choices you make here and now are what shape your fate and destiny. One new perception, one new belief, one new affirmation is all it takes to begin to experience your world differently.

**You can choose again and it is never too
late to choose to enjoy this moment
and to choose a better future.**

When I teach about the mental blocks to happiness, I use a model called the "Unholy Trinity" of the ego. The Unholy Trinity is made up of 1) *Beliefs:* the learned beliefs you identify with, such as "Happiness has to be deserved" and "Happiness must be earned". I will explore these beliefs in depth in the next chapter, "The Happiness Contract." 2) *Fears:* the learned fears that attract unhappiness and repel happiness. I will explore these fears more in Chapter 11, "Fear of Happiness". 3) *Lack:* the illusion that "something is missing" and the ego's blindness to what is already here. More on this in Chapter 12, "One Hundred Gratitudes".

The most important thing to remember about true happiness is that happiness exists regardless of your life circumstances and regardless of your state of mind. Some states of mind, like gratitude, forgiveness and humour, make it easy for you to experience the happiness of your original nature. Other states of mind, like resentment, jealousy and cynicism, make it more difficult – but they cannot wipe out your true nature. And that is why when you change your mind, you can rediscover the joy that has been with you all the while.

The intention to be happy is what changes everything. When you decide with all your heart *to be happy,* you are calling upon the grace and the power of your original nature to help you out. In truth, happiness is a choiceless choice. Why? Because your Unconditioned Self has already decided to be happy. *It wants to be what it is.* So, when you choose to be happy, you are not trying to create something that does not exist yet; rather, you are choosing to be yourself again. Happiness is a journey home from the ego-mind to the heart of your Unconditioned Self.

**Happiness is
a journey without a distance,
a journey that takes no time,
a journey that has already
been made.**

● ● ● ● ●

CHAPTER 10

the
happiness
contract

It is the night before Christmas. Little Alex, five and a quarter years old, is super excited at the prospect of getting a brand new bicycle on Christmas Day.

"Daddy, do you *really* think Santa Claus will bring me a bike?" asks Alex.

"That depends," says Daddy.

"On what?" asks Alex.

"On whether you have been a good boy this year."

Alex looks thoughtful. Taking a big gulp, he asks, "How good did I have to be?"

"Well, to get a brand new bike you would really have to deserve it," says Daddy.

"Oh," says Alex.

Later that night, just before bedtime, Alex sits beside the Nativity scene, an antique family heirloom, perfectly preserved and beautifully displayed by Alex's mother. All the main characters are there – beautiful porcelain figures of Mary, Joseph, baby Jesus, three Wise Men and also a plastic figure of Buzz Lightyear, after much lobbying from Alex.

Alex clasps his hands together, bows his head and begins to pray: "Dear God, I didn't realise I had to *deserve* the bike. Santa Claus never told me." Alex takes a very big breath and prays most earnestly, "I promise to be very good and to be completely perfect for *a whole year* if you can persuade Santa Claus to give me the bike. Please do your best. I know you have contacts. Amen."

Alex leaves the Nativity scene, but something is troubling him. He turns back. The thought of having to be good and perfect for a whole year feels like an awful lot of *pressure.* Surely, 365 continuous days of good behaviour is too much to ask of any young boy. Alex sits down again by the Nativity scene and begins to pray. "Dear God, I *so* want the bike and I promise in return to be really good for *a whole month,* starting from now. Amen."

Little Alex remains seated by the Nativity scene. He should be feeling hopeful and excited about getting a bike in the morning, but he can't help but feel the *strain* of having to be good for a whole 30 days, including weekends. It feels so exhausting and so unfair. Alex looks around the room to make sure his parents are out of sight. No one is watching him. With a heavy sigh, he picks up the porcelain figure of baby Jesus. He wraps baby Jesus up in some newspaper and puts him in his pocket. Then Alex begins to pray again. "Dear God, if you want to see your son again, make sure I get the bloody bike."

The story of little Alex is a perfect introduction to a session I present called "How to Be So Happy You Almost Feel Guilty, But Not Quite".[1] This session is an inquiry into your private beliefs about happiness. It helps you to clarify what you really believe about happiness. It addresses your hopes and your cynicism, your positive self-belief and your lack of self-worth. This session is an opportunity to wipe the slate clean and to restore your faith in yourself and in unconditional happiness.

When I coach individuals and groups on the psychology of happiness, I refer to something I call "The Happiness Contract". In truth, the Happiness Contract is just a metaphor; but its effects on your life and on your levels of happiness can feel very real. Your Happiness Contract exists beneath a pile of thoughts at the back of your mind, next to a heap of other contracts, such as "The Love Contract", "The Abundance Contract", "The God Contract", and "The Good Fortune Contract", and also "The Success Contract", which I cover in my book *Success Intelligence*.[2]

Your Happiness Contract is "a statement of belief" that determines, according to you, how much happiness is possible and how much happiness is *too good to be true.* Your Happiness Contract also asserts every condition, rule and law that you absolutely must abide by in order to be eligible for any amount of happiness. Any happiness that you experience without first fulfilling these conditions is strictly "illegal" and may result in personal penalties of guilty feelings, inner discomfort and moral foreboding.

Your Happiness Contract is a personal agreement drawn up by your superego and signed by your ego. The *superego* is the part of the ego-mind that tries to play God by constantly telling you what it thinks you need to do in order to be happy. It is the lawmaker that sets up the conditions for happiness, based upon who you think you are and what your ego thinks happiness is. I think the superego is best characterised as a blind high-court judge who has never seen your beauty, your wholeness and the truth of who you are.

Your Happiness Contract is different from everyone else's, except on one count. Every Happiness Contract has a central clause in it that states: *happiness must be deserved.* From an early age, just like little Alex, every ego adopts the belief that happiness must be, ought to be and should be deserved. This belief has led to centuries of misidentification and misperceptions about what true happiness is. It has also caused generations of unnecessary pain, suffering and struggle. The truth is, *you do not deserve happiness.* Happiness is a non-deserving issue.

**You do not deserve happiness because happiness is free –
there are no conditions.**

When you finally let yourself feel the truth of this statement, you will no longer feel guilty about being happy. Until that time, your Happiness Contract will continue to limit and deprive you of the happiness that belongs to your Unconditioned Self. When it comes to happiness, your ego is trying to strike a deal for you to purchase something that is already yours. Believe it or not, *happiness cannot be bought because it has no cost.* Happiness is a divine freebie.

The first step to experiencing more unconditional happiness is to remember that your Happiness Contract is not real. This contract is not authored by God; it is written by your superego, which knows nothing of the laws of heaven. None of the laws of happiness you believe in exist anywhere in the universe except inside your own mind. The second step to enjoying more unconditional happiness is to remember that you can rewrite your Happiness Contract at any time. You can even tear it up altogether.

Below, I have summarised nine common personal laws that are often found in the small print of a person's Happiness Contract. In each case, I outline the governing belief behind the law and also the effects that this personal law may have on your life. I also suggest a possible rewrite. As you read the rest of this chapter, notice which of the personal laws you believe in and be willing to rewrite your Happiness Contract. Simply looking at your beliefs helps replace superstition with truth and lets old fears make way for innocent joy.

Personal Law #1: Perfectionism
Superego Belief: *I must be perfect in order to deserve happiness.*

If you have written this personal law into your Happiness Contract, then not only do you have to *be good* to deserve happiness, you have to be *extra good*. Happiness is entirely permissible as long as you dress nice, speak well, make no mistakes, are a model citizen, take responsibility, think no evil and never read pornography. The deal is that *X amount of good behaviour buys you X amount of happiness points* – a bit like earning gold stars at school.

Perfectionism as a true spiritual path shows you how to see your own perfection and to celebrate the perfection of creation. Perfectionism in the hands of the superego, however, is just an extreme form of personal bullying. This is the difference between vision (to look without judgment) and perception (to look through the eyes of judgment). Unfortunately, it is very rare to meet happy perfectionists. Mostly because their self-judgment never lets them relax.

The Rewrite: Remind yourself often that *you* are the author of your Happiness Contract, not God. As such, you can rewrite it at any time without incurring divine displeasure. Remember also that the goal of your life is not to make a perfect self; *it is to see that you are perfectly made.* When you look at yourself without judgment, you rediscover your Unconditioned Self. A happy affirmation for you would be: "I accept and love my Unconditioned Self."

Personal Law #2: Martyrdom
Superego Belief: *I must sacrifice good things for happiness.*

In the spring of 1997, we held a course at one of the colleges of Oxford University. Our second workshop, which featured "The Happiness Contract", took place the day before the start of Lent – a time of prayer, fasting and sacrifice for Christians in preparation for Easter. Geraldine, a committed Christian, shared with the group how guilty she felt about being happy and doing nice things for herself, especially during Lent. I invited Geraldine to explore whether it was really true that sacrifice must always be about *letting go of good things.* Geraldine eventually decided that her sacrifice for Lent that year would be to let go of guilt.

Sacrifice as a true spiritual path is about giving up fear for love, guilt for joy, attack for peace, resentment for forgiveness, separation for oneness and the ego for God. Sacrifice according to your superego is less easy to understand. The superego deal is that you sacrifice happiness and other good things so as to be *happy-ish*. The underlying superego fear is that *happiness is selfish*. Therefore, a chief condition of your Happiness Contract must be that personal happiness is acceptable only after you have made sure that everyone else is happy first.

The Rewrite: Remind yourself who is the author of your Happiness Contract. Think in terms of positive sacrifice and be willing to give up what is unreal for what is true. If you really want to dispel the belief that sacrificing your happiness makes everyone else happier, make a list of all of the people who are truly grateful for your self-sacrifice. This list should take you all of two seconds to complete. A happy affirmation for you to investigate is: "My happiness is my gift to the world."

Personal Law #3: Earn-estness

Superego Belief: *I must earn happiness.*

If you have any major work-ethic clauses in your Happiness Contract, you will feel a constant internal pressure to *do-do-do-do* before you can *be* happy. *Doing* precedes *being* and *having,* according to the work ethic. Thus, happiness is experienced as a by-product of effort. The more effort you put in, the more happiness you *deserve* and the more happiness you *make* for yourself. Thus, the work ethic defines happiness as an accomplishment. *Happiness is not natural; it is paycheck you earn for putting in the hours first.* Happiness is a dividend you receive for completing your to-do list.

The work ethic as a true spiritual path is a rich inquiry into identifying the real work of your life. It is about letting creation and the will of God be expressed through you. The work ethic, according to the superego, is about labouring so as to earn, deserve and pay for happiness. As such, the work ethic is a cover-up, or compensation, for feelings of valuelessness and unworthiness. It can, if unchecked, lead to workaholism and it can also delay happiness indefinitely *because the work is never done.* In other words, you end up being too busy to be happy.

The Rewrite: The *joy of work* is deeply fulfilling, whereas working to earn happiness leaves you feeling empty. Remind yourself often that happiness is not something to achieve; happiness is something you accept. Also, when you choose to *be happy* first and to *be-be-be-be* before you *do* anything, all your actions will be graced with a new level of inspiration and creativity. A happy affirmation for you is: "Happiness is the purpose of my life."

Personal Law #4: Suffering

Superego Belief: *I must suffer in order to know happiness.*

If you have any suffering-ethic clauses in your Happiness Contract, you will probably be used to experiencing a lot of drama, struggle, pain, conflict and heartache. This is because, according to the superego, you have to suffer to be worthy of happiness. Your superego offers you a flexible payment plan: either you can suffer first and then be happy, or you can enjoy the happiness up front and suffer afterward. But does there really have to be a "suffering tax" on happiness? Is your superego really acting on behalf of a mean-spirited God, or is this simply some ego-superstition arising from a lack of genuine self-knowledge?

The story goes that there once was a man who suffered diligently all his life so as to buy a single moment of pure happiness. One day he packed up all of his suffering into a big heavy bag, slung it over his shoulder and headed to market. When he tried to trade in his suffering, he was told there was no exchange rate between suffering and happiness. The superego's mistake is that it believes suffering can buy happiness. It also peddles the belief that suffering can clear away unworthiness. In truth, happiness and true self-worth *are experienced when you outgrow your need to suffer.*

The Rewrite: In the past you may have attended the "school of hard knocks", but that doesn't mean you have to keep signing up for another new course in suffering or for another PhD in pain. You could enrol, for instance, in joy, or dance, or forgiveness. A happy affirmation for you to play with is: "Being happy cures the need to suffer."

Personal Law #5: Mastery

Superego Belief: *I must be enlightened to know real happiness.*

When you believe that happiness has to be deserved, there is a temptation to turn happiness into something special, mysterious and elusive. Happiness is no longer a natural experience; it is a problem to be solved. Thus the superego turns happiness into a test and you will be examined on how proficient you are and how worthy to accept the accolade of happiness. To be happy, you simply have to demonstrate world-class expertise, true mastery and an exhaustive learning about what real happiness is.

Imagine you stand before two doors: One door has a sign on it that says "Happiness" and the other door has a sign on it that says "Lecture on Happiness". Which door will you walk through? If you have a lot of expertise and enlightenment clauses in your Happiness Contract, you may well make the mistake of being a lifelong learner who never actually lets himself or herself enjoy happiness. You are like a perpetual student who constantly preps for happiness, but unconsciously always delays the experience of happiness. This delaying tactic conceals a hidden sense of unworthiness and mistrust about happiness.

The Rewrite: Remind yourself often that happiness is not a mental idea; it is the ground of your being. Happiness is not learned; it is remembered. There is no pass or fail. Happiness is not to be understood; it is to be enjoyed. *Happiness happens when you least inspect it.* A happy affirmation to investigate is: "Happiness is the key to enlightenment."

Personal Law #6: Approval

Superego Belief: *I must have 100 per cent approval that my happiness is okay.*

How much happiness can you handle before you start to worry that it's not okay to be this happy? Most of us can handle some occasional happiness, some snippets of pleasure and some sweet moments of joy. A bubble bath, for instance, with lots of bubbles, is okay, as long as it is okay with everyone else, too. The real difficulty is knowing what to do with the happiness that lasts for, say, two days in a row. The problem is that too much happiness evokes too much worry about the possible dire consequences of staying happy. And then the happiness appears to disappear.

If you find it difficult to trust that happiness is okay, you will probably look for approval from two main sources. One is approval from other people, such as your partner, your parents, your friends, your kids, your colleagues and *everyone else you know.* To compensate for this, you may make it your duty to ensure that everyone else is happy first. The second is approval from your superego. This is difficult, however, because happiness serves as a pink slip for your superego. When you are happy, the superego has nothing to do. Too much happiness literally does your superego out of a job. Too much happiness causes superegos to have panic attacks.

The Rewrite: It is impossible to trust that happiness is okay if you will not trust that you are worthy of happiness. For as long as you believe you must deserve happiness, you will look for guarantees, warranties and seals of approval for even small amounts of happiness. *And you won't find them.* The truth is, however, *that happiness is okay because your Unconditioned Self is happy.* A happy affirmation for you to believe in is: "My happiness is my gift to everyone."

Personal Law #7: Control

Superego Belief: *I must be in control.*

If your Happiness Contract has some heavy control clauses in it, then you will probably tell yourself, "I can be happy once I am in complete control of my life." In other words, you can be happy once you have sorted your life out and figured out what your purpose is and know with 100 per cent certainty what you want to be when you grow up. Meanwhile, your superego (a.k.a. "The Controller") sends you internal e-mails from its control tower that constantly pester you to be positive, rosy, certain, upbeat, smiley, confident, strong and, paradoxically, happy.

The superego's controlling commands often conceal a hidden desire to control happiness itself. Once again, this is a response to the fear that happiness is not deserved and therefore can be lost. It is good to remind yourself, however, that in truth *happiness cannot be controlled; it can only be let loose.* Ultimately, the key to more happiness is not more control; it is more surrender. It is only when you surrender your attachment to the superego and surrender the chase for happiness, that you can be more spontaneous, more receptive and more open to the happiness that is already here.

The Rewrite: If you believe that you can only be happy if you are always positive and in control, you run the risk of trying to "fake it until you make it". The problem with "faking it" is that you end up so dissociated from what you really feel that you can never know if you have made it. Happiness is about being honest *and* positive. Also, remind yourself often that happiness is not a chase; it's a choice. Try this happy affirmation: "Happiness is where I am."

Personal Law #8: Independence

Superego Belief: *I must be completely independent.*

If your Happiness Contract has a strong independence clause in it, then you will probably experience plenty of superego dictates like "I must be strong," and "I must be self-sufficient," and "I must do it yourself." The superego worships the vertical pronoun "I". It makes constant declarations of independence because it believes that independence is the key to freedom and the key to protecting your happiness. Unfortunately, the superego doesn't know when to stop and too much independence leads to increased feelings of separation, fear, defensiveness *and unhappiness.*

The superego spews out endless independence mantras like "Happiness is self-reliance" and "Happiness is an inside job" and "Happiness depends upon me." The superego misinterprets accountability, autonomy and self-responsibility to mean that "I must never ask for help" and "I should never rely on anyone else." These dictates hide a lack of self-worth – for example, feeling unworthy of asking for or receiving any help. This extreme insistence on independence leaves your ego weak, exhausted, cut off and living in exile from the strength and power and joy of your Unconditioned Self.

The Rewrite: It is important to take responsibility for your life and to be accountable, and sometimes that means *being willing to ask for help.* You will experience greater happiness each time you let go of any separation and connect wholeheartedly with life, nature, people, God and the universe. A happy affirmation to try is: "Happiness is oneness with myself and with all."

Personal Law #9: Goodness
Superego Belief: *I must be good.*

Notice how you feel when you repeat out loud the superego mantra "I must be good, I must be good, I must be good" for one full minute. Can you feel the pressure, the strain and the exhaustion that little Alex felt in the story at the start of this chapter? Does repeating, "I must be good, I must be good" make you want to rebel? Now add a few more ego messages like "I must be nice" and "I must be calm" and "I must be kind" and "I must be centred" and "I must keep myself on an even keel at all times." If you believed any of this, you would be forgiven for thinking that happiness is not worth the trouble.

The problem with a superego message like "I must be good" is that it takes all the fun out of wanting to be good. Instead of choosing to be good, you *have to be good.* Furthermore, if you "must be good" in order to be happy, you are likely to try to be agreeable at all times, never rock the boat, be a peacemaker, repress your real feelings, say "Yes" when you mean "No", give your power away and avoid conflict. You do all this to find happiness, but what actually happens is a great big disappearing act and *you* are now nowhere to be found.

The Rewrite: The superego is trying to make your ego adopt essential qualities, like *goodness* and *kindness,* that *already belong to your Unconditioned Self.* Your ego does not need to deserve happiness because your original Self is already happy. Your goal, therefore, is to let the grace of your Unconditioned Self flow through you and bless your ego, bless your psychology and bless your life. A wonderful happiness affirmation to try is: "I accept myself and I accept happiness."

• • • • •

CHAPTER 11

fear of
happiness

There is an extraordinary sense of anticipation in the room when we gather for the first time in the happiness course. This anticipation is physical. You can see it in the way people enter the room and how they search for what they decide will be "their" chairs. It's on their faces, in how they sit and in their friendly yet cautious greetings to one another. It's a big moment. We are about to take a class on happiness. This is the class that most of us wished we could have taken at school. We are about to study life's most important goal.

When I ask my students how they are feeling, I find that half the room is feeling excited and the other half is feeling nervous. People often say, "I almost didn't come," and "I nearly changed my mind," and "I've been looking forward to this course for so long, but now that I'm here I am really scared." Scared of what? Well, for some people it is simply the fear of the unknown: "I don't know what's going to happen," and "I've never done this sort of thing before," and "I hope I'm not going to be made to hug people."

For others, it's the fear of disappointment: "I've heard how good this course is, but what if it does nothing for me? What if I'm the *only one* who fails?" Many people experience the fear of failing: "What if I take this course and I'm still not happy? Where else can I go?" However, the most common fear of all is *the fear of happiness*. One student, Caroline, sent me an e-mail just before the start of a course. She wrote: "I want to be happy. I want it so much that I haven't really let myself realise this – until now. I want it so much, I'm almost too scared to let myself have it."

Everyone I have ever worked with, both in groups and in one-on-one sessions, knows something about the fear of happiness. How strange to be afraid of something so wonderful. How odd to be afraid of something you want so much. But wait, it gets stranger and more odd. Such is the nature of fear, which has its own logic and its own reasons. Not only does absolutely everyone experience a fear of happiness, they also experience a fear of freedom, a fear of love, a fear of truth, a fear of being beautiful, a fear of shining, a fear of being big and even a fear of success.

I didn't start out on purpose to study *the fear of good things*.[1] Truth be told, I had no idea that so many people experienced the fear of happiness until I started my work with The Happiness Project. Similarly, I had no idea that the fear of success was so prevalent until I began my work with Success Intelligence.[2] And yet the evidence was plain to see that there comes a point in a person's life journey when the only block left that stands between you and a whole new level of happiness is your fear of happiness.

The Ego U-Turn

The fear of happiness is not usually activated by small pleasures like a bubble bath, a Belgian chocolate or a pleasant first date. Most of us can handle these brief dalliances without freaking out. What does normally activate the fear of happiness is an experience that is judged to be *too much, too big* or *too good to be true*.

I have coached many people who have gotten themselves out of a hole and are about to be truly happy again, when suddenly they turn around and run back into the hole. Sometimes it's a different hole, perhaps a slightly more interesting one, but it is still a hole. And if it's not a hole they find, then it's a drama, or a crisis, or a health issue, or some other distraction. This looks like bad luck, and as if some external force has intervened, but I assure you what's really happened is that your ego has performed a manoeuvre that I call the "Ego U-Turn".

The term Ego U-Turn is helpful because it identifies exactly *what is afraid*, which is your *sense of self*. Technically, it's not you who are afraid; it's your self-image that is afraid. Also, it is your ego (or self-image) that judges if the happiness you are experiencing is too good to be true.

**You are not afraid of too much happiness,
but your ego is.**

I devote one entire session of the course to studying the ego's allergic reaction to happiness. This session is called "The Fear of Happiness" and it is part of the threefold inquiry into the Unholy Trinity of lack, belief and fear. I usually begin the session by naming two primary fears: 1) the "Identity Fear" and 2) the "Allowance Fear".

The Identity Fear. This primary fear anticipates that too much happiness will change you. Hence, happiness is a threat to your familiar self. Your ego generates anxiety because too much happiness does not fit with its story about you. The ego's "set point" or "familiar point" (see Chapter 9) is wavering and you are noticing the discomfort. You may also notice the fear that "Too much happiness will make me lose control of my life." Happiness changes your life. And all the familiar devils ("better the devil you know") begin to exit. Unless, that is, you invite them back.

The Identity Fear is caused by misperceptions of who you really are and also what happiness really is. For as long as you relate to happiness as a "thing", an "it" that exists outside you, you will always feel your sense of self threatened by the perceived arrival of more happiness, joy, love, grace, good fortune, abundance and success. The gift of happiness is that it challenges you to undo your misperceptions of who you are and to remember your original, Unconditioned Self.

The Allowance Fear. When you feel very happy, the Identity Fear will ask, *Is this really me?* And the Allowance Fear, which is the other primary fear, will challenge you to think, *Do I really deserve this?* Indeed, your current self-image might not be compatible with this much happiness. Too much happiness is illegal in that it exceeds your personal allowance, as stated in your Happiness Contract (see Chapter 10). Hence you will continually notice your ego's fear and anxiety until you either dismiss the happiness or rewrite your contract.

Until you interview and question both your Identity Fear and your Allowance Fear, you will continue to block unconsciously and to delay indefinitely your experience of greater happiness. Thus, you will identify yourself as someone who searches for happiness, but does not find it. And you will act like someone who is about to be happier, but never actually is. *Happiness is here because you are,* but you won't let yourself feel it. And the better your life gets, the more you will numb out, dismiss it and pretend that you are still waiting for things to get better.

The "Happy Fears"

Unconditional happiness challenges you to keep letting go of your ego until you don't have one any more. And that's called enlightenment. Until then, your day job, so to speak, is to keep committing to unconditional happiness *and* to keep facing your ego's fears of happiness. Like most fears, they prevail because you won't look at them and they disappear when you dare to meet them. Why? Because, in truth, the fears of happiness are not based on anything that is real.

I will now focus on six common fears of happiness that are an extension of the Identity Fear and the Allowance Fear. I encourage you to do your homework on these fears so as to see if they are in any way blocking your possibilities of greater happiness. My advice is to assume they are, unless you are 100 per cent sure that you can in no way identify with them. The ultimate goal is to be able to meet any fear of happiness with equanimity and nonattachment. Welcome each fear into your "guesthouse" and treat it with enough compassion and honesty that it eventually moves on without any quibble.

Loss of Suffering. The happier you are, the more your ego will potentially experience a fear of loss, particularly the loss of suffering. You might think that you would be pleased to see the end of suffering. And indeed you may, unless, that is, you have become identified with and attached to your suffering. Suffering serves to differentiate your ego from other egos. No one has suffered exactly the way you have. Your suffering is special. It is your own story. You may also believe that your suffering is what makes you interesting, complex, unique, quirky, erudite and mysterious.

Everyone has to choose between happiness and the pay-offs of unhappiness. I encourage you to take some time to identify the special rewards you get from unhappiness. Take a pen and paper and complete the following sentence 10 times: "One of the pay-offs of unhappiness is . . ." Here is what some of my students have said: "Unhappiness wins me attention," "Unhappiness drives me," "Unhappiness buys me love," "Unhappiness helps me connect to other people," and "Unhappiness makes me feel alive." Yes, unhappiness can buy you all of the above – *and happiness can give them to you for free.*

Here's the bottom line: you will find it easier to accept and enjoy greater happiness the more you outgrow the need to suffer. When you let go of suffering, you do have to let go of any unhealthy attachments to your own unique history, but, in doing so, you also open yourself up to new possibilities for happiness, love and success, starting from now. When you lose suffering, you don't necessarily lose the pay-offs of suffering; you simply receive them in an easier, gentler way. Consider this happy thought: *happiness helps me to lose my suffering and to find myself.*

Fear of Selfishness. Most fears defy common sense and that is especially true of the fear that happiness is selfish. Yet many people are afraid of happiness because they have somehow learned to believe that happiness erases your good conscience, ruins your character, makes you insensitive to others and turns you into a deranged egomaniac frothing at the mouth when you smile. The fear that happiness leads to selfish, hedonic, narcissistic behavior is perpetuated by a misunderstanding of what true happiness is. Happiness is made of love, and as such, it is not selfish.

Countless studies show a strong correlation between happiness and unselfishness.[3] For my doctorate on the psychology of happiness, I asked subjects to judge people they know as either "mostly happy" or "mostly unhappy" and also as "selfish" or "unselfish". I defined "selfish" as "not interested in other people's happiness" and "unselfish" as "interested in other people's happiness". The results were: 1) 85 per cent of "mostly happy people" were judged as "unselfish" and 2) 92 per cent of "mostly unhappy people" were judged as "selfish".[4]

In the same study, I asked the question: "Are people more selfish when they are unhappy or when they are happy?" A huge 98 per cent of people circled the answer "unhappy". Many major investigations have found that depressed people do, unfortunately, exhibit strong traits of loneliness, individualism, alienation and disinterest in others. This is in contrast to plenty of empirical studies that prove that people who are consistently happy are less self-obsessed and more sociable.[5] Some things in life you can do on your own, like anxiety and depression; but happiness is different. The experience of happiness actually increases the more you share it.

Fear of Envy. A common ego fear is the fear that *if I become too happy it will attract envy and attack.* If you were to interview this fear and ask it, "Who will be envious?" the fear would probably name the people whose love and approval mean the most to you, such as family, friends and colleagues. Is this fear true? The only way to find out for sure is to go ahead and be happy. Some "friends" are worth losing if it means being truly happy. True friends will be happy for you – maybe not always at first, but always in the end. Happiness for any one person is an invitation to all of us to be more accepting and gracious. When one of us grows, all of us can grow.

Similar to the fear of envy is the fear that *my happiness hurts and upsets others*. Caroline, a staff nurse at a busy city hospital, noticed that she was afraid to be happy because of a belief that it would upset and annoy her patients. "Would being miserable or emotionally neutral be better for your patients?" I asked. Caroline discounted that. She concluded that her happiness would be annoying only if she expressed it in a hyped-up way and was overly positive, like a character from a pantomime play. Caroline confessed she felt uneasy around people who were permanently positive and upbeat.

Every fear is a story that has a twist in the tale. This is especially true of the fear of envy. For example, Jean shared how she was afraid that if her happiness increased, her partner would become jealous and might leave her. I asked Jean to investigate whether her real fear of happiness was a fear that she might leave her partner. Jean had a history of playing small in relationships and of attracting or recruiting people who would play out her beliefs of how much happiness was safe and okay. Her inquiry led to the most honest and confronting dialogue she had ever had with her partner.

Another twist in the tale: is it the envy of others that blocks your happiness, or is it your own envy? Are you happy for your friends to be as happy as possible? Would you be happy, for instance, if your best friend became famous, started dating George Clooney, found a soul mate, moved into a dream home, dropped a dress size, won the lottery? Could you ever be friends with people who could eat all the chocolate they liked and not put on weight? Seriously! If you are envious of others, deal with it! Otherwise, you will be afraid of being attacked for being happy, successful and lucky. And you will probably play small for the rest of your life.

Fear of Boredom. There is a school of thought that fears happiness is superficial. The theory goes that happiness is best suited to intellectual lightweights, dizzy blondes and little dogs, but that the more serious-minded human should study Russian poetry and lament the hopeless suffering of the world. I understand this, and I agree in part. Pleasure, which is often confused with real happiness, can indeed be dizzy and superficial. And satisfaction with the things of the world can be fleeting. But real joy is more than just an emotion or a toy; it is an angel that brings salvation and peace.

Another fear of happiness is, *I will lose my creativity if I am happy.* This is common among actors and artists, for instance. It is born of a misunderstanding that if you are happy you can't feel anything other than happiness. The fear is that happiness is monotone, not symphonic; grey, not multicolour; smooth, not textured. On a visit to New York, my colleague Avril Carson took me to a Broadway play featuring a famous Royal Shakespeare Company actor who played every part in the story. After the show, we met for a drink and we got talking about happiness. He said, "The happier I am, the better I can play every emotion in a clean, direct and honest way."

I've heard lots of people say, "A lifetime of happiness would be boring." But I haven't heard anyone say, "I tried it and it was boring." Once again, not every fear you experience is true. Sometimes a fear is just a fear, nothing more. The reason that happiness could never be boring is that you cannot be completely in control of your life and be happy. Of course, you can still control your choices, but ultimately happiness is about openness and surrender, spontaneity and flow. Happiness is an adventure and a discovery. It is dynamic and it renews itself in each moment.

Fall from Grace. If you relate to happiness as a peak experience instead of a natural experience, you will think of happiness as a "high" that is right "up there" at "the top" of life. Thus, when you are happy you are dancing on the ceiling and your ego is likely to suffer from a sort of spiritual vertigo. This leads to the fear that *after happiness, there comes a fall* and to other similar fears like *what goes up must come down*. Once again, I encourage you to ask yourself if this fear is really true, or if it is just a misperception.

One way to avoid the fall from grace is to not let yourself be happy in the first place. The way to do this is to employ cynicism, perfectionism, pessimism and other ego defences that guard against too much love, too much joy and too much good fortune. For consolation, you can of course dream of happiness, watch happy movies and buy a dog or cat that will never let you down. It is likely that you have a precedent in your past, a time when you did experience a fall from grace after being in love, being successful and being happy. I am truly sorry for that, but I must remind you that just because something happened once before does not mean it has to happen again. The universe has no need to repeat itself and that is especially true if you are ready to tell a new story.

If your Happiness Contract has a strong sacrifice or suffering clause in it, then you are likely to fear that happiness has a cost. Hence, the happier you are the more miserable you feel, because you know you are about to be presented with a great big cosmic invoice for your pleasure. Despite your best attempts to be thoroughly rational, you secretly fear that there exists in the pantheon of gods a troop of Karma Debt Collectors who have an omnipotent ability to tax you for your happiness. This belief in a "happy tax" is enough to put you off happiness forever.

Fear of Death. Some people are afraid of happiness because they are convinced that happiness is a prelude to death. They fear that happiness is the great orgasm that happens before you leave your body. Hence, one way to deal with this is to put happiness into your future, chase it endlessly, never quite get there and keep petitioning the gods in the meantime for another extension to your life. As a result, you're never exactly happy, but you're not exactly dead. Of course, the trouble is that when you are happy, it scares you so much it nearly kills you. Unless, that is, you can perform a skilful and timely Ego U-Turn.

The fear that you might die is not the problem. One day you will die. I know that's not very positive of me, but the fact is that 100 per cent of people do die. Even positive thinkers die. But, the big but, is: no one dies of happiness. Your problem is not that you are going to die; your problem is that you fear that God is going to single you out and make you die because things are going too well. Evidently you think of the great Creator as a killjoy who has nothing better to do than spoil your fun. God gets such a bad rap. And, in truth, it's a cover for our own fears and our own self-sabotage.

Some fears do have an element of truth in them. This is why it is so important to interview your fears and to discover what is true and what is not. If you fear that happiness leads to death, a good inquiry is to ask, "Who dies?" or "What dies?" Something does indeed die when you choose to be happy and usually what dies is an old self-concept. Specifically, it might be a self-concept like "the victim", "the lost soul", "the Prodigal Son", "the betrayed one", "the unlucky one", "the martyr", and "the wounded one". The old stories must end if the truth is to be told once more.

In my course, to close the session on "The Fear of Happiness", I lead a powerful meditation, accompanied by Robert Norton's music, in which I first invite everyone to meet each fear of happiness and to investigate if the fear is based on truth or superstition. After that is done, I invite them to imagine how good their lives could be if they gave up their fears of happiness to an unconditionally loving God. I encourage you to do this too. Imagine no fears. No fears of happiness. No fears of love. No fears of abundance. No fears of being who you really are. No fears.

● ● ● ● ●

CHAPTER 12

one
hundred
gratitudes

The following story is one of my favourites and therefore I always manage to find a perfect moment to share it in every happiness course I teach.

Despite years of intensive psychoanalysis, Ted, a 43-year-old man, had still not overcome a chronic fear that monsters lived under his bed. Bedtimes were a nightmare, his sleep pattern was a mess, his work was suffering and his love life was nonexistent. It's hard to be amorous with someone when you're afraid that a monster might come out from under the bed and bite your butt. You try it.

Three times a week for five years, Ted had visited his nice psychoanalyst. He tried free association, positive affirmations and cognitive reframing. He faced his fears, he looked at his shadow and he even forgave his mother. He did countless visualisations and meditations, but none of them cured his palpitations. And still, he was afraid of the monsters. Reluctantly, Ted told his psychoanalyst he was going to stop coming. The bills had mounted up. It was time for a change. The psychoanalyst took the news quite well.

Two weeks later, Ted ran into his former psychoanalyst in a local bookstore. Ted was looking for a copy of the *Kama Sutra* when he saw his ex-psychoanalyst browsing in the Self-Help section.

"Hi, Doc," said Ted, who was positively beaming.

"My God, you look so well," said the doc.

"Thanks," said Ted.

"You look rested. You look healthy. And, I hesitate to say this without a proper diagnosis, but you look happy," said the doc.

"Doc, I am completely cured," said Ted.

"How?" asked the doc.

"I went to see another doc," replied Ted, "and he cured me in just ONE session!"

"One session!" yelled the doc. "What's his name? What does he do? Is he taking on new clients?"

"Her name is Dr Yao and she is a behaviourist," said Ted.

"A behaviorist. Wow. So how did she cure you in one session?" asked the doc.

"Easy," said Ted. "She told me to saw the legs off my bed."

I don't believe in positive thinking, not if it isn't backed up with positive action. Positive thinking changes nothing if you're not also prepared to change the way you show up in the world. For instance, you can't just hope to find love; you also have to be a loving person who performs daily acts of love. Similarly, you can't just pray for peace and think that'll do it; you also have to practise forgiveness, do no harm and share your peace of mind with others. And it's not enough just to wish for more happiness; you have to take a risk, do something different and spread your happiness.

Imagine visiting a fabulous restaurant, thinking about your order, dreaming how great the food will taste and then leaving before you eat anything. I suppose it is a cheap night out, but you never get to taste the real thing. Occasionally I get students who only want to do the theory – a bit like people who read books like this one and don't do the exercises. They think that a positive mental attitude is enough, without any practice or action. My feeling is that, if you aren't prepared to do the work, your attitude is not as positive as you think it is.

Philosophical insights can radically change your psychology and your behaviour. It is also true, however, that actually doing something can change your psychology and your philosophy. In the course, I introduce my students to approximately 25 powerful action-learning exercises. Each one has been scientifically proven to increase happiness. One of my personal favourites is called "One Hundred Gratitudes". This exercise, which I will share with you now, is potentially life-changing. Let me put it this way: If you will do it, it will do a lot for you.

Three Types of Gratitude

Before I introduce you to the exercise called "One Hundred Gratitudes", I think it is good to acknowledge the intimate relationship that exists between gratitude and happiness. This beautiful intimacy is best summed up by happiness coach Barry Neil Kaufman, author of *Happiness Is a Choice* and co-founder of The Option Institute.[1] Barry says: "Gratitude is the shortest shortcut to happiness." Heartfelt gratitude really is the fastest way to experience happiness now. It is impossible to be truly grateful and neurotic; it is also impossible to be truly grateful and not happy.

To get the best out of "One Hundred Gratitudes", I think it helps to reflect on the true nature of gratitude, the real purpose of gratitude and also the potential power of gratitude. In my experience, everyone is familiar with gratitude, but they are often unaware of what it really can do for you, if you really do it. My own inquiry into gratitude has shown me that there are three different types of gratitude. The first type of gratitude is a basic positive attitude; the second type is a philosophy about life; and the third type is a training in vision.

Type #1: An Attitude. Most people's experience of gratitude is a positive response to events that are judged as favourable. Gratitude is a conscious reaction to things, people, situations and outcomes that you deem to be "good" and "positive". This type of gratitude is very personal and highly interpretative. For example, I might be grateful that my football team beat yours, but you probably don't feel that way right now. If you're really spiritual, you may congratulate me on my team's good fortune, but you probably don't feel grateful about the outcome.

This attitude of gratitude is mostly reactive, that is, it exists because something happens first. Like the type of happiness called "pleasure", it is an effect of a cause, a response to a stimulus. There is, however, also such a thing as a proactive attitude of gratitude. Proactive gratitude is based on a decision to enjoy something before it happens. For example, *I intend to appreciate and give thanks for today, no matter what happens.* Proactive gratitude uses the power of intention to help you make the most of your day. *It is good to end the day with gratitude, but it is even better to begin the day with gratitude.*

Type #2: A Philosophy. This is an "unconditional gratitude" based on a faith that *everything that happens (or doesn't happen) in your life is for your own best interests.* It starts with the awareness that we live in a purposeful universe in which everything that happens can be used as a hint and a valuable spur for greater happiness and enlightenment. No matter what an event looks like and no matter whether you judge it as "good" or "bad", "right" or "wrong", "success" or "failure", it carries a gift of great value. This awareness of "a gift in everything" dawns slowly at first and grows eventually into an absolute faith.

This philosophy of gratitude proclaims, "Life is on my side." Life is always for you; it is never against you. Practising unconditional gratitude for your life helps you to hold a space in your mind for the possibility of blessings in every situation. It is a fact that blessings sometimes come wrapped in fear, pain and tears. In choosing to practise unconditional gratitude you are choosing to trust the process, to honour your feelings every step of the way and to place your faith in an outcome of *inevitable grace*.

Type #3: A Vision. Real Gratitude, with a capital G, stems from a holy revelation that *you are what you seek*. It is more than just an attitude or a philosophy, because it gives you a glimpse of the light that is your original, divine nature. This type of gratitude is based on a deep spiritual realisation that you were created perfectly and that everything you have chased after and longed for – love, happiness, peace – is already yours. It is, therefore, a type of salvation, a homecoming and a chance to finally rest.

This real Gratitude is based on a thanksgiving for your true identity. It teaches you that *happiness does not leave its source*. In other words, happiness does not come and go; what comes and goes is your awareness of happiness. It also teaches you that *what is truly valuable already belongs to you*. For instance, your true nature has an ever-ready capacity to love unconditionally, to be unreasonably happy and to be truly wise. You can enjoy these things now, because of who you are and because of what created you.

A Big "Thank You"

"One Hundred Gratitudes" is a journal exercise that invites you to reflect on your life, from past to present, and to record 100 entries of pure appreciation and thanksgiving. The goal is to compile a list of 100 experiences, relationships, places, people, books, songs, pieces of art, events, adventures and other moments that you are truly grateful for. These One Hundred Gratitudes add up to one great big "Thank You" for the miracle of existence. It is like a thank-you letter to God.

There are a number of ways to do "One Hundred Gratitudes". Some people compile their lists chronologically: "Dear Mum, thanks for giving birth to me. Sorry it was such a long labour." Others don't follow a timeline; they just write what comes. Some people compile the list in one sitting. Personally, I recommend that you do it over several sittings, maybe compiling 10 to 15 entries at a time. Some people do "One Hundred Gratitudes" on their own; others do it with close friends or with their partners, for instance. Sharing your One Hundred Gratitudes is as powerful as compiling them.

The one key instruction that I ask you to follow is that for each entry you include a "what" and a "why". Here is a personal example from my list. "What: a book called *A Course in Miracles*. Why: This book is my spiritual bible and my daily practice. I am truly grateful to the author. Studying this book helps me to remember my true identity, to be a more loving person and to enjoy my life even more." The "why" is as important as the "what" because the goal isn't just to create a list; it's to recognise what it is you truly value and appreciate about being alive.

On the last day of the course, you review your experience of compiling your One Hundred Gratitudes. First, I ask you, "What did you value about doing this exercise?" Second, I ask you, "What did you learn about yourself doing this exercise?" If you did it with someone else, I might also ask you to reflect on what you learned about each other. Third, I ask you, "What did you learn about happiness doing this exercise?" This exercise is a powerful meditation on happiness. And lastly, I want to know if this exercise will affect the way you live your life from now on. Will you do anything differently?

"One Hundred Gratitudes" is always one of the exercises that students rate "most useful". I can honestly say that everyone who does this exercise experiences huge value. It is a truly profound exercise. And yet not everyone chooses to do it. Lots of people appear to have a good excuse for not doing it, for example, "too busy", "no time", "feels inauthentic", and "too simple". I find that the people who don't do "One Hundred Gratitudes" are the people who have never done a gratitude exercise before. They like the theory of gratitude, but they just don't think it will have a powerful enough effect.

Joy of Gratitude

"One Hundred Gratitudes" is fun to do and it can be a real life-changer. I would go as far as to say I have witnessed miraculous effects in people who have done it. As with every exercise I introduce, I guarantee that *it works if you do it; it won't if you don't.*

Do yourself a favour and compile your own "One Hundred Gratitudes". You will be so thankful that you did. No excuses, please. Excuses are just resistance. And any resistance you may experience to practising gratitude is really either a desire to hold on to pain or a fear of joy. As you do this exercise, I honestly believe you will experience many powerful benefits along the way. Below is a list of seven common benefits to look out for, as told by past students.

Undoing Lack. "One Hundred Gratitudes" literally helps you to change your perception of the world. Comments from students include: "I can see a pattern to my life now that will help me as I consider my next steps," and "It has put my entire life into perspective," and "I am better able to focus on what is positive and good now," and "Finally, I can see a perfection to my life." One of my favourite comments is from John, a photojournalist, who said: "Doing 'One Hundred Gratitudes' showed me that my past was better than I realised; my life right now is better than I realised; and I think my future just got a whole lot better, too."

Practising gratitude is really a decision to give up all belief in lack. Phoebe wrote a personal letter to me after doing her One Hundred Gratitudes. She said, "All my life I have felt a huge sense of lack and nothing ever made it go away before. Now I realise that the lack I experienced was due to my lack of gratitude. I can see now that nothing is missing from 'here' and 'now', other than my expectations of what should be here. Nothing is ever missing, other than my acceptance and gratitude for what is." Ego perceptions give way to true vision. Through gratitude, you begin to see not just with the eyes but with the heart.

Increased Wellbeing. Doing "One Hundred Gratitudes" feels good. Students report, "It's like a tonic," and "I feel uplifted," and "I smile more," and "It's my Vitamin G," and "I notice the good stuff more." Another one of my favourite comments is, "Gratitude is free psychotherapy and every session is a good session because I always feel better about myself and my life afterward." Practising gratitude on a regular basis will change your psychology. You will notice a higher level of optimism, confidence and enthusiasm. Also, it is impossible to be truly grateful and depressed.

Gratitude is energy. It energises you, it restores you and it soothes your weariness. Professor Robert Emmons, at the University of California-Davis, has done as much as anyone to research the potential healing properties of gratitude.[2] In one study, with a group of adults with neuromuscular disease, he concluded: "A 21-day gratitude intervention resulted in greater amounts of high-energy positive moods, a greater sense of feeling connected to others, more optimistic ratings of one's life and better sleep duration and sleep quality, relative to a control group."[3] Gratitude works when you do it.

Real Values. Caroline, a senior midwife, shared how doing "One Hundred Gratitudes" was "a real shock" that forced her to reconsider her attitude toward work. She said, "I realised that what I am most grateful for in my life is what I moan and complain about the most." I encouraged Caroline to interview her "moans" and "complaints". "What is the real message here?" I asked. Caroline concluded that midwifery was her true calling, but that she needed to spend less time worrying about the bureaucracy and more time focusing on the real purpose of her work. She also realised she needed to take regular breaks and stop putting in so much overtime.

When you really master gratitude, it helps you to discern between what is important and what is not. You no longer complain about the little things with quite the same conviction. You can't be bothered to sweat the small stuff. You remember the big picture. True gratitude helps you to tune in to your timeless values. It amplifies your conscious sense of purpose. It reveals the true meaning of life, for you. Scientific research also shows that the better you get at gratitude, the less likely you are to be materialistic, acquisitive and envious and to feel like you are lacking something compared to others.[4]

Healing Perspective. Most people's One Hundred Gratitudes are a full and frank inventory of their life's most important moments. Gratitude doesn't just focus on what is positive; it focuses on what is significant. For that reason, many people include in their lists past mistakes, heartbreaks, illnesses, divorce, bereavement, failures and dark nights of the ego. "Gratitude has helped me to find gifts in the most unexpected places," wrote Clare, "like in my experience of chronic fatigue syndrome and also in my divorce last year, which at the time I thought I would never recover from."

Gratitude helps you to focus on the "positives". And it also encourages you to look again at everything you have judged as "negative", "bad", and "wrong", and to see past your judgments and beyond the appearances to the truth, the learning, the healing and the love. The power of unconditional gratitude is expressed beautifully in Alanis Morissette's song "Thank U", in which she sings of her gratitude for disillusionment, frailty and terror – for teaching her to be brave, to be strong, to stop blaming and to "enjoy the moment for once"[5]

Heart-Centred. Every exercise that I share is an exercise I have done for myself first. The first time I did my "One Hundred Gratitudes", I was surprised by just how many entries were about people and relationships. I really appreciate the people in my life, but I didn't realise how much until I made my list. Only 2 out of 100 entries were about possessions. I love "things", I'm certainly not anti-material, but I was genuinely surprised to see that I didn't love "things" as much as I thought. Doing "One Hundred Gratitudes" put me back in touch with my heart.

My list of gratitudes was a wake-up call that reminded me to keep putting relationships first. I realised how loved I really am and also how blessed I am to know my family and my friends and everyone who is part of The Happiness Project. I also noticed something interesting – that *the more grateful I am for the people in my life, the more attractive and wonderful and interesting and talented and friendly they become!* Practising gratitude also reminded me to say "Thank you" more often to the people I love. In short, gratitude is a good excuse to show more love, to receive more love and to be more yourself with everyone.

Conscious Connection. Practising gratitude helps you to feel a greater sense of connection with people, with places and with the present moment. People who do "One Hundred Gratitudes" say things like, "I am less self-centred now," and "It got me over myself,'" and "I feel less independent and cut off from life." Anna wrote, "My 'One Hundred Gratitudes' taught me that I'm not as alone as I think I am. Being all alone is just my story; it's not the truth." Isolation and aloneness are often exacerbated by a lack of conscious gratitude. It is impossible to be truly grateful and feel alone.

Gratitude also promotes a greater sense of spiritual connection with yourself, with others and with life as a whole. In another scientific study of gratitude, the researchers concluded: "Grateful people are more likely to acknowledge a belief in the interconnectedness of all life and a commitment to and responsibility to others."[6] Gratitude is one of the highest forms of prayer. Practising gratitude daily helps you to remember your divine inheritance and your original, happy nature.

Happiness NOW. At first, most people are a little daunted by the task of finding 100 things to be grateful for, but by the end they usually find it impossible to restrict it to only 100. Gratitude works in harmony with the Law of Attraction, which states that *what you focus on is what you attract.* Elizabeth, a painter, compiled her list of gratitudes while sitting outside in her favourite garden chair. She wrote, "One effect of this gratitude exercise was that my garden became more and more beautiful to me." Gratitude helps you to pay attention and as your attention grows, so too does your sense of wonder and awe.

For me, the real gift of gratitude is that *the more grateful you are, the more present you become.* Gratitude gets you back into your life. It makes you *be here now.* And the more present you are, the more abundant and alive you feel. Terry, a jewellery designer, who attented the course in 2002, wrote, "My 'One Hundred Gratitudes' showed me that I have persistently delayed feeling truly grateful for my life. Never now; always later. I now see that this delay was entirely unnecessary. My life is happening NOW and the more willing I am to be grateful as I go, the more my life naturally gets better and better." Gratitude is an angel that restores sight to those who were once fooled into believing their ego stories of separateness and lack.

There are many versions of the "One Hundred Gratitudes" exercise. It does not have to be a list from past to present. Neither do you have to do it just for yourself. On the first anniversary of our marriage, which is traditionally celebrated with a paper gift, I gave my wife, Hollie, a letter with my 100 gratitudes for her and our life together. And I did the same on the first birthday of our darling daughter, Bo. I also compiled a list of One Hundred Gratitudes for my brother David, which I gave to him on his 40th birthday. Over dinner with him, I shared several of the entries that highlighted why I feel so blessed that he is my brother.

**Gratitude is double happiness because it
blesses both the giver and
the receiver.**

● ● ● ● ●

PART IV

everyday abundance

the
daily
unconscious

"Ten Blessings" was the opening exercise in the very first happiness course back in 1992. It's so simple. And challenging. I begin by inviting everyone in the class to stand up. Then I explain that for the next 10 minutes they are to wander around the room and introduce themselves to 10 people and share one blessing they have experienced in the last week – a different blessing each time. A blessing refers to something you are grateful for, a precious moment, something you received, or something that made you smile.

I encourage you to review the last week of your life now and write down a list of blessings. Ten blessings in the last seven days. It's not much to ask, is it? All you need to find is one blessing per 16.8 hours of life. It will be even easier if you are a light sleeper. The maths would suggest that more waking hours equals more consciousness, which equals more blessings. Reflect on what you have most appreciated, enjoyed, received and noticed. Identify what you most valued and what was most meaningful. Notice also your response to doing this exercise. One response might be not to do it, but I urge you to give it a go, for the sake of personal research.

I find people's responses to this exercise are so interesting. For a start, very few people look happy. If anything, they look harassed or nonplussed. Physically, everyone stops breathing. Which is not good in the long term.

A blank look appears over people's faces. And sometimes I think I see bits of tumbleweed blowing across the empty wasteland of their minds. That's probably just my imagination. Or my projection! Next, there is a sense of growing panic. And after that, there's lots of mutual muttering: "This is difficult." "Impossible." "Can we use the same blessing 10 times?" "A *different blessing* each time!" "Can I use one of your blessings?"

The problem most people have with the "Ten Blessings" exercise is that they can't remember anything about last week. It's like they've just been given an ancient history exam. Even yesterday can feel like a distant memory. Did yesterday actually happen, or was it a dream? In the feedback after "Ten Blessings", people often say things like, "At first, I had no idea what I did last week," and "I couldn't recall anything positive, to begin with." Most people struggle through to 10 blessings eventually, but the common initial response is, "What happened?" and "Where was I?"

Recently, I gave a workshop on happiness for 150 volunteers with one of the charities that The Happiness Project sponsors. I began with the "Ten Blessings" exercise. Everyone got up, walked around and started to share their blessings. Except for Joan, that is, who was sitting in the front row and looked absolutely lost. I went over and sat next to Joan. We introduced ourselves to each other. This is how our conversation went:

"So, Joan, name one blessing from the last week."

"I can't think of any," said Joan.

"Just one blessing, Joan."

"My mind is blank."

"Remember to keep breathing, Joan,"

"Okay," nodded Joan, as she let out a smile.

"Was it a bad week?" I asked.

"No, just a normal week," said Joan.

"So, what did you do last week?"

"I can't remember."

Joan felt bad that she couldn't play along and I was tempted to give in, but something made me keep going.

"Give me one small, baby blessing, Joan."

"Oh yes!" said Joan, as her face lit up. "It was my granddaughter's first birthday last Tuesday. We had a wonderful time. She is such a joy."

"Well done, Joan," I said. "Now, can you give me another blessing?"

"Yes," said Joan, who had clearly perked up. "My husband has been off work for 18 months with a serious injury and last week he was finally given the doctor's clearance to return to work."

"My goodness, congratulations," I said.

Joan's past week was improving by the minute now, so I thought I would go for a third blessing.

"I can't think of anything else," said Joan, shaking her head.

I was about to call it quits, when Joan said, "Last Monday, I won a National Award for being Volunteer of the Year. Does that count?"

"Well, are you happy about it?" I asked.

"Well, I'm looking forward to meeting the Queen," said Joan.

"Ten Blessings" is a revelation to many people who often find that their life is a lot better than they first thought. Initially, their minds are blank. They are not conscious of any blessings at all. And then, by some miracle, the blessings appear: anniversaries, birthdays, dinner dates, family time, meetings with friends, funny moments, good news, rich conversations, a great book, a sunset, the stars at night – they all come out. An extreme lack of consciousness, a gross act of denial even, gives way to a renewed sense of everyday abundance.

The Daily Blur

Every day, the majority of us participate in a strange, hypnotic dance that I call "The Daily Unconscious". We wake up, we hit the autopilot, we lock onto our schedules and then we get going. It's a routine that the masses are familiar with: school runs, daily commute, arrive at work, check e-mail, meetings, errands, lunch at your desk, more meetings, more errands, check e-mail, school pick-up, commute home. This isn't exactly your life; this is just what you do with your time. And most of it is done unconsciously.

A certain amount of "auto" is practical and convenient. It's a good thing, for instance, that you don't have to manually boot up your autonomic nervous system each day. It's so good to know that your body can automatically monitor the movement of the earth, the moon, the sun and the stars so as to work your circadian rhythms – without any conscious help from you. Your unconscious mind can also take care of a lot of the mental bureaucracy and detail that go into running the brain. This saves you time. It frees you up. You can get more stuff done. You can earn a salary. You can get on with your day.

While your auto can help you to get *through the day*, it doesn't exactly help you to *enjoy your day*. If you send too much of your life into the unconscious, you end up barely conscious of anything any more. As a result, your life goes by unnoticed. You miss the detail. You miss your life. You see only your prejudgments, which is another word for *prejudices*. The precious present is lost in a daily blur of unconscious processes. Each brand new day is encountered like "another yesterday". Your ego is routinely blocking out the miracle of existence so that you can stay on track with your schedule.

The Daily Unconscious is, by its very nature, difficult to plot. If you are not careful, you can end up sleepwalking through the days, months and years of your life. "Our life is but a sleep and a forgetting," wrote the poet Wordsworth.[1] Here are some telltale signs of The Daily Unconscious at work in your life:

You stop to write a cheque – and you realise, all of sudden, that you have no idea what the date is today. Moreover, you are not exactly sure what day of the week it is. Is it Tuesday or Thursday? You don't even know the month. Is it June already? And you may even have to think twice about what year it is.

Another birthday so soon – and the days turn into weeks and the weeks turn into months, and so on. It feels like your children have at least two birthdays a year. You can't help but feel that Christmas Day would be a lot more practical if it was biennial. Every year is shorter than the one before. You literally do not know where the time goes. You have as much time as everyone else, but it doesn't feel that way.

The weekends are a blur – and when a friend or a colleague asks you "How was your weekend?" you may say "Great!" but truthfully you have no idea what you did, whom you spent it with or what about it you enjoyed. Monday morning comes around so fast it's like you missed a whole Sunday or something. There is no stopping. There is no sabbatical. Your life is one swift swoosh.

Another week of vague busyness – and "Thank God it's Friday!" goes the weary worker's prayer. You know you have been busy all week and you know how tired you are now, but you have no idea what you have been busy about. If someone were to ask you to name five successes in the last week – just one success a day – your mind would go blank and you would struggle to name any.

You get lost in roles and duties – and, if you are not careful, you forget to appreciate and enjoy your most intimate relationships. For instance, you are so busy taking care of the mortgage that you miss out on your children's upbringing. One minute they were in nursery and the next minute they want to rent their own apartments. Relationships need conscious attention.

You open your credit-card statement – and you wonder who has been spending all your money. Your first thought is, "Someone must have stolen my credit card and gone on a spending spree." As you examine the bill more closely, you are gradually able to account for most of the spending. Some of it still remains a mystery, though. You literally do not know where the money goes.

You demand to know who ate your muffin – and then you figure out that it was you. You munch unconsciously. You convince yourself that you only eat 1,500 calories a day, that is, until you start to keep a daily food journal. Many of us are so unconscious about our relationship to food. Reading a food label is a good start to enjoying the pleasure of conscious eating.

The real problem with The Daily Unconscious is that you stop checking in with yourself. Before long, you have no idea what you really think, how you really feel and what it is you really want. There is no interior awareness. You have no idea who the real you is. You feel vacant inside, but that's only because you have not been paying attention. You know it would be good to stop and wake up, but the fear of stopping drives you on and keeps you unconscious. Your ego, the unconscious controller, is afraid of what you might see, what you might feel and what you might have to deal with.

Happiness returns when you wake up from the routine of your life and actually start to live again. Consciousness returns when you start to listen to yourself again. You start to read the internal memos and you take notice of the whispers of your heart. You begin to feel alive again, after a long, unconscious winter. You are available once more to the people in your life. You find your life again in each new moment. It turns out that the truth wasn't hiding from you; you were hiding from it. You went unconscious and now you are awake again. What was once a blur becomes clear. You remember who you are and you remember what really matters.

A Daily Practice

I recommend to everyone who takes the course that they have a daily spiritual practice. It does not have to be a long, extravagant, religious affair. It needs only to be simple and sincere. The purpose of having a daily practice is to help you to wake up. It should make you feel grounded, centred and strong. It should help you to focus. And it should enable you to be open and receptive. A daily spiritual practice helps you to connect to your joy, negotiate your ego and show up even more in your life.

Having a daily spiritual practice is a very personal thing. You have to choose one that fits you. And the best fit is a practice that you actually enjoy doing. Also, the enjoyment should be implicit and instant. In other words, you don't do the practice because you hope to get a reward one day. *Doing the practice is the reward.* It improves your life *now*. It makes a difference *today.* It helps you to be more *here.* There are many great practices to choose from. Here are four practices that we experiment with.

Greeting the Day. "Please do not say, 'It is morning,' and dismiss it with the name of yesterday. See it for the first time as a newborn child that has no name," wrote the Indian poet Rabindranath Tagore.[2] A spiritual practice helps you to greet each new day in the same way you would greet a new life or a new person. Greeting the day can take many forms. For instance, a morning prayer, some meditation time, lighting a candle, a daily affirmation, inspirational literature, or a physical movement like the sun salutation performed by yoga students.

When I appeared on an episode of *The Oprah Winfrey Show* called "How Happy Are You?" Oprah introduced five people, with a one-minute film on each and then asked the audience to guess who had scored the highest in a well-known happiness test. The winner was David, a 53-year-old funeral director. "But you look at dead people all day long," Oprah jested. David and I spoke at length and he shared that one of his keys to happiness is to "name the day". He talked about "Marvellous Mondays" and "Terrific Tuesdays" and "Wonderful Wednesdays". He was both positive and sincere about doing this. So I tried it for myself and I found it really works.

I had a chance to speak to David again a few weeks later when I interviewed him for an *Oprah & Friends* satellite radio show. He told me, "Naming the day helps you to be present." He said, "My job as a funeral director teaches me that life is an immediate proposition. Either you live it or you don't." Even just taking a moment to register today's date can be a powerful spiritual practice if it actually helps you to be more present. Herb Gardner, author of the play *A Thousand Clowns,* had the character Murray Burns say,

> **"You have got to own your days and name them,**
> **each one of them, every one of them,**
> **or else the years go right by**
> **and none of them belong to you."[3]**

Setting an Intention. Your day does not happen at random. As soon as you wake up, you make decisions that affect how your day goes. Some of these decisions are conscious, but most of them are not. Some of these decisions are "to do" decisions, but the most important decisions of all are your "to be" decisions. Deciding to *be present,* to *be kind,* or to *be loving,* for instance, helps you to engage your power and to participate more creatively in your life today. Try it. Set an intention to be happy. *Decide to make today even more enjoyable than you thought it was going to be.*

One of my favourite intention-setting practices is a short prayer from *A Course in Miracles*. I have recited this prayer every morning for many years now and I find that it helps me to be open to the Unconditioned Self, which really knows how to live. First I say the prayer and then I listen for a couple of minutes. Guidance, wisdom and joy flow naturally. It sets up my day perfectly. The prayer is:

> **What would you have me do today?**
> **Where would you have me go?**
> **What would you have me say and to whom?**[4]

A Single Purpose. You only have to watch your mind for five minutes to realise how scattered and unfocused it normally is. One reason for this internal chaos is a lack of unified purpose. In the course, at the start of each workshop day you receive an Inner Smile card.[5] Each of these cards has a single word on it, like "generosity", "receive", "honesty", "spontaneity", and "defenceless". The idea is that you use your Inner Smile card to help set a conscious purpose for your day. You can go online to www.behappy.net right now and pick an Inner Smile card.

You also receive a daily e-mail that helps you to set a conscious focus for each day. These daily messages are written specifically for each new class. They are designed to help you make each day a creative event. They feature inspirational sayings, affirmations, poetry, meditations and also prayers like this well-known Navajo prayer:

> Happily may I walk.
> May it be beautiful before me.
> May it be beautiful behind me.
> May it be beautiful below me.
> May it be beautiful above me.
> May it be beautiful all around me.
> In beauty, it is finished.[6]

Practising Readiness. The whole point of a daily spiritual practice is to help you *be ready now* for more love, more happiness, more success and more of everything that you truly want. In *A Course in Miracles* there is a line that reads: "Prepare yourself for miracles today."[7] I love the sound of these words. I find that every page of *A Course in Miracles* helps me to be more open and available to what is on offer now. Later on in the text, there is a passage that reads:

> Each day a thousand treasures come to me with every passing moment. I am blessed with gifts throughout the day, in value far beyond all things of which I can conceive. A brother smiles upon another and my heart is gladdened. Someone speaks a word of gratitude or mercy and my mind receives this gift and takes it as its own. And everyone who finds the way to God becomes my savior, pointing out the way to me and giving me his certainty that what he learned is surely mine as well.[8]

To be happy, all you have to do is *be ready to receive more happiness than you thought was possible.* Your happiness awaits you, just as soon as you are ready. Be willing, therefore, to give up your theory of how the universe works and simply be ready. Proclaim, "I am ready to enjoy my life today." Be ready to be happy now. Allow yourself to be happy for no good reason. Be ready to be so happy you almost feel guilty but not quite. Be ready to forgive your past. Be ready to give more of yourself. Be ready to receive. Be ready for a miracle.

· · · · ·

CHAPTER 14

ready,
steady,
NOW

It's official – the pursuit of happiness has speeded up! We are chasing after happiness faster than ever. As a result, we work faster, we speed date, we shop online and we generally live life on the run. The latest advances in science, the new era of global speed merchants, the real-time bankers and the information superhighway mechanics have all contributed to the acceleration of everything. We can now travel fast-forward, nonstop, to a land called "there", which is, apparently, better than "here". We are going so fast you would think we would have arrived by now. But, it seems, we are still trying to *get there*.

"The pursuit of happiness" is a central tenet of the US Declaration of Independence. The American forefathers described it as an "unalienable right" of mankind, and many people the world over subscribe to it today. It was also described as a "self-evident" truth, which suggests that its meaning is obvious. But that is not so. Thomas Jefferson wrote the phrase "life, liberty and the pursuit of happiness", which was based on the previous writings of English philosopher John Locke, who wrote about "life, liberty and estate".[1] Jefferson never publicly explained his alteration and so we can only speculate about what he meant by it.

The word *pursuit* has, according to the American Heritage Dictionary, two distinct meanings. The first meaning is the act of "chasing" or "striving".

This meaning turns "the pursuit of happiness" into a *chase after happiness*. As such, happiness is seen as a finish line, a destination that must be reached. And you, therefore, relate to happiness as something that exists outside you, in the future, somewhere else. Also, there is no indication that the *race to happiness* ever ends. You go faster, but you get no closer.

The second meaning of the word *pursuit* is "an activity, such as a vocation or hobby, engaged in regularly". This meaning turns "the pursuit of happiness" into something that you focus on, are inclined toward and engage in regularly, like a *literary pursuit*, for example. Now, if this is what Thomas Jefferson meant by "pursuit", he was surely advocating that it is your right to enjoy as much life, liberty and happiness as every other person on this planet. Happiness is your equal right and that means *right now*. There is no indication in this second meaning of "pursuit" that any distance exists between you and happiness.

Ultimately, it doesn't matter much what Thomas Jefferson meant by the phrase "life, liberty and the pursuit of happiness". What is important, however, is what *you* make it mean. The American Declaration of Independence is as much a contemplation as it is a set of rules. Thus, *the pursuit of happiness* is for your self-inquiry. The meaning you give to *the pursuit of happiness* will influence your relationship to happiness, your relationship to your life today and your relationship to your life overall. Be conscious, therefore, of the meaning you give it.

Happiness Pension

Jennifer attended the course in 2006. At the time she was 39 years old, married, a mother of two and the human resources director of a well-known international company. Jennifer agreed to do an exercise called "The Happiness Walk-Through" with me after her name was pulled out of my magic "volunteer hat". She came to the front of the room and stood in front of a line of numbers from 0 to 10 laid out before her on the floor. I began by asking Jennifer to stand next to the number that was her answer to this question: *From 0 to 10, how happy am I in my life at present?*

Jennifer immediately went and stood next to the number 6. I noted how quickly she had moved to this number and so I asked, "How often do you feel 60 per cent happy with your life?" Jennifer replied, "I would say I am 60 per cent happy most of the time." We had found Jennifer's "familiar point", which is the figure she most easily identifies with. After a couple more questions, we identified that her "familiar range" is between 5 and 7 out of 10. "Sometimes I dip down to about 5, but hardly ever below," said Jennifer, "And if something nice happens I would say I can go to 7."

Next, I asked Jennifer to stand next to the number 7 and then I asked her to close her eyes, take a deep breath and answer the following question: *For me to be 70 per cent happy, what would have to happen?* Still with her eyes closed, Jennifer replied, "A raise or paying off the mortgage. More financial security."

I noted Jennifer's answer and then I asked her to stand next to the number 8 and I asked her to reflect on the following question: *For me to be 80 per cent happy, what would have to happen?* Eighty per cent happiness was out of Jennifer's "familiar range", and so she took a little longer to answer. Eventually, Jennifer said, "Both my daughters would be at university. And happy."

Again, I noted her answer and then Jennifer stood next to the number 9. Here, Jennifer contemplated the question, *For me to be 90 per cent happy, what would have to happen?* After a minute or so, Jennifer answered, "I would own a vacation home somewhere by the sea. And I would paint with my oils all day long. And I would read great literature. And I would enjoy *every* sunset with my husband."

At this point I stopped Jennifer's Happiness Walk-Through. I asked her, "Are you aware of how all of your answers are based far off in the future?" "I wasn't conscious of that until now," she said. Jennifer clearly enjoyed a strong sense of anticipation about future happiness. Anticipation can be a positive thing. For example, anticipating how good your vacation will be is part of the fun of booking in advance. The enjoyment of anticipation doubles the pleasure of every good thing.

That said, there is also "obstructive anticipation", which is when your sense of anticipation becomes so constant and excessive that it obscures your chances of being happy now. Obstructive anticipation is so future-focused that you end up constantly planning happiness instead of actually being happy. Happiness is never now; it is always "if", "when", and "after" something else has happened first. Hence, you end up simultaneously preparing for and *delaying* your happiness. The French philosopher Blaise Pascal wrote this caution to us:

> Let each one examine his thoughts and he will find them all occupied with the past and the future. We scarcely ever think of the present; and if we ever think of it, it is only to take light from it to arrange the future . . . So we never live, but we hope to live; and, as we are always preparing to be happy, it is inevitable we should never be so.[2]

Interestingly, scientific research shows that when people dream about the future, they tend to imagine themselves happier and more successful.[3] Just like Jennifer, they score themselves higher on the happiness scale in the future. For example, the score is 6 out of 10 for now and 8 out of 10 in the future. The reality, however, is that when you arrive at your future, you do so with a 6-out-of-10 mindset or "familiar point". So what do you do then? Well, either you change your mind and enjoy your new "now", or you create yet another happy future and you engage once again in an unending pursuit of happiness.

I asked Jennifer to do "The Happiness Walk-Through" again. And this time, when she stood next to the number 7, I asked her to answer this question: *For me to be 70 per cent happy, what would have to happen* now? On number 8, I gave her the question, *For me to be 80 per cent happy, what would have to happen now?* And on number 9, it was, *For me to be 90 per cent happy, what would have to happen now?* Interestingly, none of Jennifer's answers was about the world being any different; they were about her being different.

Jennifer said things like, "I will enjoy watching my daughters grow up," and "I promise to take all of my vacation days this year," and "I am going to start painting again," and "Tomorrow evening I will take my husband out on a date, down by the river, to watch a beautiful sunset together." At the end of this short 20-minute exercise, Jennifer was back in her life again. She was no longer chasing happiness; she was simply making conscious choices – creative choices – that would help her to enjoy more happiness now.

A few days later, Jennifer sent me a beautiful calligraphy card with a famous saying on it: "Happiness is not a destination; it is a manner of travelling." She also wrote these words inside the card: "Robert, you have just saved me 20 years of my life. There I was, busy saving up for some imaginary happiness pension and dreaming my life away in the meantime. What 'The Happiness Walk-Through' has shown me is that to have a happy future I have to start now. Happiness isn't a pension you save up for; it's an inheritance you are meant to enjoy now!"

Happiness Ticket

If you take *the pursuit of happiness* to mean "a chase" or "a striving," then it is most likely you will relate to happiness as a "thing", "reward", or "place" that must be won or arrived at. If this is so, you will start to look for the "big tickets" that will win you your prize. Eventually, you will forget that happiness is a way of being and something you can choose; you will convince yourself that happiness can only be experienced "if", "when", and "after" something has happened first.

So, what do you have to do to win the prize? In the course I give students a piece of paper called "The Happiness Ticket". This ticket has three columns on it and the goal is to complete the sentence at the top of each column. The sentence for Column One is: "I'd be happy if . . ." For Column Two it is: "I'll be happy when . . ." And for Column Three it is: "I'll be happy after . . ." I give the group 10 minutes to fill in their Happiness Tickets. The goal is to find out *what you have told yourself must happen first before you can be happy.*

On average, I would say most people complete a total of 10 entries across the three columns. I encourage you to take some time now to identify your own happiness conditions of "if", "when", and "after". Here are a few examples of what people write:

"I'll be happy when I have a loving partner."

"I'll be happy after I have found my next job."

"I'd be happy if my talents were more recognised."

"I'll be happy when I have enough money."

"I'll be happy after I sort my life out."

"I'll be happy when I have lost 10 pounds."

Whenever you enter a competition, you probably take a quick glance at the rules and also note when the prize-giving ceremony will be. The problem with making happiness into a big-ticket prize is that once you create a list of conditions for happiness ("if", "after", and "when"), the list never really gets any shorter. Why? Because as soon as you wipe off one condition on your list you add another condition in its place. You have entered into a conditional mindset. Thus, there will never be a grand-prize draw. Which means, you will never win.

This is not just conjecture on my part. In one famous 16-year longitudinal study, conducted by the Roper-Starch Organization, a cross-section of the American population completed a happiness survey first in 1978 and then again in 1994.[4] Participants were given a list of 24 big-ticket items that are commonly associated with the "good life", such as a home, a car, a swimming pool, foreign travel and a vacation home. They were then asked the following questions:

1. When you think of the good life, the life you'd like to have, which of the things on this list, if any, are part of that good life as far as you personally are concerned?

2. Now, would you go down that list and call off all of the things you now have?

The research found that in 1978, the mean number of items people owned was 1.7, but the mean number of items they desired was 4.4 – a discrepancy of 2.7 items. In 1994, the mean number of items owned was now 3.1, but the mean number of items desired had grown to 5.6 – a discrepancy of 2.5 items. So, after 16 years of chasing after happiness, the finish line was still roughly the same distance away. Psychologist Daniel Nettle summed up the research well. He wrote:

> Over the early part of their adult lives, people go from having few if any of these big-ticket items to having several of them. The trouble is that their ideal of what would be needed for the good life recedes at almost exactly the same rate as they advance. When they are young, a house, car and TV seem enough. Later on, a holiday home comes to seem just essential.[5]

Present Happiness

Some people chase happiness; others choose happiness. It all depends on how much time you want to save.

Chasing is a mindset. To chase after happiness is to misunderstand who you are and what happiness is. You only chase after what you think is not already here. Whatever it is you pursue – be it peace, happiness, love, abundance or God – is what you won't yet accept. You chase after what you fear you are not worthy of. Chasing keeps away what you will not let yourself receive. At some point, if you really want to be happy, you have to be willing to give up the chase. And you have to let happiness chase after you.

The more you chase after happiness, the further away you move from the *here and now*, and the more alienated you feel from yourself. Chasing is both a cause and an effect of self-alienation. When you lose your conscious mooring to your Unconditioned Self, you will chase after anything that looks like it might make you happy again. But the more you chase, the more "out of sync" you feel with yourself. And the faster you run, the longer the race becomes. Chasing is a never-ending mindset.

Constant chasing is not a happy lifestyle. Centuries ago now, Saint Augustine wrote, "Man wishes to be happy even when he so lives as to make happiness impossible."[6] Never has that been more true than today. The modern world is a breathless society. We are so manic. We are so hyper. We are pathologically fast. We are so distracted by the chase that we are barely present. Each day is a new rush, another unconscious adventure, that fails to touch us. We miss out on the joy of slow. We don't integrate anything. We never stop *to be happy*.

> **"I try to take one day at a time, but sometimes several**
> **days attack me at once."**
> – Ashleigh Brilliant[7]

We are a busy generation in danger of being too busy to be truly happy. Happiness research shows that most of us feel our lifestyles are too busy, that we work too hard and that we are constantly living on the edge of exhaustion. We are, quite literally, *missing in action*. Our lives are overcomplicated and overscheduled. This is true even for our children. A recent report by the UK charity The Children's Society warns that young children have such packed schedules today that they are not getting enough time to play, to relax and to enjoy themselves.

When the pursuit of happiness becomes an addiction, you get so busy trying to make life better that you forget how to enjoy your life. So preoccupied are you with the pursuit that no time is convenient enough for you to be happy. You definitely plan to enjoy your life one day, but chances are you will die before that happens. You are so busy you have erased yourself from your life. Your schedule means more to you than your life. You are living in the not-now. And you tell yourself you can't stop, yet. And you can't relax, yet. And you can't feel good, yet.

As you become even more strongly addicted to the pursuit of happiness, you are in no way prepared for happiness when it arrives. You miss out, because you are psychologically absent. Happiness is here, but you are not. At some point on your journey, you will have to give up the pursuit of happiness in favour of actually being happy. You will stop using the present merely as a means to get to the future and you will actually start to enjoy the present. Someday now, you will be present in your life. Any moment now, you will start to enjoy yourself.

Stop! Your life changes when you stop chasing happiness and you decide to be happy. The spiritual teacher Gangaji wrote a beautiful book called *The Diamond in Your Pocket* that I recommend to everyone who takes the course. Her teaching is a call to end the search and to give up the chase. She writes, "If you will stop all activity, just for one instant, even for one-tenth of a second and simply be utterly still, you will recognise the inherent spaciousness of your being that is already happy and at peace with itself."[8]

Unless you stop and be present, you cannot recognise what is already here. But there is a fear of stopping. The ego is afraid that if it stops it loses ground on the future. It tells you, "You will be overtaken," and "You won't get there," and "You will lose out." Are these fears true, or are they just fears? I believe they are based on the erroneous belief that the future will make you happy. The truth is, the future will not change you, it will not change your psychology and it will not change your life. Why? Because the future is just another now.

Another fear of stopping is precisely that you will be more present. And being present means facing up to your life. All of it. Including hopes and fears, blessings and wounds, triumphs and mistakes, your ego and your Unconditioned Self. Sometimes chasing happiness is really a covert operation, a concealed attempt to run away from unhappiness. At some point, you have to stop living your life on the run. At some point you have to be present. And when you are, you will find more support than you imagined. You couldn't see it before, because you weren't present.

"Enlightenment is but a recognition, not a change at all." This is one of my favourite lines from *A Course in Miracles*. Substitute the word *happiness* for *enlightenment* and you have discovered one of the most simple and profound secrets to happiness. When you decide to be present, you recognise how much you really have and it changes your life. The more present you are, the more abundant you will feel. The more present you are, the richer your day will be. The more present you are, the more you will enjoy your future.[9]

The real goal of life, then, is to be happy now *and* in the future. And the key to future happiness is present happiness. Giving your best to your life now improves your chances of future success in everything you do. Again, this is not just fanciful conjecture. Longitudinal happiness studies show over and again that *present happiness is the best predictor of future happiness*. In other words, your attitude toward now is what determines your capacity to enjoy your future.

Psychologist Daniel Nettle, whom I quoted earlier, sums up very well the scientifically corroborated relationship between present happiness and future happiness. He writes:

If you want to know how happy Bob will be in 10 years' time, don't bother to think about the fact that he will then be in his 40s, or that he is a man. Don't consider the fact that he is a dentist who will by then be in the top 5 per cent of wage earners and have a huge house in the country. Don't even factor into your deliberations the beautiful and voluptuous wife he will meet or the three children she will bear him. Instead have him take a personality inventory. Alternatively, for the best estimate of all, simply ask him how happy he is right now.[10]

CHAPTER 15

the
real
more

I was only 21 years old. It was my first visit to New York City. And it wasn't my fault. At least, that's how I saw it. Here's what happened:

It was about 9 P.M. I was in my apartment. And I was alone. After another busy day in the metropolis, I needed to relax and switch off. So I turned on the TV. It was a big TV. Bigger than the one I owned in England. It also had more channels. Approximately 250 more channels. I started to channel-hop, switching channels every five seconds or so. Making instant decisions: "No," "No," "No," "Maybe." One of the problems with channel-hopping is that you end up seeing *all* of the commercials on *all* of the channels. It was during this hopping session that I discovered, for the very first time, the shopping channel QVC.

The great thing about QVC is that it has no commercials. QVC got my attention immediately. I stopped hopping. And I started watching. The item on offer was an 11-piece professional stainless-steel cookware set. I didn't cook, but I was impressed by what I saw. The cookware set was presented by an attractive woman with very white teeth. The stainless steel gleamed beautifully beneath the television studio lights. The woman with white teeth told me that professional chefs had endorsed the cookware. She didn't mention any names. I didn't need pots and pans anyway, but they did look nice.

The price was $199, which was out of my range. But, then, all of a sudden, the woman announced there was a special offer for the next 24 hours. She told me that today the cookware set could be mine "not for $179" and "not for "$159" and "not even for $99". I was captivated. I thought to myself, "I could save over $100 if I get this." But, then again, I was returning to England soon and I didn't cook and I didn't need it. Then, the woman with white teeth said, "Today, I can offer you this item for $29.99." Oh my God. That was a saving of $170. This was truly awesome, not in a landing-on-the-moon way, but in a bargain-of-the-century way.

Finally, the woman with white teeth told me that if I purchased the item in the next hour, I would receive "completely free" a fabulous set of kitchen knives worth $99. "My God, I am technically making money on this deal," I thought. So I dialled the number on the screen. I had a short conversation with a phone operator, who was nice, but not as friendly as the woman with the white teeth. I paid on credit. An instant purchase. The cookware set and kitchen knives were now mine. And they would be with me in 28 days – approximately one week before I went back to England.

Fast-forward 20 years: I'm in Manhattan again. I'm in a hotel room. This time it's nearly midnight. I had just given a public talk and had enjoyed a late dinner with friends. I needed to wind down before going to sleep, so I started to channel-hop. And I found the QVC shopping channel again. Amazingly, the item on offer was a cookware set. I smiled to myself, remembering what had happened to me once before. I kept watching. I told myself, it's okay. I'm older now. And wiser. And I meditate every day. But I also love to cook now. And I had to admit that the cookware set did look awfully nice.

As before, the cookware set was professionally presented by an attractive woman with white teeth. The set was definitely superior to the one I had first bought. For one thing, it was a 17-piece set. The design was sleek and space age. Apparently, a scientist who had worked on the first Apollo spacecraft designed the set. The material was tougher and lighter. And bulletproof. The diamond finish was awesome. This wasn't just cookware; it was jewellery. You could practically wear this stuff. And I had to agree with the woman with white teeth who said that this beautiful item would indeed enhance any home.

The initial price was $299. I could afford that now. But I also knew the price was about to drop. And it did. So I stayed calm. But when the price settled at $39.99, I must admit I was sorely tempted. "I could buy an extra suitcase and take it home that way," I thought. Another voice in my head said, "Customs might stop you." "Pay the duty," I replied to myself, "it's still a bargain." The woman with white teeth then announced that the free gift, *for the first 500 callers,* was a three-piece, clear-view kitchen steamer set. Oh my God. I could feel myself rapidly losing consciousness. Not to sleep, but to desire.

I'm ashamed to say I reached for my credit card again. And I so nearly went ahead with the purchase. But I returned to my senses just in time. My inner voice saved me. Twenty years of meditating daily, 15 years of practising *A Course in Miracles,* countless repetitions of Louise Hay affirmations and many other spiritual practices had managed to save me from another mindless purchase. But only just.

In "The Happiness Interview". which is part of the advance work you get when you enrol in the course, one of the tasks reads: "Reflect on your life and list the possessions, achievements, relationships and events you hoped would bring happiness but didn't. What have you learned from this?" Just like everyone else, you will have convinced yourself many times that you "must have" and "absolutely need" a thing or a relationship to make you happy, only to find that when you got it, happiness wasn't there. It happens. And it happens to us all.

One short life, so many desires. What to do? The world is a marketplace, full of influences and persuasions. Your task is to discern between a burning desire that only brings short-lived pleasure and a heartfelt wish that opens you up to true joy. You have to learn to listen to your *real thoughts* – to think with God, to hear your inner voice – and not be swayed by the things you don't even want or need or like. Ultimately, you have to discern between what is valuable and what is valueless. Why? Because when you lose sight of what is truly valuable, you start to crave more of everything else. One key to happiness, then, is to spend some time with a good question like:

What do I really value?

Daily Onslaught

Every day sees a new product launch, a new advertising campaign and the birth of a new object of desire. In every major city of the world, even while you sleep, they are hard at work – the marketing wizards, the cunning wordsmiths, the PR gurus and the doctors of desire. These brand builders and brand developers are masters in the art of knowing how to make you want more. Together they create a daily onslaught of messages: Up, bigger, better, more. Up, bigger, faster, more. Up, bigger, smaller, more. Up, bigger, thinner, more.

Monthly magazines in every category work especially hard to bring you news of the latest fashion, new looks, accessories, gadgets, beauty buys, "It" things and other "must-haves". From time to time, just for a bit of fun, I conduct an informal survey of randomly selected monthly magazines to see who is offering "the most of more" right now, this month. Here are the results from the survey that I shared in the most recent course:[1]

6th Place: *Company*: 235 items
The *Company* mantra is: "More Fun for Your Money". In this month's issue they featured "235 high-street buys with attitude". They also have a special feature on "The New 'IT' Bags".

5th Place: *Cosmopolitan*: 302 items
The *Cosmopolitan* mantra is: "For Fun Fearless Females". This month they offered "302 hot fashion buys you'll never regret". They also promise to help you "SHOP like a *genius*".

4th Place: *Lucky*: 794 items
"794 items we want now". This month included a Bonus New York Section. And also "The First Annual *Lucky* Shopping Awards". Plus 150 shopping sprees to be won.

3rd Place: *Marie Claire*: 827 items
Marie Claire believes in "Fashion with Heart". This month they offered "827 great fashion and beauty buys". One headline reads: "Goodbye bling, hello happiness. Why simplicity is the new luxury".

2nd Place: *New Woman*: 867 items
"As Smart and Funny as You Are" is the *New Woman* mantra. This month they featured "867 cool new looks". The headline in pink reads: "Kiss your 2007 wardrobe goodbye!"

1st Place: *Glamour*: 1083 items
The 100% high-street Issue. This month the editors compiled a survey-topping list of "1083 great buys – to make you look like you splurged when you didn't".

Advertising is omnipresent. Every available space is a potential advertising space. Billboards, bumper stickers, ATMs, your T-shirt, your Facebook profile, all try to sell you something. One day even the individual trees in your local park will be stamped with Nike swooshes or big yellow *M*s for McDonald's. The constant aim is to make you want more, shop more and buy more than ever before. A recent advertisement from the cosmetics company Molton Brown sums it all up. The headline message is: "Everything is never enough!"

The real value of the happiness course is that it offers you a temporary retreat from the daily onslaught. It's your chance to stop the world and to remind yourself what is really important to you. The course is like a spiritual spa in which you can rinse off any unhealthy attachments to the messages of "want", "must", and "more". These messages don't just come from advertisers; they are also from your parents, from your teachers, from your politicians, from your culture and from your peers. It is essential that you give yourself time to make proper sense of what these messages are really telling you.

Over the years, I have found that you can stop anyone in his or her tracks with one simple question. The question is, "What do you want?" Your answer to this question is essential to your relationship to happiness and to the overall quality of your life. In *A Course of Miracles* there is a passage that reads:

> The question "What do you want?" must be answered.
> You are answering it every minute and every second.
> And each moment of decision is a judgment that is
> anything but ineffectual. Its effects will follow
> automatically until the decision is changed.[2]

Contrary to the popular messages, the goal of your life is not *to have it all*. Nor is it *to have everything*. As the comedian Steven Wright once remarked, "You can't have everything. Where would you put it?"[3] Also, you're going to have to give it all back anyway – at some point. Your goal is not just to accumulate. You are not a *consumer*. You are not here on earth just "to get". If you think only in terms of "getting" or "doing," you will be constantly afraid and you will also be haunted by a mistaken sense of inner lack.

Earlier, I shared one of the main principles of my work: *most people do not need more therapy; they need more clarity.* This is especially true when it comes to exploring your personal goals and desires. One powerful *goals exercise* we do in the course is called "The Three Envelopes". The idea is that you are given three envelopes, each with a question inside. You have 10 minutes to answer each question. This exercise can either be done in pairs as a conversation or on your own with pen and paper.

In Envelope 1 the question is: *What do I want?* In Envelope 2 the question is: *What do I really want?* And in Envelope 3 the question is: *What do I really, really want?* I know this sounds like a Spice Girls song, but don't let that put you off. The purpose of this exercise is to help you be honest with yourself and to be clear about what really matters to you. In the review session afterward, I invite you to reflect on, for example, how many of your answers are about "having", "getting" and "being". I also ask you to notice the balance in your answers between "things" and "relationships". And I invite you to appreciate how much of what you really, really want is already in your life.

There is great freedom and happiness in getting clear on what it is you really, really want. Brian, a filmmaker in his 40s, attended in 1998. At the end of the course, he put a letter in my hand and said, "This is a 'thank you' from me." Here is a short excerpt from his letter:

> When I signed up for the happiness course, I expected it to work. I was ready. I wanted to be happier. And I am. I feel free again, young again and more alive again. What I didn't expect, however, was how it happened. Honestly, I expected my breakthrough to be more esoteric. A flash of light. A cosmic meditation. Singing angels. Hearing the voice of God. Instead, you pulled my name out of your magic hat and in front of everyone you hit me right between the eyes with the question "What do you want?"
>
> Initially, I had no answer. I thought what I wanted was what everyone else wanted, plus a little bit more. All my life I have gone with the flow. But really, I can see now that I was just unconscious and that I wasn't really in my life. I became a filmmaker and my life became about watching other people's lives. The focus was outside myself, not inside. And now with your help, I am pointing the camera at me and I am noticing who I really am, what I really think and what I really want. And for that, I will be forever grateful.

Getting Real

From time to time, you will be called to meditate on the essential truth of your life. To coin a phrase, you have to *get real*. You have to assess what the real currency of your life is, what you are really shopping for and what you truly want your life to be. I have described my work with The Happiness Project as a meditation on "What is happiness?" I have also described my work with Success Intelligence as a meditation on "What is success?" And I have described both projects as a meditation on the question "What is real?"

The problem is not that we do not have enough; it's that we don't enjoy what we have. I refer specifically, here, to those of us who live in high-income First World countries – like the United States, the United Kingdom, Japan, Australia and countries in the European Community, for instance. Economists and happiness researchers report consistently that the top one per cent of the wealthiest people in these nations display high levels of depression, anxiety and aloneness. Clearly, we are successfully proving to ourselves and to the world that happiness cannot be bought. Happiness is not a commodity. It is not for sale at any price.

Rich people seldom *feel* rich. They do not perceive themselves to *be* rich. In a Gallup Poll, conducted in the United States, the average person judged that 21 per cent of people, approximately one in five, are in the "rich" bracket. And yet not even one-half of one percent of people put themselves in that bracket.[4] In other words, less than one person in a hundred can identify with the phrase "I am a rich person." Most people relate to terms like "rich", "wealth" and "abundance" as something you eventually experience when you finally, one day, you hope, enjoy something more than you have now.

Rich people often feel poor. "When they are asked how much income they need, richer people always say they need more than poor people," writes Lord Richard Layard, the British economist.[5] In his book, *Happiness: Lessons from a New Science,* Lord Layard collated research on the economics of happiness back to the early 1970s. He writes, "Although real income per head (corrected for price inflation) has nearly doubled, the proportion of people who say they are pretty well satisfied with their financial situation has actually fallen."[6]

Clearly, something is missing. "I cannot afford to buy everything I really need," say 4 out of 10 Americans who earn an annual salary of between $75,000 and $100,000. Imagine how this must sound to the three billion people on our planet who earn less than $2 per day. It doesn't add up. More money is needed in the Third World; but in the First World countries, more money is clearly not the answer to happiness. In fact, research confirms that people who value money above other life goals report they are less satisfied not only with their financial status but also with their lives overall.[7]

So what is the real more? This is one of the central inquiries. One of the goals of the course is to identify what it is you really long for. It is to identify your *holy longing,* so to speak. To put it another way, it is to identify the *real hunger* of humanity. This important inquiry leads, I believe, to a profound and life-changing revelation. But to enjoy that revelation, you must first shift your inquiry from being extrinsic and externally focused to being more intrinsic and Self-focused. Why? Because discovering the real more is not about getting more, it is about getting real.

True happiness requires honest self-reflection. The more honest you are with yourself, the greater happiness you will experience. Eventually! Initially, more honesty can feel painful, particularly if you have been out of touch with yourself for a while. Greater self-honesty may mean you need to look at old mistakes, self-deceit, self-neglect and old wounds. As Werner Erhard famously said, "The truth will set you free, but first it will piss you off."[8] But you must not give up on honesty, because without honesty you cannot experience authentic happiness.

I encourage people to *get real* with themselves by focusing their self-honesty inquiry on three main parts.

Part #1: Self-Awareness. It is essential that you know this: *you will always feel inadequate and you will always feel like something is missing, until you learn to know yourself better.* To be happy, you have to know the difference between your ego and your real, Unconditioned Self. The ego is a separate self, based on biology and bones, personality and psychology. It is a learned self, caught up in conditioning and fear and guilt. Your real, Unconditioned Self is more the *spirit of who you are.* And the more you identify with your spiritual wholeness, the less you feel like something is missing.

Life isn't about *getting more;* it is about *being more* of who you really are. Being more honest is threatening to your ego's defences, but the fact is you can't be defended and happy. Greater authenticity is the key to being happier with you and with others. Authenticity is also the perfect antidote to split desires, to envy of others and to negative comparison. And the more real you are with yourself, the more you will realise what you really want. This is important, because as Eric Hoffer put it, "You can never get enough of what you don't need to make you happy."[9]

Part #2: Self-Acceptance. *For as long as you do not accept yourself, you will always want more than you have.* If you will not accept that happiness is your true nature, you will search for happiness for the rest of your days. And if by some chance you discover some happiness, you will not let yourself enjoy it unless you have learned to accept yourself. Is that paradox enough for you? The fact is, *more of anything or everything will not be enough until you choose to be happy.* The choice to be happy is what opens your eyes to the happiness of your real nature.

Part #3: Self-Accountability. Okay, so now it's time for the profound and life-changing revelation that I alluded to earlier. This revelation is the key to any experience of lack in your life right now. The revelation is this:

**If you think something is missing in your life,
it is probably you.**

Do you get it? Is this real enough for you? The idea that something is missing in your life, in your relationships, in your work, or in any given situation, is a projection. The projection is based on the fact that you are not fully present. In other words, *you think something is missing here because you are not here.* Somehow you are not being real enough, honest enough or authentic enough.

True happiness requires you to participate fully in your life *now.* Therefore, if you feel like something is missing, you would do well to stop searching outside yourself and to attend to the following self-inventory. This inventory is based on three key questions:

Question #1: *What am I not being?* If you want to be happy and yet you are not feeling happy, you should reflect on what you are not being. For example, not being honest, not being kind, not being loving, not being forgiving, not being grateful. Identify *what you could be more of* or *less of.* This is not a "should-be", good-behaviour exercise; it is about being more unconditional, more open and more true to your real nature.

Question #2: *What am I not giving?* When you feel like something is missing, the common search is to look for what you are not getting; but the real search should be for what you are not giving. In *A Course in Miracles* there is a line that reads, "Only what *you* have not given can be lacking in any given situation."[10] This includes both what you are not giving to yourself and what you are not giving to others.

Question #3: *What am I not receiving?* Maybe the only thing that is missing is what you are not allowing yourself to receive. One of my favourite mantras is, "There are no shortages, only a lack of willingness to receive."[11] This might not always be true, but it is always worth checking out, just in case your attachment to pride, to cynicism, to independence, or to unworthiness is getting in your way. Becoming a better receiver certainly helps to dispel illusions of lack.

● ● ● ● ●

CHAPTER 16

the
receiving
meditation

*"*The Receiving Meditation" happens at the halfway point of the happiness course. This extraordinary exercise has proven to be a defining moment for many people who take the course. It works as a catalyst that helps to turn honest intentions into real, tangible results. The Receiving Meditation is a moment of grace. It activates new possibilities. It offers you a better way. I love this meditation because, for many people, myself included, this is when *shift happens*.

Everything you have looked at so far has been, in part, a preparation for "The Receiving Meditation". The session on "Following Your Joy", for example, is designed to help you understand what happiness is and who you really are. The session on "The Fear of Unhappiness" is designed to help you let go of old wounds and blocks. The session on "The Happiness Contract" is designed to help you open up your mind to grace and joy. And the session on "The Daily Unconscious" is designed to help you be more present in your life.

You are ready now –
readier than you have ever been –
to receive and be happy.

"The Receiving Meditation" takes up one whole session. In the coffee break before this session, everyone is asked to leave the room so that the Happiness Project team can prepare it. All of the chairs are removed. A space is cleared. The room is decorated with flowers, fragrances and candlelight. Robert Norton, our musician, begins to play. There is a stillness that comes over the room that is just beautiful. We are ready to receive the students.

Outside the room, the students gather. I explain that the room has been prepared for their delight. The room is now a symbol for *a world that is full of gifts to enjoy*. The floor is covered with over 100 beautifully decorated signs – like golden leaves, cherry blossoms, red hearts – each of which carries a theme. The main themes are 1) "acceptance", 2) "love", 3) "success", 4) "creativity", 5) "wisdom", 6) "grace", 7) "joy", 8) "freedom", and 9) "peace." Other themes include "miracles", "healing", "money", "God", "abundance", "inspiration", "help", and also some blank canvases.

The actual meditation takes one hour. I explain that when you enter the room, you should go to any theme you are drawn to. You may then sit, stand or lie down on the sign that represents that theme. If nothing appeals to you, I encourage you to go to one of the blank canvases and to write your own theme on it. I also explain that you are free to move around the room at any point in "The Receiving Meditation". For example, you may wish to spend 20 minutes on "joy", 20 minutes on "abundance", and another 20 minutes on "God". Or you may wish to visit as many themes as possible in 60 minutes.

Of all the themes I have mentioned above, w*hich theme would you pick first?* Hold this theme in your mind as you continue to read. Carry it in your heart as I share with you what we do next. As soon as everyone is settled on a theme, the meditation begins. I encourage you to start by taking a deep, long, full breath in. Deepening the breath is symbolic. The in-breath represents your willingness to breathe life in. We are a generation of shallow breathers and this reflects a consciousness of lack. By breathing more deeply, you become more conscious, more present and more receptive.

On the next inhalation, imagine you are breathing in the essential qualities of your chosen theme. Imagine that joy, for instance, touches every cell of your body, lights up every part of your mind and blesses your heart. The out-breath represents letting go. On the next exhalation, imagine yourself letting go of any old resistance to joy. The out-breath also represents radiance and sharing. Imagine, therefore, breathing in joy and breathing out joy, receiving and giving in equal measure. As you do this, I encourage you to *connect* consciously with your theme, to *visualise* yourself being with it and to *welcome* it wholeheartedly into your life.

The rest of the instructions for "The Receiving Meditation" remain very simple, because the art of receiving is not about a technique; it is about intention. Receiving is not about hard work; it is about willingness. It is not about *making it happen;* it is about *letting it happen.* To receive is not about labour, effort and sweat; it's about surrender.

Stories of Receiving

The best way to describe "The Receiving Meditation" is to share some stories of people's experiences over the years. Selecting which stories to share with you is the most difficult decision I have had to make in writing this book. I could share with you a hundred life-changing stories, all of which I am certain you would find deeply inspiring. Instead, I have picked just five, each of which illustrates an important lesson on both the real meaning of receiving and how to be a better receiver.

Story #1: Giving Up Struggle. Ben Bartle, a property developer in his late 40s, chose "money" as his theme for "The Receiving Meditation". He stood on the same spot for the entire meditation. Two days later, he applied to enter the TV game show *Who Wants to Be a Millionaire?* He was accepted. He won his qualifying round. And he went on to win $250,000.

Ben brought his winner's check with him to our next session. When I asked him to identify what had been the real key to his success, he replied, "I consciously gave up my old addiction to struggle." Ben shared how he had used a "struggle story" most of his life to reinforce some unworthy self-concepts. He said, "In the meditation I realised like never before that no one benefits from my sense of struggle and lack. I visualised myself being free of struggle and being the truly generous person I want to be in this world."

Ben discovered in "The Receiving Meditation" that *to receive is to be willing to give up all unnecessary struggle and lack.* Ben was very generous in publicly thanking the course for playing its part in his good fortune. His generosity caused a nice problem for us in that the phone lines at our offices did not stop ringing for days. Ben decided that the happiness course works! He has since served as a team member on several courses.

Story #2: Giving Up Sacrifice. Julia, a nurse at a London hospital, focused on "abundance" and "miracles" for her meditation. Two days before, Julia had sold some personal articles, including a pair of silver earrings, to help finance her mother's treatment for cancer. After doing "The Receiving

Meditation", Julia went across town to a nurses' gala ball. She entered the prize drawing. She won second prize. Her prize was a pair of silver earrings made by Tiffany & Co.

When I asked Julia to identify the real miracle of her experience, she came up with two miracles. The first miracle was that she entered the drawing at all. "I normally don't enter anything", she said, "because I always think I will lose. But having just done 'The Receiving Meditation,' I went for it." The second miracle was about giving up sacrifice. Julia said, "In my professional and personal life I often take on the role of 'helper', and then I neglect myself and I am of no help to anyone. In my meditation I visualised myself being free of self-sacrifice – and it felt so good that I almost felt guilty, but not quite."

Story #3: Giving Up Resentment. Tanya, a concert pianist, chose "forgiveness" and "love" in "The Receiving Meditation". The main focus for her meditation was her relationship with her estranged father, whom she had not been in contact with for 18 years. That night, as she opened the door to her apartment, the phone began to ring. She picked it up. "Tanya speaking", she said. The caller said, "Hello darling, it's your father here." It was the first time her father had called in 18 years.

When Tanya shared her story with us, she acknowledged she had to decide if the timing of her father's call was either a random bit of synchronicity or the miraculous effect of her meditation. Tanya said, "In 'The Receiving Meditation' I witnessed with total clarity how parts of my life will continue to remain on hold until I forgive my father. I prayed for forgiveness and I made up my mind to make contact with my dad. I also prayed for help with the fear of doing this. I believe my prayers were answered, because he made contact with me first." Tanya learned that receiving sometimes starts with letting go. She also discovered that *shift happens when you let go!*

Story #4: Giving Up Fear. Andrea won a free place in the course after entering a competition in a magazine. Clearly, Andrea already displayed a healthy capacity to receive. During "The Receiving Meditation" she focused on "purpose", "success", and "joy". A week later she saw an advertisement for a senior editor position at a national magazine. She applied for the job. "I almost didn't do it," she said. Much to her surprise, she got an interview. She was then asked back for a second interview and a third. She got the job, plus a 300 per cent pay increase.

Andrea identified that the real gift of her meditation was "giving up the fear of rejection". "I have been so afraid of rejection that I have only been to three interviews in my entire life," she said. Andrea got every job she was interviewed for, but she also recognised that she hadn't aimed very high because of her fear of being rejected. In her meditation she saw how the fear of rejection was blocking her chances of receiving. "This happiness course has given me the strength to stop rejecting myself, to stop hiding and to be more present in my life," said Andrea. Andrea had decided to show up more in her life and the world had expressed its thanks.

Story #5: Giving Up Pride. Louise focused on "healing" and "help" in her meditation. And it saved her life.

When I invited the class to share any stories of receiving, Louise was the first person to raise her hand. Louise shared that she had suspected for a while that her health was suffering. "But I kept ignoring the messages," she said, "until I did 'The Receiving Meditation', and that's when I got a strong internal message to book a doctor's appointment immediately." Louise was diagnosed with breast cancer. Her doctor told her she had very nearly left her appointment too late for her treatment to be effective.

When I asked Louise to identify any lessons she had learned from doing "The Receiving Meditation", she named two. The first lesson was "giving up unhealthy independence". She said, "I have always been too independent for my own good. I know that this ultimately holds me back from being a better receiver." The second lesson was "giving up unhealthy pride". Louise explained how she felt too proud to ever ask for help. Her pride had to do with wanting to feel strong, but it was in fact a weakness.

Louise's treatment for breast cancer was completely successful. She allowed herself to receive the best possible help every step of the way. On the 10th anniversary of The Happiness Project, I received a congratulations card from Louise. She wrote in the card:

> The happiness course taught me to give up separateness in return for greater happiness. I often think of your mantra: 'If you are alive, you need help.' Thank you for helping me to receive. Thank you for helping me to live more fully – and for longer!

Unconditional Receiving

The purpose of "The Receiving Meditation" is to help you live your life with an open heart and to welcome wholeheartedly what you most want to experience in your life. The more you are truly willing to receive, the happier you will feel and the more you will enjoy your life.

In the introduction to "The Receiving Meditation", I like to explore the real meaning of receiving. I give my students this simple question: "What does it really mean to receive?" The art of inquiry is to take the *blindingly obvious,* like the meaning of receiving and explore it as if for the first time. The goal of inquiry is to find a hidden gem, an unearthed treasure, that gives you a new sense of clarity and appreciation. And the joy of inquiry is knowing that you can connect at any time with an innate intelligence that wants you to see the truth and beauty in every situation.

My inquiry into the art of *unconditional receiving* has revealed what I call the "Three Levels of Receiving". Here is what they are:

Level #1: Acquisition. On this *action level,* "to receive" sounds like a verb, an action and something that you do in order "to get" something. This level is transactional. It is about a gain, as opposed to a loss. Something is offered to you, given to you, sent to you; and you have to receive it, accept it and take it in. When people first do "The Receiving Meditation", it is a common experience to start receiving, for instance, more compliments, gifts, prizes, good fortune, free parking spaces, green traffic lights, job offers, financial rewards and other good things.

To acquire more "good things" you have to be willing to be a better receiver and also to let go of unhelpful behaviours and roles. For example, bouncing compliments: when someone tries to thank you for something you did, don't dismiss it with a comment like, "Oh, it was nothing." Other blocks to receiving include being too manic, too busy and too hyperactive. An unhealthy attachment to roles like "the independent one", or to insisting on always being "the leader" and "the helper", will block your capacity to receive.

Level #2: Recognition. On this *mental level,* "to receive" is about a shift in perception. This level has nothing to do with getting a FedEx package, or any gift, that appears to arrive from somewhere else. It is about being present and mentally receptive, to everything that is *already here* and that is *always here.* When you make a decision to be a better receiver, it is as if your sight is restored and you suddenly recognise all manner of gifts that are awaiting your appreciation and welcome. Interestingly, the Latin word for "receive" is *recipere,* which means "to regain or take back".

How good a receiver are you? Make it your intention today to be more open and receptive to the people you meet, the places you go, the things that happen. *Notice how the more receptive you are, the more wonderful your life appears to be.* Be willing to open your mind to the possibility that happiness is here, abundance is here and heaven is here. Give this day as much appreciation as you imagine you would give to the best day of your life. If you do this, even for just one hour, you will surely "regain" and "take back" all of the gifts you could so easily have overlooked. Remember the saying from *A Course in Miracles:* "Enlightenment is but a recognition, not a change at all."[1]

Level #3: Identification. On this *being level,* "to receive" is about being in tune with your true self. This level is more than just getting and seeing; it is about letting yourself experience the gifts of your own original nature. It is about enjoying the love in your heart, your lightness of being, your natural wisdom and the miracle of your own existence. This level is not about "out there"; it is about who you are. It is about tuning in to the real self that will outlive your ego, your personality, your self-image and every other learned self-concept. Hence, to receive is to give up all ego thoughts of unworthiness.

This level of receiving is like a meeting point with your Unconditioned Self. *To receive means to know who you are.* It is to see yourself as a *receptacle* that welcomes all of God's gifts. It is to see yourself as a *receiver* who allows all of creation to flow through you. *To receive is the beginning of creativity in all its forms.* Receptivity is an act of creation. Ultimately, to receive is to realise that not only is the world full of gifts for you, but you are also full of gifts for the world.

An inquiry into the true nature of receiving also reveals that *receiving is a prelude to giving.* Receiving and giving are two sides of the same coin. They are the *yin* and *yang* of creation. They are the *vice versa* of abundance. In other words, your capacity to receive is what determines your capacity to give; and the more freely you give, the more freely you are given to.

> **For as long as you do not receive, you will
> be afraid that giving equals loss.**

If you are not good at receiving, you will not give yourself fully to a relationship or to a job, for instance, because you will be afraid that giving will deplete you. The only way to keep giving and not receive is to be in sacrifice. And that can only last so long before you feel like you have nothing left to give. Also, in truth, no one can give what he or she has not received. So, what now? Well, you are not receiving and you are not giving, and so you are barely living. The prognosis does not look great. Unless, that is, you make a decision to receive. This one simple decision, made several times a day, is the perfect restorative for taking back the happiness of your true nature.

A Happiness Journal

When you enrol, you sign up for a journey that happens 24/7 for eight weeks. Your whole life becomes your teacher. What happens outside class is as significant and valuable as anything you experience in the class. Every day you experience another lesson, a new gift, a wonderful conversation, a profound realisation. You are, literally, a full-time student. On day one, you are given your own personal Happiness Journal to help you fully receive all of the lessons and gifts that you will encounter.

The idea of the Happiness Journal is to set aside 15 minutes every day, for the full eight weeks, in which to record all your personal notes, reflections, scribbles, doodles, inquiries and epiphanies. Personally, I always start a new journal each time I run a course. While I like to meditate every day all through the year, I prefer to journal more intermittently – for example, eight weeks on and one month off. Why? It just feels more fun that way and less like an endless, routine obligation. Each time I return to my journal after a short break, the experience is somehow richer.

The Happiness Journal is a gift you give yourself. If you have ever kept your own daily journal, you will know very well how rewarding this process can be. Scientific studies on journaling have produced a wealth of evidence that shows that writing regularly about your personal experiences can have many beneficial effects on your wellbeing and mental health.[2] Journaling can make your whole life richer, particularly if you set specific goals for your journal. For example, keeping a Happiness Journal while you take the course, or doing your morning pages while you read a book like *The Artist's Way*.[3]

The Happiness Journal helps you to stop the world for 15 minutes a day and check in with yourself. It is your chance to catch up on your own news. It is a precious opportunity to review your life and to give yourself the gift of your own attention. Your journal is a "letter to self" in which you listen to how you really feel and hear what you really think about what is happening right now. Journaling helps you to stay in contact with yourself. Whenever you lose this contact, you feel like something is missing. You feel like you are not enough, and you begin to crave something more. Journaling puts you back in touch with yourself.

The Happiness Journal helps you to listen to your real thoughts. It is a chance to dialogue with your natural wisdom. It is an opportunity to be extra honest with yourself. One way to journal is to ask yourself specific questions like, *What is my life teaching me about happiness at present?* or *What is my unhappiness trying to teach me?* Studies on journaling show that writing about happiness and sadness, joy and pain, love and fear, can help to enhance your levels of physical and mental health.[4] The key is to express yourself freely, without editing or censorship. Self-honesty leads to greater happiness.

The Happiness Journal can also help you to be a better receiver. For example, you can use your journal to focus on the daily gifts and blessings you experience in your relationships and your work. Or, for example, you can use your journal to record one big gratitude per day. The more you do this, the more it transforms your psychology and your experience of your life. Your journal literally helps you to write and rewrite the story of your life in a way that is more meaningful and enjoyable for you. Every day you can write more happiness back into your life.

I like to use my Happiness Journal to set positive intentions. The following three questions provide a great focus for each new entry: 1) *How am I being?* For example, are you being the partner you want to be, the parent you want to be, the colleague you want to be? If not, what could you be more of or less of? 2) *What am I giving?* For example, are you using all of your strengths and talents at present? Could you be giving more of yourself to a certain person or situation? 3) *What am I receiving?* For example, are you being as open as you would like? Notice how present you are and how receptive you are being to your life.

The Happiness Journal can also help you to make requests and prayers. For example, "Dear God, help me today to be a better receiver." And "Dear God, please help me to enjoy myself today." Simple, honest requests like these can produce such powerful results. One of my favourite prayers is by Nancy Spiegelberg, who wrote, "Oh God of second chances and new beginnings, here I am again."[5] Your Happiness Journal can be a most helpful companion to you. The dialogue you record can help you to understand true happiness. It can help you to create a life you love.

PART V

love and happiness

CHAPTER 17

the
family
story

The family you are born into is your first point of reference in this world. As such, your family is your first classroom. It is where you learned, and continue to learn, many of your major life lessons. Your family is your first romance. It is where you experienced your first love and also your first yearning for more love. Your family is your first happiness. The first smile, the first laugh and the first connection happened here, even if only for a fleeting moment. Your family is also your first great disappointment. It is where you had your first fight, your first fall from grace and your first experience of unhappiness.

Your relationship to happiness is influenced greatly by your family's story about happiness. For that reason, I devote a significant amount of time in the course to a deep inquiry into "The Family Story". This is the part of the course in which many people encounter the biggest blocks to happiness and also the greatest breakthroughs. Here is where you meet your inner child and also your Unconditioned Self. It is here that you may unearth your primal resistance to happiness. And it is here that you may also discover a golden chance to be as happy as you had, once upon a time, hoped to be.

When you are willing to understand your family better, to heal an old family wound, or simply to express more gratitude and love for your family – you literally *grow up* and *grow into* another level of freedom and abundance in your life. Your willingness to understand your family helps you to realise who you really are and what your life is really for. Your courage to heal old family wounds helps you to undo the last remaining blocks to your own happiness. And when you can honestly wish every member of your family true happiness, you can go confidently (and unimpeded) in the direction of your dreams.

Consider this question, then: *Generally speaking, what is my family's story about happiness?* This open question is designed to let you answer however you like. A broad question like this one is helpful at the start of an inquiry as you begin to sense and tune in to the real truth. The goal is to get clear on what *your* story is about your family's story about happiness. So, I encourage you to listen to your thoughts, to feel your deepest feelings and to go with your gut instinct. Getting clear on your story about the family story will enable you to live an even more authentic and powerful life.

So what exactly is a family story? Well, you could replace the word *story* with *experience*. So, now the question is, what is your family's experience of happiness? Are you from a "happy family"? Yes or no? If a movie producer were to make a film about your family, would he or she make a comedy, a drama, a love story, a horror story, or something else? How prominently does happiness figure in your family story? Is happiness a major goal of your family? Is it a central theme of your family story? Or are there other goals and themes that are more important – for example, work, financial security, academic success, or social status?

The family story is also about your family's philosophy of life. For example, would you describe your family's philosophy as "seize the day" or "save for a rainy day"? And would you describe your family's attitude toward life as optimistic or pessimistic, loving or fearful, abundant or wanting? If you were to sum up your family's philosophy about happiness in one sentence – like having a family motto – what would it be? Take a moment to come up with the one sentence that best describes your family's beliefs about happiness.

The family story is also about how your family expresses its joy. For some families, joy is most commonly associated with family mealtimes that are full of conversation, laughter and sharing. In musical families, joy is expressed through song and dance and impromptu performances and plays. In artistic families, joy is associated with paints and hobbies and magical bedtime stories. In sporting families, joy is a football, joy is a pony, joy is family games and joy is adventure holidays. In families with strong spiritual faith, joy is grace at mealtimes, prayers of gratitude at night and an infusion of deep love that is expressed in lots of ordinary moments. How does your family express its joy?

An inquiry into your family's story should also look at family roles. A family role is the position a person takes in the family system. For example, was there anyone in your family who was the entertainer or the star? Did you grow up in a family in which someone played the martyr? Is there a loner in your family? In many families, the roles are polarised. For example, one parent plays "good cop" and the other parent plays "bad cop". Or one sibling plays the happy mascot and another plays the Goth misfit. Or one sibling plays the extroverted socialite and another plays the introverted studious one. What role did you take on in your family and how has playing this role affected your relationship to happiness?

Your family story – and also your interpretation of the story – can be found in the library of your subconscious mind. It sits on a shelf next to lots of other stories, symbols, metaphors and myths that also influence your experience of the world. The family story and the story you tell about yourself are deeply entwined. Which came first? Was it the family story or your story about you? Either way, when you heal one, you can heal the other. When you get more honest about one story, you get to the truth about everything. *Beyond the story, true happiness awaits.*

Family Lessons

Your family story is unique and therefore it has its own unique curriculum of specific lessons. The story is unique because the ensemble is unique. Also, each storyteller has his or her own special perception of how the story goes. Indeed, members of the same family can have such a different take on the family story that they may seriously doubt that they grew up in the same family. Also, the family system has its own special form that may feature absent parents, foster parents, stepfamily, family bereavements, family illness, sibling dynamics, family secrets and more. All this must be taken into account when exploring the family story.

As we begin to dive deeper into the family story, the question I like to ask is, "What was your mother's (or mothering influence's) definition of happiness?" The same question goes for your father (or fathering influence). As I have already mentioned in Chapter 3, "Defining True Happiness", your definition of happiness is significant because it influences your life in so many ways. That said, your parents' definition of happiness is especially significant because not only will it have influenced their life, it will have also influenced yours. Are you fully aware of how both your parents' definitions of happiness have influenced your own definition?

Some people live their entire lives in reaction to their parents' definitions of happiness and they never discover what true happiness is for them.

Another powerful question is, "When is your father (or fathering influence) at his happiest?" The same question goes for your mother also. These questions often draw a hush from the class. Most people have little or no idea how their parents define happiness or when they are at their happiest. Exploring these questions can give you a precious insight into who your parents really are. You get to meet them adult to adult and soul to soul. You see past the role they played for you and appreciate more of their original nature. In doing so, you move beyond the story of your relationship to an even greater experience of love.

Francis, a TV producer in her 30s, took the course in 2002. She wrote me a letter soon after we did "The Family Story". She told me how the question about her father's definition of happiness had stopped her dead in her tracks. She wrote, "I knew that my father wanted me to be happy. But we never talked about happiness. It was a common goal that we pursued in private from one another." In her very moving letter, Francis told a story that I have her permission to retell in my classes today. She wrote:

The inquiry into my family story taught me how little I still know about my dad. Growing up, I didn't even know my dad's name until I was about 16 years old. He was just "Dad". I only ever saw him on evenings and weekends and for the most part he was quiet, tired and miserable. Then, one day, when I was 13 years old, he invited me to a Bring Your Child to Work Day. I had no idea what my dad did or where he worked. I agreed to go, but only so that I could skip school for a day.

To my amazement, my dad was the life and soul of the party at work. He greeted everyone by name. He was like best friends with the car-park attendant. The girls at reception lit up when he walked through the doors. He even hugged Hilda the West Indian coffee lady. My dad was popular. People actually liked him. He was funny. He was cool. And when we got back home he acted quiet, tired and miserable again.

It was a shock. I felt angry about it. I wondered why he was friendlier with "them" than with "us", his real family. But I never asked. When I was 19 years old, my mother told me that my dad had had a younger brother who died in a car accident. I never knew that. It was unspoken. Was this why my father was so unemotional with his family? I knew that my dad loved me, but the fact is we just didn't know about each other. You could say it was a "strange love".

One of the big complaints of my life has been that my dad didn't really know me, but what this happiness course has shown me is that I don't really know my dad. I guess it's time for me to grow up now and to start a conversation I wish I had had a long time ago. Not just with my dad, but with my mother and with my sister. Robert, I have heard you say many times now, *It is never too late for a new beginning.* This is especially true for my family and me. Better late than never. Better now than not at all. On behalf of all my family, thank you.

Every family story has enough lessons in it to last a lifetime. Here is another question to consider: *Growing up, what did my mother (or mother influence) teach me about happiness, e.g. through her example and her attitude?* Once again, the same question also goes for your father (or fathering influence). Your mother and your father are your first teachers. They are usually the people who give you the first big messages about happiness. If you identify with these messages, they become internalised and you write them into your Happiness Contract. Of course, you can rewrite your Happiness Contract at any time. But until you do, these parental messages will shape and influence your relationship to happiness.

If your mother played the role of a martyr, for instance, you may have learned to believe that *happiness is selfish.* If your father subscribed to the work ethic, he may have taught you the mantra *easy come, easy go.* They may also have taught you that *the stork brought you.* And that *doing homework is fun.* And that *if you keep playing with "it" it will fall off.* And that *all artists starve to death.* And that *there will be tears before bedtime.* Alternatively, they may also have taught you that *you have a right to be happy.* And that *happiness is being true to yourself.* And that *happiness is your gift to the world.*

Here are two more questions to help you identify what your family story has taught you about happiness. The first question is, *Who is (was) the happiest member of my family? And what has this person taught me?* Many people say that their parents worked so hard to raise them that they had no energy left over for happiness. Material needs came before emotional and spiritual needs. Interestingly, many people often name a grandparent as the happiest member of the family. Another very common answer is, "My cat" or "My dog". And from time to time, people say, "Myself".

The second question is, *Who is (was) the unhappiest member of my family? And what has this person taught me?* Everyone can teach you something about the true nature of happiness, either through their joy or their pain. When you respect that this is so, it allows you to live with a greater sense of appreciation and compassion for the people in your life. Your family may be teaching you that *this is the way to do it* or that *this is* not *the way to do it.*

Either way, they are teaching you something. When you learn the lessons, you graduate to a new level of possibility and joy.

Family Gifts

The inquiry into your family story includes a meditation called "Family Gifts". I think of this meditation as a true gift because it has helped so many people, myself included, to experience healing and happiness in key family relationships.

"Family Gifts" is designed to help you discern between the *story* and the real *purpose* of a relationship. The story is what happens on the surface of a relationship, at "see level". It is about the roles you play, your personal history together, your interactions and how well (or not) you get along. The purpose of a relationship is much deeper than the story. It is about the real reason why you are in each other's lives. Understanding what this "soul-level" purpose is can make the story of a relationship sweeter and more loving.

Every relationship has a purpose. And one of the real joys of relationship is to identify and appreciate exactly what that purpose is. Usually, the purpose of a relationship involves an exchange of gifts. These gifts can be many and varied and they may have no particular form. For example, they may include the gift of unconditional love, the gift of companionship, the gift of laughter, the gift of romance, the gift of forgiveness, the gift of self-acceptance, the gift of giving each other confidence, the gift of a shared purpose and so on. These gifts bless both the giver and receiver.

The "Family Gifts" meditation is so healing because, in essence, it is about appreciating people as they are, not as you want them to be. The dramas in relationship are usually caused by power struggles and by fruitless attempts to change one another. The joy of relationship is found in deep acceptance, in unconditional love, in really seeing each other, in valuing each other, in offering mutual support, in showing appreciation, in giving trust and in really being here for each other. Regardless of what your story is together, *happiness is found in loving the truth in people.*

The meditation can be done in one of two ways. The first way is a general contemplation that is based on the following invitation:

Imagine you chose your family. And imagine that you chose your family because this family has three major gifts about happiness to give you. Name those three gifts.

The emphasis here is on positive gifts, that is, things you are truly grateful for. You may notice that you associate each gift either with one particular family member or with the family as a whole. Either way is okay. Also, you may find that the most valuable gifts have come from the most difficult relationships in your family. This is very common.

For example, Rachel attended the course in 2008. Both of Rachel's parents had committed suicide when she was in her teens. Rachel is now in her 50s and two years ago, her husband committed suicide. In her "Family Gifts" meditation, Rachel discovered that one of the gifts of her family story is to make sure that, in her words, "I face my own demons with courage, I overcome my own death temptations and I am as close as is humanly possible to being 100 per cent alive in my life." I think everyone who met Rachel in that course was deeply inspired by her honesty, her courage to grieve and her commitment to living a full life.

The second way to do the "Family Gifts" meditation is to do it as a visualisation in which you focus on each individual member of your family. For example, you may begin by visualising your mother (or mothering influence) standing before you. First, on an ego level, you acknowledge the story of your relationship and your personal history together. Then, on a soul level, you ask, *What is the real gift my mother has come to give me?* And you listen and receive. And then you ask, *What is the real gift I have come to give my mother?* Again, you listen. And then you visualise yourself giving this gift.

People's experience of doing the "Family Gifts" meditation this way does vary. Some people are good visualisers and they have a very graphic, visceral experience. Other people are more kinesthetic and they tend to feel the meditation and to experience it energetically. And others are more auditory, so they often experience the meditation as a dialogue in which a meaningful exchange happens. Also, many people include family members who are deceased. This is perfectly okay, as relationships live in the mind and the heart. Death changes the form, but it does not end the relationship.

The willingness to go beyond the story to a greater sense of truth and purpose is what makes every relationship more meaningful and joyful. It is an invaluable key to healing and happiness.

**Happiness is the willingness to choose the truth
instead of staying stuck in a story.**

Family Healing

A research study conducted in 67 countries interviewed parents from diverse cultures, faiths and income levels. One question asked what they most wished for their children. The number one answer, by a long shot, was *happiness*.[1]

Every parent wants his or her child to be happy. When you become a parent, you know how true this is. Unconditional love is only interested in happiness. However, parenting can be challenging, relationships can be challenging, personalities *are* challenging and life can also be full of challenges. In the midst of these challenges, you can lose sight of your best intentions. You can overlook the true purpose of your most loving relationships. A love story turns into a drama. We literally *lose the plot*. Happiness is forsaken for some other goal.

Most family stories are full of gifts and dramas. There is usually plenty to be grateful for and there is also much to forgive. We each encounter grievances and upsets in even the most loving relationships. Communication is usually the problem *and also the solution*. Something said, some misunderstanding – or no communication at all – play a part in most unhappy situations. Sometimes it will be your turn to apologise for a transgression or hurt you have caused. And, of course, you will want to apologise, if, that is, you value happiness more than some ego defence or drama.

The final part of "The Family Story" is a focus on communication and healing. This usually takes the form of an assignment, which is to have a conversation about happiness with someone in your family. I normally recommend at least two conversations. One conversation is with a member of the family that you grew up in – for example, your mother, your father, a grandparent, a sibling, a godparent, or an aunt. The other conversation is with your partner, your children, your sister-in-law, or, if you like, a best friend.

In this inquiry, when I ask people to reflect on the best conversation on happiness they have ever had with a family member, the most common answer is, "I haven't had one." As Francis said about her relationship with her father, "We never talked about happiness. It was a common goal that we pursued in private from one another." One reason why family members won't start a conversation about happiness is because they have *never* had a conversation about happiness. Another reason is an old wound or grievance. All I know is that communication *is* healing. When you are willing to communicate from an honest and loving place, something wonderful happens.

Your life evolves through conversation. It evolves both through the conversations you have and through those that you don't. One single conversation can open up a world of immediate possibility. This is particularly true for conversations about happiness. Make a date, therefore, with your father, your mother, or someone else you love and start a conversation about happiness. You will probably feel some initial awkwardness, but you will get over it if you let yourself remember what is really important.

Mark, a lawyer, attended in 2000. Here are the last two paragraphs from an e-mail that he sent me the morning after his "date" with his father. The setting was a top New York restaurant. The purpose of the meeting was to talk for "the very first time" about happiness.

There we were: a 40-year-old gay man and his 70-year-old straight father. Neither of us had ever been so nervous. Happiness was a totally new conversation for us. I was convinced this was going to be even more difficult than "coming out". Father started by ordering a bottle of red wine. As the wine flowed, the conversation got going. Over the course of the evening, we talked about our definitions of happiness, our beliefs, our fears, our disappointments and our hopes.

Robert, I can honestly say that I never really felt like I had a father – not until last night. What happened last night was a miracle between two strangers who have lived in the same family for four decades. What we discovered is that we both want happiness – not just for ourselves, but for each other. We are completely different and we are exactly the same. I love my dad, and my dad loves me.

● ● ● ● ●

CHAPTER 18

the
relationship
questionnaire

Every day at the Happiness Project office we receive another request to participate in a survey, documentary or interview on happiness. The most common request is on the subject of *happiness and relationships*. Enjoying happy and loving relationships is one of life's most sought-after goals, and as such it represents our most important work. Relationships are the heart of happiness. They are also the heart of your life. Your relationships are what help you to grow and evolve into the person you most want to be.

It is painfully clear that one of the great challenges still facing the human family (a.k.a. humankind) is to learn how to be happy with each other. The fact is, we are not very good at it yet. Instinctively, we know that relationships represent our best opportunity to experience love and happiness, and yet all too often our experience of relationships is that they end up as a pyre for our broken hopes and expectations. Some relationships help you to discover something more about true happiness; other relationships can tempt you to give up on happiness altogether.

Over the years, The Happiness Project team has researched the subject of *happiness and relationships* more than any other. The whole team, and especially my co-director Ben Renshaw, have participated in national studies on family wellbeing, conferences on relationships and mental health, television documentaries on relationships and happiness, and even a campaign to create a government Ministry of Peace, for example. Our research has centred on two main themes: how positive relationships can increase personal happiness and how personal happiness can attract and enhance positive relationships.

The first major scientific review of happiness was conducted by Warner Wilson in 1967. In his research, Wilson asked the question, "What really determines happiness?" His exhaustive review eventually identified 16 "dichotomous items", which included a good income, good health, high job morale and education. Most of all, he concluded, "The most impressive single finding lies in the relation between happiness and successful involvement with people."[1] A generation of scientists took note and set about testing for proof that *relationships can make you happy.*

Countless studies of relationships and happiness were conducted in the following decades. The most significant studies focused on the key differences between "happy people" and "very happy people" – in other words, between people who consistently reported they were either "happy" or "very happy". These studies identified one chief external element that distinguished the two groups, and that was the enjoyment of "rich and satisfying social relationships".[2] Thus, more conclusions were drawn that marriage makes you happy, friendships make you happy and relationships make you happy.

These conclusions are only half true, however. And they are half true on two counts:

First: It is too deterministic and too simplistic, to say, for example, "Marriage makes you happy." Happiness studies have indeed found that if you can say, "I am happily married" (and really mean it!), you are more likely to enjoy more happiness than those who are unmarried, divorced, separated, or widowed.[3] However, if marriage is so good, why do more people choose to marry later or not at all?[4] And why has the divorce rate spiralled in recent years?[5] Marriage is not all joy; it can be stressful and it can break down. To say that "marriage makes you happy" is to paint only a half-picture. What really needs to be studied is, *what is it that makes a marriage happy?*

Second: It is too one-sided to draw the single conclusion from the positive correlation between happiness and relationships that *positive relationships make you happy.* Surely the other side of the coin, so to speak, is that *happiness makes for positive relationships.* In other words, the whole truth is that

loving relationships may increase your chances of being happy; but being happy may also increase your chances of enjoying loving relationships.

In the happiness course we run an in-depth inquiry into the reciprocal relationship between personal happiness and positive relationships. We do this using a method called "The Relationship Questionnaire". This "questionnaire" is not a paper-and-pen exercise in which you simply check some boxes. It is a dynamic experience that includes questions, conversations and exercises designed to help you enjoy even happier and more loving relationships with family, friends, colleagues and everyone else in your life. In the rest of this chapter, I will introduce you to six of the main topics we cover in "The Relationship Questionnaire".

Predicting Happiness

Question: What would you say is the most powerful key to enjoying happy and loving relationships?

As you reflect on your answer, please consider every type of relationship, including marriage, friendship, family, colleagues and neighbours. Draw upon every experience of your life to date and name one, two or three of the most powerful keys that you know with all your heart really do help to create rich and rewarding relationships. Common answers include shared interests, mutual respect, honest communication, quality time and joint investment in the relationship. It is so important that you are clear on your answer(s) to this question. Why? Because if you understand what really makes a relationship work, you can keep it working.

It just so happens that one of the best predictors of happiness in relationships is *happiness itself*. Happiness research has found a very strong correlation between life satisfaction and happy relationships. Thus, if you agree with the phrase "I am very happy with my life," you are more likely to be able to say, "I enjoy happy and loving relationships." In one of the largest happiness studies, 6 out of 10 couples who rated their marriages as "very happy" also rated their lives as "very happy". However, those who declared that were not in "very happy" relationships also reported that they were not "very happy" with their lives.[6]

Several studies on happiness and marriage also conclude that *the best way to make a marriage really work is to be happy already.* One German study, conducted with 24,000 people over a 15-year period, found that those who got married and stayed married were happier at the outset.[7] In other words, they were already happy. It wasn't that marriage "made them happy"; rather it was that marriage "added to their happiness". Also, there is evidence here to suggest that being happy already is what actually attracts a loving and lasting relationship into your life.

Your relationship to happiness influences all your other relationships in life. How so? For example, if you define happiness as an "it" or a "thing" that you "chase" and try to "catch", you are also likely to be someone who "searches for love" outside yourself. If you believe happiness is outside you, then you will surely believe that love exists elsewhere too. This definition of happiness "out there" must inevitably lead to relationships that become transactional, needy, manipulative, inauthentic and unsatisfying.

As you clarify your relationship to happiness, you will automatically increase your chances of attracting and retaining relationships that are healthy, happy and loving.

Unconditional Love

Question: What do you believe is the secret to unconditional love?

In this question, the word *secret* alludes to an *essential truth* that you have personally discovered about unconditional love. This *essential truth* is what you ultimately aim to put into practice day to day. Clearly, your answer to a big question like this will have a big effect on your experience of love and happiness. Your willingness to learn about love, and not just search for love or just hope to be loved, is what undoubtedly helps you to be a genuinely more loving person.

In "The Happiness Genie" (see Chapter 1), when people are asked to choose between a wish for happiness and a wish for love, most people ask for two wishes. When pushed, 7 out of 10 people choose the wish for love. As one student commented, "Whether you choose love or choose happiness, you are really choosing the same thing." Love is happiness, and happiness is love. And for that reason, all of the major wisdom traditions, religions and philosophies agree that

**the more loving you are,
the more happiness you will experience.**

Your beliefs about happiness also influence what you think is possible or not possible in love. For example, if you don't believe in unconditional happiness, you won't find it easy to believe in unconditional love. If you think happiness has to be earned and deserved, you probably won't let yourself receive unconditionally all of the love that is available to you. And if you don't believe that happiness can last, you will find it impossible to believe that love can last. Fortunately, however, when you change your mind about happiness, you can also have a completely different experience of love. Happiness is the key to love as much as love is the key to happiness.

My work with The Happiness Project has taught me that *people who are good at happiness are also good at loving.* What it takes to be happy is what actually helps you to be a loving person. For example, to be happier, you have to dare to be even more authentic and more present in your life. If you do this, you will also experience more love. Similarly, happiness increases when you are less self-obsessed and more sociable; so too do your chances of love. And happiness grows as you give more unconditionally and as you become kinder and more generous; so too does your ability to love.

To be happy you have to be willing to receive unconditionally, and being a good receiver is what helps you to enjoy intimacy and appreciation in all your relationships. The happier you are, the less prone you are to suffering from negative comparisons, envy and jealousy. Also, you are better able to manage conflict and to forgive. Clearly, your ability to be happy is what helps you to attract and participate in loving relationships. The better you are at happiness, the better you will be at love, and vice versa.

Real Joy

Exercise: Make a list of five important relationships in your life, and then next to each person you've named, write a sentence that best describes the "real joy" of that relationship.

Allow yourself to interpret the words "real joy" however you wish. For instance, with one person the *real joy* of the relationship may be a deep appreciation for a defining quality or characteristic. With another person, the *real joy* may be the sense of connection and oneness you feel with each other. With another person, the *real joy* may allude to a sense of purpose and meaning. And with another person, the *real joy* may come from all you have been through together, the ups and downs and the lessons learned.

Beyond Pleasure. If a relationship has no other purpose than just "for pleasure", it can never really flourish beyond a certain point. And maybe it isn't meant to. But for our most intimate and precious relationships, it is vital that you be willing to go "beyond pleasure" so as to discover the real gifts and treasures of the relationship. Giving a relationship a higher purpose than just "for pleasure" is what helps to create a greater sense of intimacy, joining and real love. Beyond pleasure, a whole new level of joy and connection awaits you.

Beyond Personality. When you look for the "real joy" of a relationship, you find yourself looking beyond a person's ego, beyond his or her personality and right into the heart of who he or she really is. Appreciating the "real joy" helps you to witness the person's essence. You discover this person's eternal loveliness, secret beauty and Unconditioned Self. The "real joy" helps you to appreciate that people are not just their egos, their personalities, or the way they act. This healing perspective is helpful for the moments when egos and personalities are difficult to love.

Beyond Pain. Just as the term "happy people" is misleading if you make it mean "people who never experience sadness or pain", the term "happy relationships" is misleading if you make it mean "a relationship that never experiences conflicts or challenges". Every relationship that lasts longer than a weekend will encounter happiness and sadness, love and fear, gratitude and hurt. Identifying the "real joy" of a relationship can help you both to stay on course, to remember what is really important and to keep committing to the true purpose of why you are together. Joy increases resilience and it can help your relationship to flourish.

Relationship Strengths

Exercise: What makes you so good at relationships? Name your top five relationship strengths. Also, identify which one of those strengths you could be using more right now and with whom.

Everyone acknowledges that relationships can be an abundant source of shared happiness, love and purpose. Yet few people seem to work consciously on the essential talents and strengths that help to make relationships work. Most people appear to adopt a passive attitude of hoping a relationship will be fulfilling and that their next soul mate will know how to make a relationship work. For this reason, many people find this exercise difficult at first. I recommend you try it. Notice how easy or difficult it is for you to identify your relationship strengths.

Are you fun to be with? Fun is definitely a relationship strength. When people are asked what first attracted them to a partner or a lifelong friend, they rarely mention "her abject cynicism", "his workaholism", or "her Goth look." No, the answer is usually, "his smile", "her sense of humour", and "his zest for life". Relationships are not just about constant fun, but neither are they just about "getting through the day" or simply "staying together".

Remembering to have fun helps to bring energy, creativity and renewal to a relationship. Happiness is attractive. And fun makes way for love.

Making a conscious intention to enjoy each other helps to make a relationship thrive. It can also help to break the spell of a melancholy routine, wake you up from the daily unconscious and birth some much-needed spontaneity and aliveness. Psychologist Janet Reibstein interviewed hundreds of couples for her research into happy relationships. In one paper, she identified making time for pleasure (e.g. play, humour, games, joking, touching, hugging and relaxing in each other's presence) as one of the "defining and strengthening key factors in successful partnerships".[8]

Relationship Lessons

Exercise: What is your major relationship lesson at present?

Every time you make a new friend or begin a new romantic relationship, you sign up for a new batch of lessons on how to be a happy and loving person. Every relationship is a teacher. Every relationship has its own special curriculum. And every relationship will give you an opportunity to learn something about happiness or healing. So, you grow and evolve through your relationships. We can't do this on our own. We need each other. That is what relationship is for. The ultimate purpose of relationship is to become the most loving person you can be.

As you review all of your most important relationships, notice if one particular relationship lesson stands out at present. Another way to do this is to pick two relationships: one that feels healthy and happy and another that feels stuck or painful. Now, with each relationship, see if you can identify what lesson you are being asked to learn. In the happy relationship, notice what you are doing well; in the unhappy relationship, look for any mistakes you may have made, for ways you could communicate better, or any defenses you could drop.

One of the most important lessons to learn about relationships is that *it is not another person's job to make you happy.* Your happiness is not someone else's job. Until you realise this, you will always be dissatisfied with your relationships. Happiness research shows that while a romance, a marriage and even having children can dramatically increase happiness in the short term, it does not make you happy forever. Habituation sets in. The familiar set point restores itself. Ultimately, your relationship with others mirrors your relationship to happiness. In the long run, no one can *make* you happy; but everyone can *encourage* you to be happy.

Relationship Success

Question: How could you, starting today, make all of your relationships sweeter and more loving? Identify one, two or three practical ways you could enjoy greater relationship happiness and success.

Think about how you are *being*. Remember your intentions. Think about what you really want, then be what you want. In other words, if you want more love in your relationships, be more loving. If you want richer, deeper communication, be more open and be more honest. Do you want to be happy or in control? Do you want to be happy or safe? Do you want to be happy or defended? Do you want to be happy or do you want to hold on to your favourite complaint about relationships? *To be happy, you have to be willing to be the goal that you most want to experience.*

Think about what you are *giving*. The joy of commitment is that the more you give of yourself in a relationship, the better the relationship becomes. True giving is not sacrifice. On the contrary, when you decide to give of yourself fully in a relationship, you discover more about what you really have to offer. Through giving, you become fully engaged. Through giving, you find yourself. Through giving, you grow and evolve. When you commit to giving a relationship more of your best attention and energy, it instantly feels more attractive and rewarding.

Think about what you are *receiving*. Sometimes the reason a relationship wobbles is because you do not give it every opportunity to thrive and prosper. Perhaps you are too busy, too tired, too scared, too independent or too cynical for your own good. Relationships become more attractive and more wonderful when you let people in, when you open up and when you let yourself receive. So, do you want to be happy or independent? Do you want to be happy or superior? Do you want to be happy or proud? The more you let yourself receive, the more gifts you will find in all your relationships.

● ● ● ● ●

CHAPTER 19

making
the
connection

This is the story of a minister and a mystic. They met at a lecture on Michelangelo and enjoyed each other's company very much. So the minister invited the mystic to his home for a cup of tea and a spot of theology. The mystic was happy to accept.

The minister lived in a magnificent home in the middle of the city. Each room was adorned with fine furnishings. The minister and the mystic took tea in the library, which was lined with row upon row of leather-bound spiritual texts. On the ceiling was a most beautiful replica of *The Creation of Adam,* painted by Michelangelo for the Sistine Chapel in the 16th century.

As the minister and the mystic began to talk theology, the mystic noticed a golden telephone sitting on a table in the corner of the room. The mystic asked, "Is that what I think it is?"

"Yes," smiled the minister.

"Is it a hotline to God?"

"Yes," confirmed the minister.

"How wonderful," said the mystic.

"Would you like to make a call?"

"Yes, please."

The mystic picked up the phone and said, "Hello."

"Hello," replied God.

The mystic and God had a great chat, as old friends do. It was a beautiful connection. Afterward, the mystic thanked the minister profusely.

"My pleasure," said the minister.

"How much do I owe for the call?" asked the mystic.

"$10,000, please," said the minister.

"Gosh," said the mystic, who hadn't reckoned it would cost so much.

"Well, it is a long-distance call," explained the minister.

The mystic asked if the minister would accept a credit card. The minister said he preferred cash. They agreed that payment would be made when the minister visited the mystic's home for a cup of tea and a spot of theology.

The minister and the mystic met up a week later. The mystic's home was deep in the heart of the countryside. It too was very beautiful. Interestingly, there were no books anywhere. But every room was decorated with the most inspiring religious art from every faith. The minister and the mystic took tea in the meditation room. Coincidentally, on the ceiling of the room was a most beautiful replica of *The Creation of Adam* by Michelangelo. Also, in the corner of the room on a table sat a golden telephone. The minister asked, "Is that what I think it is?"

"Yes," smiled the mystic.

"Is it a hotline to God?"

"Yes," confirmed the mystic.

"How wonderful," said the minister.

"Would you like to make a call?"

"Yes, please."

The minister picked up the phone and said, "Hello."

"Hello," replied God.

The minister and God had a great chat, as old friends do. It was a beautiful connection. Afterward, the minister thanked the mystic profusely.

"My joy," said the mystic.

"How much do I owe for the call?" asked the minister, tentatively.

"$1, please," said the mystic.

"Gosh," said the minister, who hadn't reckoned it would cost so little.

"Well, it is a local call," explained the mystic.

In this story, the minister represents the part of your mind that has learned to believe in a theology of separation. Thus, heaven is outside you, God is distant and happiness is somewhere else. The mystic represents the part of your mind that believes in a theology of connection. Hence, there is no separation and there is no distance between you and heaven, you and creation, or you and others. Everything, including happiness, wisdom and inspiration, is really just a local call.

Both the minister and the mystic own a replica of *The Creation of Adam*, which is my favourite work of art. It is the painting in which a slight distance separates Adam's finger and God's finger. One hypothesis is that this separation is literal; another is that it is purely artistic, as Adam is in easy reach of God. Thus, separation and connection are choices that Adam can make. Interestingly, some scholars see that God is airborne, sitting in a cloud; others see that the cloud is an exact replica of the human brain. Thus, God is not far away up in the sky; God is in you. It all depends on how you see it.

In the happiness course, we research in depth the relationship between self and happiness, as well as the dance between perceived separation and connection. One of the chief causes of unhappiness is the sense of separation, or anxious apartness, we feel from our true self, our real heart and the rest of creation. In these moments, the distance between happiness and us seems insurmountable. And yet, this aloneness can disappear in the blink of an eye. Connection is a conscious choice. Connection is easy. Connection already exists. It is only your resistance that creates the illusion of distance and delay.

Happiness is in the connections we make with ourselves and with each other.

Self Connection

The central principle of my work with The Happiness Project is called the Self Principle.[1] This principle states that *the quality of your relationship with yourself determines the quality of your relationship with everyone and everything.* Who you think you are and what you think you deserve, is what creates the happy or unhappy dynamics you experience in your relationships with family, friends, colleagues, God, the taxman and everyone else in the world. Your relationship to yourself is the key to how you connect with others – or not.

The quality of your relationship with yourself also determines the quality of your relationships with important life goals like love, success and happiness. It influences, for example, how abundant or lacking your relationship to money is. It also shapes your relationship to time, including such things as how much "me time" you allow yourself, why you are always running late and your ability to make time for what is most important. The Self Principle is so precise that it even affects your relationship to luck and good fortune. When you are aware of this connection, you can start to change your experience of the world by changing your relationship to yourself.

At the start of each course, I invite people to talk for 60 seconds about why they have enrolled. In the last course, Sandy, a woman in her late 30s, stood up and proclaimed with a wry smile, "I am here to meet someone special." Evidently, she thought the course was a dating service. Applause broke out around the room. I smiled to myself, because it is certainly very common for people to make deep connections and lasting friendships in this course. But Sandy hadn't finished yet. She still had another 50 seconds to go.

Sandy continued, "Ever since I can remember, I have hoped to meet someone special. It got worse when I was a teenager and after I watched Olivia Newton-John and John Travolta in *Grease*. The desire to meet someone special has been a lifelong obsession. Recently, I finally realised that the reason I am so obsessed with meeting someone is that I have never ever met myself. So, I am here in this happiness course to meet myself. I want to learn about who I am, what I really think and what would really make me happy."

The course is a chance to connect with yourself. It takes you past your ego, past your personality, past old self-concepts and past the roles you play and reconnects you to who you really are. This conscious reconnection with your Unconditioned Self is the key to happiness. The reason you search for happiness is that you have temporarily lost your conscious connection with your true nature. The reason you are bored with your life is that you are estranged from yourself. The reason you feel so lost in this world is that you have not consciously found yourself yet. Make this connection and you will begin to lead a happier life.

One of the goals is to help you to connect with the part of your mind that is in constant communication with the joy of your original nature. There is a part of your mind in which truth abides and in which peace reigns, whether you are aware of it or not. This part of your mind is in constant communication with God and with the wisdom of creation. Happiness is a local call. Wisdom is a local call. Peace of mind is a local call. When you turn down the neurotic static of your ego-mind and consciously connect to your original nature, you rediscover an original joy that does not ever leave its source.

Social Connection

We are living in the Communication Age. Technology and invention have transformed our experience of the world. In 1930, a three-minute telephone call from London to New York cost about $300 at today's prices. By 2000, the cost had dropped to about $1.[2] Soon it will be free. Distance is dead. It doesn't matter where you are. We can all connect all the time. It takes only an instant to fax, e-mail, text, Skype, iChat, or "poke" someone anywhere in the world. Telecommunications mirrors what we know, which is that connection is our true reality.

We can connect more easily with each other than ever before and yet an increasing number of people report that they feel alone and cut off from the world. Ironically, the major illnesses of the 21st century will be diseases of loneliness and isolation.[3] According to the World Health Organization, the major health epidemic affecting the world now is not starvation, not AIDS, not even heart disease; it is depression.[4] The root of depression is an excruciating sense of separation and abandonment. All sense of connection with self, and with creation, is lost. Happiness feels distant and impossible.

Happiness research reveals that personal happiness flourishes when you invest in a rich and enduring social life.[5] On the other side of your ego, a lifetime of exciting connections awaits you. The key is to make relationships a priority. Everyone agrees with this, but many just don't do it. In research, when people are asked this question – "Do you invest as much time, energy and attention as you would like in your most important relationships?" – a staggering 90 per cent of people say no. So, what is the block? Here are three considerations:

Increased Mobility. We live in an increasingly mobile society in which we enjoy greater personal freedom, but also less enduring connections. This is reflected in the results of a relationships poll I take in each course. For example, in the last course, only 10 per cent of the group still lived in the same town, city or village they grew up in. And only 30 per cent of the group had lived in the same house for the last 10 years. And only 40 per cent of the group had worked for their current employer for more than five years. Personal freedom without deep and meaningful social connection can cause us to feel less happy and more alone.

Increased Independence. Today, more than one-quarter of households are occupied by a single person. This number has increased with rising separation and divorce rates. Here are some more statistics from the last poll I conducted: 1) only 30 percent of the group knew their neighbours' names; 2) only 20 per cent counted their neighbours as friends; 3) only 10 per cent had invited their neighbors for dinner, lunch or coffee; and 4) 25 per cent had best friends who did not live in the same town, city or village as they. Beware dysfunctional independence – a mental state that, in the name of freedom, leaves you feeling less open and less connected to the world you live in.

Increased Busyness. More of us are seeing less of our closest friends than ever before. The main reason people give for this is *busyness*. In a recent survey, more than 60 per cent of adults claimed that their relationships were more important to them than career or money.[6] And yet our most important relationships usually have to compete with our permanent busyness, and the busyness often wins. And, as a result, we are less happy. This is particularly true for men. Personally, I believe that excess busyness is a smokescreen that covers up an assortment of old wounds, disorientation and a lack of true connection with ourselves. It is also a symptom of dysfunctional independence.

In individualistic cultures like the United States and the UK, where prescription rates for the treatment of depression, anxiety and other diseases of loneliness are soaring, people spend more time home alone watching TV than connecting with friends. Today, the average home has more TV sets than people in it.[7] Professor Robert Putnam, the author of *Bowling Alone,* has alerted the world to the unhealthy effects of excessive individualism.[8] In the BBC *Happiness Formula* TV series, Putnam states, "If someone asked me, 'How can I be happier?' I would say, 'Turn off the television and spend a little more time with friends.' You will be happier. The evidence is overwhelming."[9]

Things are changing now. The "Me Generation" is giving way to a new "We Generation" in which more of us are making more time for connection and friendship. And modern digital technology, which is more participative and less passive than the old analog technology, is playing an important part in this change. For example, new online social utilities like Facebook, Friends Reunited and Flickr help us to keep up with family and friends and share in each other's lives. Through global technology we can think together, offer each other support and connect across vast distances that once appeared to separate us.

In one social study, it was found that participants who could list five or more close friends were significantly happier than those who could not.[10] In the course, I invite you to make a list of the first five people who come to mind. I then encourage you to reflect on the quality of your connection with them. Which of these people would you like to connect more with? Whom could you be listening more to? Whom could you acknowledge more? Reaching out, beyond your busyness, your independence and your defences, will make you happier. Happiness is in the connections we make.

Nature Connection

The venue for the courses in London overlooks Hyde Park, which covers 365 acres of historic and beautiful landscape. Students go to Hyde Park for breakfast meetings, lunchtime walks, summer picnics and time for personal reflection. Hyde Park is one of nine major Royal Parks in London that are described as "London's personal space". Londoners enjoy their parks in much the same way New Yorkers enjoy Central Park, Sydney's residents enjoy their harbour and the people of Kyoto enjoy their botanical gardens.

One of the reasons why I appreciate nature so much is that *there is no psychology in nature*. Natural spaces are empty and free of common human anxieties. The trees don't think in the way we do. There is no social comparison among the flowers. A rose shows no obvious signs of self-doubt. A daffodil rarely, if ever, appears cynical or forlorn. A bluebell does not fear it should be doing more with its life. The animals do not look like they are searching for a meaning or purpose. The river is not late or behind schedule. And the birds sing and hum, but they don't speak, which is what I love.

Nature has a different pace. One of the reasons why nature is so healing and restorative is that it returns you to the rhythms of your original nature. In nature, we can stop. In nature, we can breathe more deeply. In nature, we can tune in to a stillness that is beyond all space and time. There is no sick hurry, no neurotic busyness, no looming deadlines and no penalty for being late. "Nature does not hurry, yet everything is accomplished," said the Taoist mystic Lao-tzu.[11] In nature, we do not strive after the future as we do when we are in the city.

Connecting with nature somehow helps us to connect more fully with our natural aliveness. Nature is not mental; it is pure energy. Nature is not emotional; it is symphonic. Nature encourages us to inhabit more fully each present moment. Lying on the grass, listening to birdsong, looking up at the stars, we remember our place in the grand scheme of things. When we lose touch with this connection, we experience the effects of what journalist Richard Louv calls nature-deficit disorder.[12] These effects include a loss of connection with ourselves and with each other.

In nature you can connect with something bigger than your ego. Various philosophers have described both nature and the human soul as having a centre that is everywhere and a circumference that is nowhere. In nature, there is one life and you are part of that oneness. Artists and inventors describe nature as a teacher. Spiritual thinkers say that God delivers sermons through the flowers and trees. When you dialogue with nature, you learn something. You also connect with your heart and with the natural joy of your Unconditioned Self.

Spiritual Connection

Happiness researchers have consistently found that people who attend a church are more likely to have higher happiness scores than those who don't. Also, churchgoers tend to live longer, are less likely to divorce, enjoy good mental health and are also less prone to drug abuse, committing crimes, being violent and choosing suicide.[13] However, if going to church makes a person happy, why is it that fewer and fewer people choose to visit church?[14] Just as it is too simplistic and deterministic to conclude that *marriage makes you happy,* the same applies to concluding that *going to church makes you happy.*

In recent times, happiness researchers have refined their focus so as to study people who have strong spiritual faith. These people may or may not visit a church, a temple, a synagogue or a mosque, but they do identify themselves as having strong spiritual commitment and a rich spiritual life. In one major study, conducted by The Gallup Organization, people who described themselves as "highly spiritual" were twice as likely to say they were "very happy".[15] Also, sociologists like Professor Christopher Ellison have shown that people who pray and meditate regularly also experience good mental health and high levels of wellbeing.[16]

Although church attendance is down in recent years, there has been a strong increase in spirituality. In one recent poll, the number of Americans who feel the need to "experience spiritual growth" rose from 54 per cent to 82 per cent in just five years.[17] More and more people describe themselves as having "spiritual interests" as opposed to "religious interests". This reflects a growing dissatisfaction with how traditional religion has conducted its affairs. It also reflects a desire to dial direct to God as opposed to just "having a faith".

So, what are the key components of a happy, spiritual faith? This is something happiness researchers will have to explore more in future. I believe one key is *connection.* Religious leaders and philosophers have often described the chief ailment of humanity as a feeling of separation. Separation is misery. The Indian mystic Sri Anandamayi Ma wrote, "The sole purpose of all spiritual endeavour is to abolish the distinction between 'you' and 'I'."[18] Beyond the ego, there is oneness. Happiness is oneness.

If you can honestly say that your spiritual faith helps you to be a more loving person, then I believe that your spiritual faith will also increase your experience of happiness. Some religious teachers preach a theology of love; others preach a theology of fear. It is my experience that the more loving and less fearful you are, the happier you will be. Moreover, if you agree with the idea that "God is unconditional love", then I also believe you will feel less guilt, less fear and less neurosis about being happy. Happiness is love.

Erich Fromm, the German-born psychologist who authored classic works like *The Art of Loving* and *On Being Human,* once wrote, "It would be better to say that one *is in* faith than that one *has* faith."[19] This difference is more than semantic, if you let yourself feel it. A spiritual faith *has you;* you don't *have it.* It is bigger than your ego or your personality. Words become inadequate at this point. The best I can do is to say that at some point in your inquiry into happiness, you will discover that God is happiness.

Therefore, that which created you (God, Brahma, Source, Spirit, Allah or any other name) must naturally want you to be happy too.

● ● ● ● ●

CHAPTER 20

the
joy of
forgiveness

True happiness has nothing to do with either forgiving or being forgiven. This is perfectly true until you experience your first wound. After that, it is your willingness to forgive and be forgiven that enables you to remember who you are and what happiness is. Forgiveness is now essential if you are to be happy and free again. To be happy, you have to be willing to choose forgiveness.

Some people demonstrate a consistent capacity to be very happy. What is clear is that these people don't necessarily enjoy better circumstances than you, but they do exhibit certain happiness traits that help them to be happy. In the happiness course, we examine these happiness traits in detail. They include self-honesty, being present, proactive gratitude, being kind, unconditional receiving, being loving and good humour. For me, the one stand-out happiness trait is *forgiveness*. Over and over again, I find that people who are good at happiness are also good at forgiveness.[1]

Anyone who has a past probably has enough reasons to be unhappy for the rest of his or her life. Anyone who has a birth certificate has experienced some personal loss, deep grief, dashed expectations, romantic heartbreak, career setbacks and more. I don't have to be psychic to know that you know what it is like to carry a wound. We have all made mistakes, put our worst foot forward, suffered disappointment, felt personally cursed and endured many dark nights of the ego. And this is why *forgiveness is the key to happiness*.[2]

Even in a happy life, there are sad days. What my work has taught me is that beneath every sadness, problem or conflict, there is usually an opportunity to forgive something. It might be self-forgiveness for a mistake, some selfishness, or a hurt you may have caused someone. Or it might be forgiveness of another. Whichever it is, I have learned that *unhappiness is a call for forgiveness*. In other words, when I am unhappy I am being asked to practise forgiveness. Forgiveness is the remedy. In *A Course in Miracles* it is written that

> **there can be no form of suffering that fails**
> **to hide an unforgiving thought.**
> **Nor can there be a form of pain**
> **forgiveness cannot heal.**[3]

So what is forgiveness? In essence, *forgiveness is the decision to be happy.* In practice, this means that when you are faced with a life challenge, you make happiness more important than any other outcome. For example, if you are hurt, you choose personal happiness over a lesser goal like revenge or righteousness. Here is the question: *do you want to be happy or right?* Whatever situation you are faced with, you have to decide what is most important to you. For example, will you choose the past or the present, a story or the truth, a grievance or happiness, an attack or freedom?

Forgiveness is also a realisation. It is the joyful discovery that no single person or event can take away your happiness forever. Life happens and there are times when the pain feels endless and the choice in favour of happiness feels impossible. The dark nights of the ego can run into weeks and months and years. Even so, the possibility for happiness remains. Even so, the choice for forgiveness exists. And when you choose either happiness or forgiveness, you set in motion what can only be described as a miracle, an act of grace, that brings about healing and enlightenment.

I teach a set of forgiveness exercises in the course that can be used on a daily basis. By doing these exercises regularly you will discover for yourself how practical and beneficial an attitude of forgiveness can be. "Forgiveness is not an occasional act; it is a permanent attitude," said Martin Luther King, Jr.[4] I devote the remainder of this chapter to three powerful forgiveness exercises, which I believe can *with regular practice* increase your experience of love, peace and joy.

No Past

I often begin the session on "The Joy of Forgiveness" with an exercise called "The No Past Meditation". The instruction is to sit comfortably, close your eyes, breathe deeply and imagine yourself without a past. In round one, you do this meditation for just one minute. In round two, you sit for five minutes. And in round three, you sit for 10 minutes. For the really curious students, I assign optional homework – a one-hour meditation. In each round, I invite you to imagine even more vividly that the past is not here and that you do not have a past.

In the group discussion that follows "The No Past Meditation", people share their experiences. In round one, people often experience some disorientation and discomfort. They may encounter anxiety and fear, for example, *Who am I without my past?* In round two, people's experience is often more pleasant. They describe a growing sense of "peace", "calm", "relaxation", "emptiness" and "timelessness." In round three, people start to enjoy the meditation. Common reports include feeling "energised", "egoless", "freed up", "more present", "younger" and "happy".

Intriguingly, "The No Past Meditation" reveals how impossible it is to feel any pain or fear without a past. Can you feel that? This is quite a revelation. I encourage you to test it for yourself. Imagine you do not have a past! Really imagine it. And feel how impossible it is without a past to be cynical, to be pessimistic, to be defended or even to be tired. Without a past, there is no story. Without a past, there is nothing to forgive. And, without a past, there is virtually nothing that blocks your happiness.

Everyone has to let go of their past eventually. You have no choice about this. Everyone has something in their past they need to let go of if they are to be truly happy. You have no choice about this either. Not if you really want to be happy. No one's past has been entirely satisfactory. We have all lodged our complaints, claimed compensation and sought damages. And some of us are still fighting for a fairer past or a better past. To be happy, you have to be willing to let go of your past suffering. Happiness is letting go. Forgiveness is letting go. When you choose one, you choose the other.

To keep choosing happiness, you have to keep choosing to let go. Specifically, this means letting go of your hopes for the past, your story of the past and your disappointments in the past. Certainly you can honour the past and learn from the past, but you are not meant to live in the past. The one great truth about the past is that it is not here any more. The past is over. The only place it exists now is in your mind. Now, the past is just a memory.

**Sometimes in order to be happy in the present
moment you have to be willing to give up all
hope for a better past.**

Learning to let go and be happy again can happen in an instant. The instant
in which that happens may be today or in a few years' time. It can take great
courage and willingness to let go and be happy again. Initially, you will
have to encounter the full force of your identification with and attachment
to feelings like anger, grief and guilt. You will encounter your resistance to
letting go. You will even meet the pleasure of holding on to resentment or
grievances. Indeed, there is a certain pleasure in holding on. It is nowhere
near as great as the joy of freedom, but your attachment to this "unhappy
pleasure" may well delay your decision to let go.

You may meet the fear that you will not be able to let go. By yourself,
you will not; but with help, you will. You may also meet the fear of letting
go and the fear of forgiveness. The fear of forgiveness usually stems from
misconceptions about forgiveness. Be assured, forgiveness is not about
repression, pretending to forget or keeping quiet about something. You do
not forgive in order to "be good" or to "be spiritual"; you forgive so as to be
free of hate and free of pain. Forgiveness is not a cover-up; it is a letting go.
Forgiveness is not meek; it is strong. Forgiveness is about truth.

Another fear that you may encounter in the process of letting go is *the
fear of good things*. For example, you may fear being happy again (just in case
you lose it again); you may fear being open again (just in case you get hurt
again); and you may fear trusting in life again (just in case you get betrayed
again). Your fears whisper to you, "Keep your broken heart" and "Keep your
defences" and "Keep away from happiness." At some point, however, you
will want to forgive because you know that the future does not have to
equal the past. By changing your mind, you change your future. By letting
go of the past, you literally create a new future.

The joy of forgiveness lies in realising that you do not have to be a
victim of your past. Through forgiveness, you can give your past a different
meaning. Through forgiveness, you can learn your lessons and let go.
Through forgiveness, you discover new ways of responding and moving on.
Happiness research also proves that people who are willing to forgive are
better able to create a happy future instead of wasting time and energy on
wishing for a different past. Thus, the joy of forgiveness is that it returns you
to the present. It puts you back into your life. You can live again now.

No Grievances

"The No Grievances Meditation" is an invitation to imagine yourself to be totally free of any grievances. No grudges. No gripes. No grumbles. No laments whatsoever. The instruction is to sit comfortably, close your eyes, breathe deeply and imagine your mind is empty of all grievances. The meditation lasts for approximately 10 minutes. During the meditation I invite you to notice what it feels like to let go of all your most cherished grievances. Do you find it easy or difficult? Does it feel pleasant or odd? Do you feel happy, or sad, or both?

My students often report that they experience two opposite responses to "The No Grievances Meditation." The first response includes feelings like "resistant", "awkward", "adrift", "bored", "flat" and "dead." As one student once put it, "I barely recognise myself without my grievances." The second response includes feelings like "lighter", "brighter", "cleansed", "purified", "radiant" and "alive." When you are prepared to let go of all your grievances, without any exception, it does feel as if something dies and also as if something comes to life.

The Armenian mystic G. I. Gurdjieff once wrote, "A man will renounce any pleasures you like but he will not give up his suffering."[5] The first time I read these words, they made no sense to me. And yet the words stuck in my mind. I couldn't forget them. Slowly, I began to see what Gurdjieff meant. The more you hold on to a grievance, the more you start to identify with that grievance. Eventually, the grievance becomes so familiar to you that your ego integrates it into your self-image and your life story. If you were to give up this grievance now, it would feel like a personal death and the end of your life.

When you hold on to a grievance, you create a "self" (or a self-concept) that feels like a victim, that feels very hurt and that is less than who you really are. To hold on to a grievance is a sign of a mistaken identity. You suffer from a spiritual amnesia in which you forget who you really are. Eventually your ego feels more real to you than your Unconditioned Self. Unless you let the grievance go, you will probably end up playing small in your own life. If, however, you can forgive and let go of the "special grievance", you can rediscover the radiant nature of your true self. You can be happy again.

The more you hold on to a grievance, the less good you feel about yourself. You may feel justified in holding on to a grievance, mostly because you are still in pain, but the point is that you will continue to be in pain for as long as you don't let go of the grievance. Holding on to a grievance attracts the very things you are trying to repel: It attracts fear, it accumulates guilt and it increases pain. You identify with "small thoughts" of revenge and punishment. And your attachment to these ego thoughts hurts you even more. They hurt because they are unloving, unhappy and inauthentic. They do not represent who you really are.

Holding on to a grievance is not the purpose of your life. Your purpose is to forgive so that you can let go of the thoughts that hurt you. Through forgiveness, you can be happy again. Thus, the willingness to forgive is what helps you to get on with the real purpose of your life. Until you are willing to forgive, you will be in an emotional stranglehold. Your life, your relationships and your work will not move forward. Everything grinds to a halt. You are now one of the living dead. The only way to kick-start your life is to choose forgiveness.

Forgiveness is a decision to stop hurting yourself. Carrying a grievance does not hurt anyone as much as it hurts you. Grievances offer nothing of any value. There is no worthwhile revenge in holding on to a grievance. You win nothing of value. Forgiveness is the best revenge. Forgiveness frees the forgiver. The joy of forgiveness is that the forgiver receives the gift of happiness again. Your past is over, but now your future is just beginning. Forgiveness is a new beginning. Forgiveness is the present. Forgiveness is new life.

One exercise I give my students is to identify the one "special grievance" from their past that holds them back from experiencing greater happiness now. This "special grievance" is your reason for staying unhappy. This "special grievance" is your excuse for giving up on happiness. This "special grievance" betrays a self-concept that doesn't believe you deserve happiness. This "special grievance" reveals a basic misunderstanding about who you are and what happiness is. This "special grievance" is a story, not the truth. Interestingly, I find that everyone can find one "special grievance".

To let go of your "special grievance" is like a crucifixion to your ego. Fortunately, the resurrection follows quickly. Forgiveness is like a resurrection in that it restores you to your Unconditioned Self and to the happiness of your true nature. The ultimate joy of forgiveness is that you come to realise that the truth of who you are is still okay. Your ego got hurt, your hopes and expectations were ruined, the picture of your life has changed irrevocably, but who you really are – your real self – has not been diminished in any way. Through the grace of forgiveness what once was lost has been found again.

**Forgiveness is restoration. It returns you
to yourself.**

No Complaints

I introduce the "No Complaints" exercise to my students just before the lunch break. The goal of the exercise is to have absolutely no complaints about anything for approximately one hour. The invitation is to adopt a mindset of complete acceptance of everything that you see. It is to let go of setting any expectations or demands for how things ought to, must and should be. You are invited to give up your plan for what the weather should be like, how fast the traffic should move, how people should treat you and what should be available on the lunch menu.

The purpose of the "No Complaints" exercise is to make you more conscious of your psychology and your attitude toward life. It is to watch your mind in action, to notice your relationship with your thoughts and to check which thoughts you most identify with. In the feedback session after lunch, my first question is, "How long did it take before you made your first complaint?" The most common answer is approximately five seconds. This is because most people went into a mental sulk at having to do the exercise. The next complaint after that normally follows quite quickly. Also, I sometimes fail to stop exactly on time for lunch, which can cause another slight peeve.

I ask my students to estimate how many complaints they made during "No Complaints". I am looking for two estimates. One estimate is for the number of "silent complaints", which are the complaints you think but don't say out loud; the other estimate is for the number of "noisy complaints", which are the ones you share with others. For the "silent complaints", the average answer is about 10 complaints, which is one every six minutes. The count of "noisy complaints" can also be quite high. Some research suggests that nearly half of all conversations begin with a criticism or a complaint.

Some people object to the "No Complaints" exercise. "I have a right to complain," they say. "No one has the right to take away my right to complain." I point out that the exercise is an invitation, not an order. Also, I'm not asking them to stop complaining forever; it's just for one hour. People also share their fears of not complaining, such as, "If I didn't complain nothing would improve," and "If I won't complain people will walk all over me," and "If I stop complaining I will get taken advantage of." Although these fears feel very real, they are usually untested. In other words, no one has stopped complaining for long enough to see if the world really will end.

When complaining becomes a habit, you end up not being able to see past your judgments. You are fixated, your vision is distorted and you no longer see the world as it really is. The more you like to complain, the more you will find to complain about. Why? Perception is projection. You always see what you look for. Thus, the first rule of perception is, *Be careful what you look for, because you will find it.* Hence chronic complainers end up living in a world of their own making. They literally create their own illusion and it is an illusion that is simply not good enough.

When complaining is your dominant mindset, you become blind to the beauty, the perfection and the reality of what is already here. As a result, your life doesn't flow well. Your natural talents and gifts feel blocked. Your relationships suffer from your hypercriticism. The people in your life fail to bloom and prosper in your presence. The more you complain, the more frustrated you feel and the angrier you get. Complaining is meant to make you feel stronger and to make things work better. But there comes a point when too much complaining disconnects you from your true power. And now you are struggling to enjoy anything.

Chronic complaining is often caused by an inner tantrum, by frustration that the world does not devote itself to making you happy. Your ego demands and expects the world to make you happy. But that is not the job of the world. That is your job. Ultimately, in order to stop complaining you have to be willing to forgive the world for not doing what you won't do for yourself. Amazingly, when you decide to be happy, it shifts your perception and you discover you have less to complain about. The decision to be happy literally makes the world a better place. Your happiness changes the mix of things. A new intention creates new outcomes.

Chronic complaining is caused, at the deepest level, by a fear that you are not enough and that you do not have what it takes to make your life better. This is just a fear; it is not really true. The less you complain, the more you take responsibility for your own happiness. When you do this, you connect more consciously to your true creative power and then you naturally experience more happiness. Also, the happier you are, the more life seems to go your way. This is because there is a natural flow between how you feel and the way the world is.

The real purpose of the "No Complaints" exercise is to recognise that complaining is not a solution. Complaining does not make the world a better place and it does not make you happy. At best, a complaint is an alarm bell and a call to action. The teacher Eckhart Tolle says, "Whatever the present moment contains, accept it as if you had chosen it. Accept – then act."[6] Notice the complaint and be the solution. When you see that something is missing, let your love, your presence, your good humour and your joy make a difference. This is how to be happy in the world.

I honestly believe that if you could clear your mind of any grievance, complaint, or judgment – for as little as 60 seconds – you would have an experience of happiness that would be so profound and delightful that you would remember it for the rest of your life. The key is to forgive and let go. To forgive is to be happy.

● ● ● ● ●

PART VI

finding
the present

CHAPTER 21

the
open
road

The happiness course is a roadstop on your life's journey. It interrupts the busyness of your life and it offers you a chance to rest, to take refreshment and to review everything. You are encouraged to honour your past, to attend to what is most present now and to commit to taking the next step in the direction of true happiness. What will that next step be? For some, it is about getting back on track; for others, it is a minor course correction; and for a few, it can be a complete change of direction. The key is to remain open, to look for the signs and to let your life show you the way.

"The Happiness Timeline" is an exercise that charts your relationship to happiness past, happiness present and happiness future. It is a drawing exercise that uses a special graph paper. This graph paper has a horizontal axis and a vertical axis. The horizontal axis runs across the bottom of the page from left to right and it measures your life in five-year intervals. It starts at birth and then goes to 5 years old, 10 years old, 15 years old and all the way into your future. The vertical axis runs up the left side of the page and it measures your happiness score. It starts at the bottom at zero and then it goes up the page in 5 per cent intervals: 5 per cent, 10 per cent, 15 per cent, all the way up to 100 per cent.

The first task of "The Happiness Timeline" is to draw a single continuous lifeline that plots your happiness scores across the entire journey of your life – past, present and future. Your lifeline starts at birth, goes into your early childhood, your teenage years, your 20s, your recent past and right up to your present age, then into the near future and then the rest of your life. At each five-year point, you record a happiness score from 0 to 100 per cent. Your past scores are based on memory, the present score is based on what you feel now and your future scores are based on what you imagine and hope for.

It is rare for someone to draw a lifeline that is entirely straight. Most people's life journey is a long and winding road with forks and bends, twists and turns, highs and lows. On pages 283–4 there are three real examples of Happiness Timelines. Monica's timeline has a roller-coaster shape, with lots of ups and downs. Karen's timeline is more dramatic; it looks like a rapid heartbeat on an EKG. Jeff's timeline is U-shaped. Research studies confirm that most people's relationship to happiness is U-shaped.[1] We are naturally happy at first; then comes the fall and we lose our way; and eventually we remember what happiness is and our stock rises again.

The second task is to mark your happiness lifeline with five "life stars". Each star denotes a time in your life that has had a significant influence on your relationship to happiness. A star may signify a specific event or the start of something. It might be when you met someone or when a life change occurred. In the review that follows, you reflect in depth on each life star. This review can be done either in silence or in conversation. Both types of review are good. Either way, the process is the same. First, you give each star a name or a title and then you reflect on these questions: What exactly happened? Where were you? Who else was involved? What did you learn? What did you decide? What was the gift? Specifically, how has this influenced your relationship to happiness today?

Interestingly, most people's life stars don't include just the high spots and the happy times. Certainly, people often nominate important graduations, career successes, wedding days, significant journeys and family births; but they are just as likely to include childhood traumas, family breakups, romantic heartbreak, nervous breakdowns, personal rock-bottoms, money troubles, bereavement and cancer diagnoses. "The Happiness Timeline" teaches you to respect your whole life. It helps you to see that happiness is an open road and that *every moment can teach you something about happiness.*

I usually close the session on "The Happiness Timeline" with a reading of a poem by Walt Whitman called "Song of the Open Road".[2] It is a long and winding poem that is approximately 60 stanzas, 17 verses and 3,000 words long. Every line is a record of Whitman's life journey, in which he encounters grief and wonder, pain and passion, life and death. Through it all, Whitman proclaims, "Happiness is here." He realises that the potential for joy (which is the *Soul of happiness*) accompanies him on every step. The first three stanzas of Whitman's epic poem read:

> Afoot and light-hearted, I take to the open road,
> Healthy, free, the world before me,
> The long brown path before me, leading wherever I choose.
>
> Henceforth I ask not goodfortune – I myself am good fortune;
> Henceforth I whimper no more, postpone no more, need nothing,
> Strong and content, I travel the open road.
>
> The earth – that is sufficient;
> I do not want the constellations any nearer;
> I know they are very well where they are;
> I know they suffice for those who belong to them.

Walt Whitman's life journey is a "profound lesson of reception" in which he learns to have "neither preference nor denial". He insists that the potential for happiness exists in every step and in every place along the open road. As such, happiness is neither remote nor mysterious. It is an immediate possibility. Happiness is the journey and not just the end. And the open road is not really a physical path; it is your open mind and your open heart. Your openness is the key. Your openness reveals all.

**Happiness makes itself available to you
when you make yourself
available to it.**

Great Expectations

Consider this question: *From 0 to 100 per cent, how open am I to happiness?* What is your honest answer? Is your answer closer to 25 per cent? 50 per cent? 75 per cent? Or 100 per cent? Your answer is significant because it indicates how much happiness you are likely to enjoy today and also how much happiness you will block and reject.

In "The Happiness Timeline," people often score 100 per cent for how happy they were on day one of their lives. Most people start out very open to happiness. As newborn babies we don't have much to be cynical about. Nothing "bad" has happened yet. We have no expectations yet. We have no plans yet. We are, therefore, naturally optimistic and open to enjoying a happy life. In happiness research, when college students are asked, "Do you think you will live a happy life?" the answer is, "Yes." No one expects to live an unhappy life. The future is bright. The future is positive. The future is spotless, at least in the beginning.

When college students are asked, "Do you expect to be happier than your parents?" the answer is an emphatic "YES." Young people have great expectations. They expect to be happy. They expect to be successful. They expect to make good money. They expect to fall in love. They expect to be healthy. And, in spite of the statistics, which they may or may not know about, they do not expect to get divorced, or to be fired, or to have to take out a second mortgage, or to have a car accident, or to get cancer, or to experience depression, or to suffer any serious setbacks. And they probably don't expect to die either.

Young people's optimism about happiness is so high that it poses a statistical dilemma, which is that *the majority of young people believe they will be happier than the statistical average.* It seems that everybody expects to be happier than everybody else. Happiness researchers find that people of all ages often score themselves above average when it comes to future happiness and wellbeing. But young people in particular have especially high expectations these days and they expect to be happy, to be famous, to win the lottery, to have a gifted child and, basically, to have it all.[3]

So at first there is great hope. And then puberty happens. And the need for strong deodorants. And acne. And school exams. And passing grades. And failing grades. And first dates. And no dates at all. And parking tickets. And failed job interviews. You may have started out being 100 per cent open to happiness, but that may not be how you feel now. So, the real question now is, *From 0 to 100 per cent, how open am I still to happiness?* In the tough times, your optimism and openness will be sorely tested. And in the especially tough times, you may even find that your openness drops down into negative equity, into the minus numbers.

On your life's journey, you will meet the temptation to close down and to give up. In every moment of your life you are presented with the choice to contract or to expand, to separate or to connect. To be happy, you have to choose openness in spite of everything. This can feel like such a hard choice, an impossible choice, even. That said, the more you close down, the harder your life gets and the harder it is to feel happy again. The challenge then is to meet the temptation to close down with courage and openness.

The willingness to be open and to stay open is the key to both happiness and healing. It is what helps you to stay alive *for your whole life*. Openness creates possibility. Openness invites help. Openness gives you strength. The willingness to be open and to stay open is what releases you from the past. Opening up again is what gets you back into your life. It is what generates new beginnings and a change of fortune. Your openness enables others to share themselves fully with you. Your openness allows life to look after you and to help you take the next step.

To be happy, you have to be open. This is a big challenge, because the nature of personal psychology is to help your ego feel contained, secure and in charge. An ego achieves its sense of identity by closing down options, by restricting choices and by making up your mind about things. If you want to be even happier than your ego is right now, you have to be willing to be even more open than your ego is comfortable with. Happiness cannot be contained within your ego's comfort zone. Happiness is a great big *let go*. Happiness is giving up your ego. In practical terms, this means being willing to do the following three things:

Letting Go of Plans. There is an old saying, "If you want to make God laugh, tell Her your plans." Making plans and sticking to plans can be very productive and rewarding. Planning is a great discipline that can help to create successful outcomes. That said, life does not always go according to plan. You may have a plan for your life, but life may also have a plan for you. This is not always such a bad thing. For example, I find that most people agree with the statements "I am glad that not all of my plans have worked out" and "Some of the best things in my life were not part of my plan."

Everybody makes plans, but not every plan works. Just because your plan for happiness does not succeed, it does not mean that happiness is impossible. *Your* plan is simply not *the* plan. Perhaps your plan for happiness has not worked because there is a better plan waiting for you. Maybe there really is a better way. And anyway, who ever said that happiness needs a plan? When coaching people, I find that a common cause of unhappiness is holding on to an old plan for happiness that is too limited, too small, too future-focused and not imaginative enough. To be happy, you have to be willing to let go of your plans for something better.

Dropping Your Expectations. Expectations are commonplace. In fact, I believe that if you tried to count all of your expectations, you would lose count before you finished. For example, you expect to wake up tomorrow. For example, you expect all your loved ones to still be alive. For example, you expect to get to work safely. For example, you expect your computer to work. For example, you expect people to do their jobs well. Like everyone, you have a lot of expectations about everything, and that is absolutely okay, as long as you don't expect them all to happen.

Expectations create a mental picture of how you want things to be. Expectations create wants and desires. This is okay, unless you convince yourself that you cannot be happy if your expectations are not met. When expectations become demands, you cause yourself much harm. When expectations become demands, your relationships will often suffer. When expectations become demands, your life becomes an endless power struggle. When you drop your expectations, healing happens, you feel more peaceful and happiness returns.

Giving Up Ego Tantrums. When your plans don't work out and your expectations are not met, you can either accept that this is so or you can have a tantrum. A tantrum is a complaint. It is an incredible sulk. It is homage to a grievance. It is your ego's "middle finger". It is revenge against God or someone. Tantrums in children are always obvious, but in adults they can be more subtle and sophisticated. For example, a tantrum can be a decision to withdraw, either ever so slightly or ever so obviously, from a person or from a situation. A tantrum can be a decision never to open your heart 100 per cent to anyone ever again.

Anything less than 100 per cent openness to happiness is a sign of a possible tantrum. Cynicism is a tantrum. Depression is a tantrum. Pessimism is a tantrum. Tantrums try to block pain, but they also block happiness. Tantrums are a form of holding on that keep you stuck in the past. They are a fear that your best chance for happiness has just passed. Holding on to tantrums does not make you happy. Tantrums require personal attention and self-compassion. They are signs that you need to grieve the passing of an old plan and to mourn the demise of a dashed expectation.

Basic Trust

When your plan for happiness doesn't work out, it is difficult to know what to trust next. To trust again in anything feels hopeless because trust didn't deliver the results you had hoped for. To trust again feels frightening. You fear that trust makes you an easy target. To trust again feels foolish. You believe that trust is a trapdoor that will let you down again in the most unceremonious of ways. To trust again feels unworkable. And yet you know in your heart that to be happy again you have to trust in something.

So, what now? In the course I run a session called "Basic Trust". This session is particularly useful for people who are at a point on their life journey where they feel lost, stuck, blocked, bored, trapped, down a blind alley, in a hole, at a crossroads, in transition, or ordering another round of drinks at the last-chance saloon. In this session, I explore four types of basic trust, each of which has the power to turn your life around, improve your fortunes and help you take the next step.

Type #1: Trusting in Yourself. When your plans go awry, and you feel lost and unhappy, you will meet a temptation to give up on everything. This temptation is like a shadow figure in your mind that invites you to give up on happiness, to give up on life and to give up on yourself. This grim reaper wants you to sign a sworn statement that reads, "I am not happy. I can't be happy. I won't ever be happy." This is the ultimate ego tantrum. It is a total rejection of who you really are. Your ego is in despair, but basic trust helps you to remember your true identity:

> **There is a place in you where there is perfect peace.**
> **There is a place in you where nothing is impossible.**
> **There is a place in you where the strength**
> **of God abides.**[4]

When you hit a personal low (a divorce, a diagnosis or a bereavement, for instance), the chances are that your ego won't survive, but that who you really are will. Self-trust has healing qualities. If you stick with trust, it will restore you to your Unconditioned Self. In "Song of the Open Road", Walt Whitman discovers the joy of Self-trust. He sings, "Henceforth I ask not goodfortune – I myself am good fortune." Trust gives you the courage to meet pain, but not to identify with it. Trust takes you beyond a psychology of fear and cynicism. Trust puts you in touch with your true power.

Type #2: Trusting in Others. *From 0 to 100 per cent, how trusting are you of others?* Happiness researchers like to ask questions about trust. They have discovered a positive correlation between personal happiness and trusting others. Their findings show that the happier you are, the more likely you are to be open, to be sociable, to trust others and to enjoy strong social connections. Happiness increases your willingness to trust and trust increases your capacity for happiness. Trust is vital, then and yet social research has found that social trust has declined rapidly in recent years. This is particularly true in individualistic cultures where independence and self-reliance are championed.

Happiness is your responsibility and in order to be happy it is wise to get all the help you can. People who are dysfunctionally independent won't ask for help because it breaks the Oath of Independence – it violates their motto, "Do It Yourself." This "I strain" is a big handicap, especially in tough times. When life is difficult, when you feel tired, when you want to give up, it is a sure sign that you are trusting only in your own strength. Ironically, it is your failure to trust others that makes it look like no one can help you. Basic trust in others helps to dispel this stubborn illusion. The truth is, the people in your life want to help you and they can. Indeed, it is their joy to do so.

Type #3: Trusting in Life. Albert Einstein asked the question "Is the universe friendly?" Another way of phrasing this question is, "Is life for you or against you?" People who are dysfunctionally independent set their psychology to a default position of "me against the world". This is why basic trust is so hard for them. But what if life is for your benefit? To adopt the attitude that all things, events, encounters and circumstances are helpful puts you in a very powerful position. A basic trust in a friendly universe helps you to be courageous and authentic. Imagine how happy you would be if you adopted the creed of basic trust, which is:

Life doesn't happen to you; it happens for you.

A basic trust in life invites you to believe that *you are always in the right place at the right time.* This basic trust helps you to be fully present, fully receptive and fully committed to your whole life. Without basic trust, you withhold yourself, you subtly reject each moment and you wait for a better "here" and a better "now". With basic trust, you relax, you let go and you literally make the best of every place and every moment. Basic trust shows you that truth is here, inspiration is here, love is here, peace is here, help is here, God is here, joy is here, because you are here. And if one door closes, another one will surely open.

Type #4: Trusting in God. The name I give to this type of trust is *spiritual dependency.* It is a radical faith that is the absolute opposite of dysfunctional independence. Spiritual dependency starts with the idea that *God's will for me is perfect happiness.* This idea suggests that That which created you loves you, adores you, is deeply interested in you and wants the best for you. The idea that *God's will for me is perfect happiness* also suggests that God will do everything possible to help you to know true happiness.

Spiritual dependency can be a lifesaver when you are experiencing dark nights of the ego. It can be so hard to stay open when plans fail, expectations are broken and your sense of self is rocked. In these moments, if you can pray a prayer such as "I am willing to have a miracle here," it can be enough to release you from the psychology of your ego so you can receive extra help. Spiritual dependency is a faith that help is always at hand and for that reason you can ask God to help you with everything you set your mind to. You can even ask God to help you to be happy.

The Open Secret

The happiness course enjoys a well-earned reputation for being very successful at helping people to become happier and to make positive changes in their lives. Over the years, we have been visited by independent psychologists, professors, scientists and journalists who have all taken and tested the course. Their verdicts have always been positive. Because of this, I am often asked in interviews to divulge "the secret" of the happiness course: what makes the happiness course work? The answer I give is always the same: people's openness.

The course can encourage you to be happier, but it can't make you happy. Nothing can make you happy, except you. On the first day I tell my students, "I'll provide the entertainment, if you bring your willingness." I explain that the more you commit to the course, the better it gets. Isn't this true of most things in life? I also tell my students, "Don't wait for this course to get good." The invitation is to *put your whole self in* from the start. Openness expands possibilities. You are more present. You participate more. You give more and you also receive more.

Over the eight weeks we hold a number of "open sessions" in which people can review their progress. In these, we celebrate our successes, we share any blocks we face and we make requests for help. It is in these open sessions in particular that we get to experience a wonderful sense of community and mutual support. As time goes by, we become more and more open with each other. We are here to be seen and we really show up for each other. We are deeply aware that although we are each on our own life's journey, we are not alone.

In the open sessions, the one question we always return to is, *From 0 to 100 per cent, how open am I to happiness?* What a confronting question! But it has to be asked, because your answer to this question reveals how much happiness you are likely to allow yourself and how much you will reject.

The next question isn't for the fainthearted either. It is, "What will it take for you to be 100 per cent open to happiness?" The hush in the room is so loud it burns my ears. Here is the moment of truth. Here is the moment of decision. Here is the next step in the journey of your life.

Sometimes this step feels just a bit too big. So, as an act of compassion, I introduce "The 10 Per cent Game". To play this game, you pick a day in which you set an intention to be 10 per cent more open to life. The basic instruction is to set your intention at the start of the day and then to reset your intention every hour on the hour. The purpose of "The 10 Per cent Game" is to notice what effect your intention has on you, on everyone else and on your day as a whole. Why not try it for yourself? Are you open? Here are nine suggestions for you:

10 Per cent More Accepting
"Today I will be 10 per cent more accepting of myself,
of others and of my life."

10 Per cent More Receptive
"Today I will be 10 per cent better at receiving help,
love, and support from others."

10 Per cent More Honest
"Today I will be 10 per cent more honest with
myself and with others."

10 Per cent More Authentic
"Today I will be 10 per cent less edited and
10 per cent more real."

10 Per cent More Optimistic
"Today I will be 10 per cent more willing to
walk on the bright side of the street."

10 Per cent More Trusting
"Today I will be 10 per cent better at recognising
all the ways that life supports me."

10 Per cent More Grateful
"Today I will be 10 per cent more grateful for
everything that is happening in my life right now."

10 Per cent More Open
"Today I will be 10 per cent less independent
and 10 per cent more open-hearted."

10 Per cent More Present
"Today I will be 10 per cent more open to the
idea that I really am in the right
place at the right time."

● ● ● ● ●

CHAPTER 22

the
beautiful
ordinary

A weary traveller in search of happiness approaches the gates of a monastery. The monastery is called The Gateless Gate. It is ancient. It was built before there was any record of time.

A happy-looking old man, who is nearly as ancient as the monastery, is sitting by the gates. He greets the traveller.

The traveller asks, "Does this monastery have a teacher?"

"I am your teacher," says the old man.

"In that case," says the traveller, "will I find happiness here?"

"Where have you come from?" asks the old man.

"From the monastery over the hill," replies the traveller.

"What was it like there?" asks the old man.

"Disappointing. I expected more. Not very mystical. Food wasn't vegan. The teachings weren't very deep. There were no meditations on the chakras. The students weren't very advanced."

The old man listens with kind ears. He says, "You are welcome here. But in answer to your question, I don't think you will find happiness here."

With that, the traveller leaves.

Soon after, another traveller in search of happiness approaches the gates of the same monastery. The monastery is still called The Gateless Gate. It is still ancient. It really hasn't changed much from a few moments ago.

The happy old man, who is nearly as ancient as the monastery, is still sitting by the gates. He greets the traveller.

The traveller asks, "Does the monastery have a teacher?"

"I am your teacher," says the old man.

"In that case," asks the traveller, "will I find happiness here?"

"Where have you come from?" asks the old man.

"From the monastery down the road," replies the traveller.

"What was it like there?" asks the old man.

"Beautiful. I had no expectations. I enjoyed myself. The food was cooked with love. The teachings were very simple. There were no meditations on the chakras. I really liked the people there."

The old man listens with kind ears. He says, "You are welcome here. And in answer to your question, I think you will find happiness here."

With that, the traveller enters The Gateless Gate.

In this story, the first traveller is on a journey "to happiness"; the second traveller is on a journey "of happiness". The difference in semantics between "to happiness" and "of happiness" might seem slight, but in reality it makes all the difference in your life. At the start of each course, I explain that what I teach is not the *way to happiness* but a *way of happiness*. The course doesn't aim to make you happy eventually at the end of your life's journey; it aims to help you to be happy now and along the way.

Happiness is a journey, but it is a journey without a distance. Your journey may take you to many different places in the world, but the real destination is a place inside yourself. The journey *to happiness* makes you search outside of you. You are future-focused and most intent on "getting there". Each new "here" and "now" is seen merely as the next set of stepping stones to get you to the future. Unfortunately, on the journey *to happiness* you never stop, you never arrive and the journey makes you weary. On the journey *of happiness* you gradually realise that true progress isn't about moving forward faster; it is about being here more. Happiness is here, because you are here.

The journey *to happiness* defines happiness as an "it" and a "thing". Thus, happiness becomes something you search for – an external object of desire that you hope to find one day in another relationship, another place, or another job. This search for happiness creates a "travel blindness" that means you constantly overlook the possibility that happiness is here and that your true nature *is* happiness. The journey *of happiness* is not just about different landscapes; it is also about a different way of looking and seeing. It is more a discovery than a search. It is a realisation that in order to find happiness, you have to bring happiness with you.

The journey *to happiness* implies some sort of delay. As a result, you end up living in the "not now" and the "not yet". Reality is happening right now and happiness is in your face, but you can't see it. This is because you are waiting to be happy. The journey *of happiness* is more immediate. Reality shouts its head off: "Choose happiness!" Again Reality shouts, "Choose now!" When you finally make this choice, you discover the wonder of what I call *the beautiful ordinary*. The more you choose happiness, the more you see the potential for happiness that is all around you. You find happiness because you choose happiness.

At some point on your journey, you will give up the search for happiness in favour of actually being happy. You will give up all hopes for a happy future, and you will choose happiness now. One day now, you will do this. Any moment now, you will make the choice.

A 24/7 Invitation

The happiness course helps you to choose happiness. For eight weeks, you are asked to set a daily intention to be happy and to see how this choice affects the rest of your day. In every moment, there is a choice. Sometimes your choices help you to be happy; other times your choices block happiness. In every moment, you can choose again. The choice for happiness may not always be easy, but it is always here. And the more you choose happiness, the easier it gets.

"The Happy Choice" is a daily meditation that helps you to make the shift from a journey *to happiness* to a journey *of happiness*. Ideally, you practise the meditation in the first five minutes of the day, or as close to that as possible. The goal is to find a quiet space, to centre yourself and to reflect on the sort of day you would like to have. The focus isn't so much on what you want to have happen to you; it is more about how you want to be, what you want to do and how you can best enjoy your day. The question I set for "The Happy Choice" is:

> ### How can I make today even more enjoyable than
> ### I thought it was going to be?

"The Happy Choice" is an experiment in the power of intention. The theory is, *the more you are willing to enjoy the moment, the more beautiful each moment of your life will be.* In other words, when you choose happiness, it changes the way you see things. Your job is to test if this theory has any truth to it. Can choosing happiness actually help you to find happiness? The one constant invitation in your life – what I call the 24/7 Invitation – is to *enjoy the moment*. The question is, which moment will you choose to enjoy? And how many moments?

"The Happy Choice" encourages you to *choose your life*. You do this by being present in each moment. The present moment is here; the question is, *where are you?* "The Happy Choice" puts you into the middle of your life and asks you, *what are you going to do with it?* It encourages you to put your whole self into the smallest things you do. The goal is to show up. Be present. Be authentic. Be YOU. *You didn't come here to be normal; you came here to be YOU.* This is your life – and it is your turn to live now. And the prize is *happiness*.

"The Happy Choice" encourages you to be intimate with each moment of your life. If your day seems dull, or flat, or boring, maybe it is a sign that you need to put more of yourself into each moment. Remember this principle: *If you think something is missing in your life, it is probably you!* The poet Rainer Maria Rilke said, "If your daily life seems poor, do not blame it; blame yourself, tell yourself that you are not poet enough to call forth its riches; for to the creator there is no poverty and no poor indifferent place."[1] "The Happy Choice" really is a decision to show up.

"The Happy Choice" is a note-to-Self that reads, *Remember to enjoy the miracle of existence today.* The choice for happiness helps you to find the miracle in each moment. Asking yourself the "Happy Choice" question helps you to exercise possibility thinking, to make creative choices and to open yourself up to happiness now. "The Happy Choice" helps you to say "YES" to each moment. In doing this you discover that *the more you give yourself to each moment, the more each moment gives something back to you.* Happiness is here now, because you are here now.

NOW is the journey's end.
NOW is the end of the search.

NOW is a new beginning.
NOW is a happy discovery.

NOW is where you find yourself.
NOW is a happy Inn.

NOW is a place in your mind.
NOW is a place in your heart.

NOW is happiness.

The Flower Meditation

The Buddha said, "If you could see the miracle of a single flower clearly, your whole life would change."[2] Is this true? Or was the Buddha just having one of those flowery, spiritual moments? We put the Buddha's idea to the test in an exercise called "The Flower Meditation". Everyone is given a single long-stemmed red rose. I then explain that their task is to look at the rose for one hour. Just look, no talk. Just see, no do. For the next 60 continuous minutes they will give their roses their undivided attention.

Most people are happy to receive a red rose, but they are less than excited by the prospect of having to look at it for an hour. For the first 30 minutes or so, people experience resistance to just looking. They fidget, they twitch, they feel bored, they are easily distracted, the hands on the clock start to go backward, they can't see the point of the exercise, they experience impatience and their scattered perception makes the exercise difficult. "Nobody sees a flower, really, it is so small. We haven't time – and to see takes time like to have a friend takes time," said the artist Georgia O'Keeffe.[3]

The aim of "The Flower Meditation" is to see the rose as it really is. This is difficult to do, because what you see is that your perception is full of projections, associations, thoughts, meanings, stories and ideas gathered from the past. You don't see anything as it is now; you see the past. Therefore, to really see the rose and to have a direct experience of it, you have to be willing to clear your mind and to be completely present. You have to put yourself in the moment and look. You have been given a rose and now you are giving yourself to the rose.

After one hour, everyone agrees that the rose they are looking at is the most beautiful rose they have ever seen. One of my students, Laura, a part-time mental-health nurse and a single mother of two children, gave me some flowers (roses, of course) shortly after we did "The Flower Meditation". The flowers came with a card that read:

> Dear Robert. These flowers are to say thank you for "The Flower Meditation" and for the happiness course. The first 45 minutes of "The Flower Meditation" were so difficult. It felt like I had been sitting for hours. I felt bored, angry, irritable and fed up. And then, for no reason, I decided to surrender. I did what you said and I became completely present. Almost instantly, a miracle happened and the rose I was looking at became the most beautiful rose I had ever seen. *I didn't just see what the rose looked like; I saw its essence.*
>
> I might never have known how beautiful a rose is unless I had really looked. And I might never have known how beautiful my life is if I had not

signed up for the happiness course. I see things differently now. In front of the mirror, I look at the person I see with love. When I'm with my kids, I try to see who they really are. At work, I see my clients in a whole new way. Thank you for opening my eyes. Thank you for helping me to "find the present". With appreciation, Laura.

The Happiness Prayer

Dear God,
So far today I've done all right.
I haven't gossiped. I haven't lost my temper.
I haven't been greedy, moody, nasty, selfish or narcissistic.
And I'm really glad about that.
But in a few minutes, God, I'm going to get out of bed,
and from then on I'm going to need a lot more help.
Thank you.
Amen.[4]

"The Happiness Prayer" is an invitation to write some words that help you to live well, to be present and to enjoy each day of your life. The words can take any form you like. It can be a personal prayer, an affirmation, a sutra, a poem, a mantra, a song, or simply some prose that inspires you and helps you to be happy. You don't have to be a poet to do this exercise. You don't even need an A in English. All you have to do is create something that you can identify with and that feels real to you.

Many people find the process of creating their Happiness Prayers both difficult and valuable. I usually give people two weeks to do it. That is enough time, but most people don't get around to doing the exercise until the night before it is due. For some people, the task is made harder because they know they're going to be asked to share their Happiness Prayer. However, the whole point of a prayer is not that you say it for our benefit, or even for God's benefit; it is that you say it for yours. This is a prayer to help you and support you to fully inhabit your own life.

The benefit of any personal prayer or affirmation is that it can act as a touchstone for each day of your life. These touchstones can help you to raise your intentions to a whole new level. They can help you to set a vision, to bless your psychology, to receive help and to live your best possible life. They provide support and inspiration. They help you to stretch and grow. They take you beyond what your self-image thinks you are capable of to the true unconditioned potential of your real Self. The more you use your touchstone, the more powerful it becomes.

Most of my students create three types of Happiness Prayer. The first type is a *gratitude prayer*. "If the only prayer you say in your whole life is 'Thank you,' that would suffice," wrote Meister Eckhart, the medieval German philosopher.[5] The second type is a *service prayer*. In essence, this is a "Use me" prayer. A good example is the Prayer of Saint Francis, which begins, "Lord, make me an instrument of Thy peace."[6] The third type of prayer is a *petition prayer* in which you might say "Help me" and "Show me" and "Guide me." The following words, by Mary Jean Iron, are a beautiful example of a petition prayer. She writes:

> Normal day, let me be aware of the treasure you are. Let me learn from you, love you, bless you before you depart. Let me not pass you by in quest of some rare and perfect tomorrow. Let me hold you while I may, for it may not always be so.[7]

I have written many Happiness Prayers for myself over the years. It is my experience that life *with a prayer* is much better than a life *without a prayer*. Here is the very first one I ever wrote:

> Dear God,
> May Your JOY be my angel today.
> May Your JOY be my muse today.
> May Your JOY be my teacher today.
> May Your JOY be my healer today.
> May Your JOY be my purpose today.
> Amen.

More Fun per Day

Are you having fun yet? Are you enjoying your life now as much as you plan to one day?

"Most of the time I don't have much fun. The rest of the time I don't have any fun at all," wrote Woody Allen.[8] Can you identify with this statement? One of the effects of *not* making a daily intention to be happy is that you forget to have fun. Your schedule is so full that fun gets lost in busyness. You are in such a rush that you forget to smile. You have jobs to do and so you promise yourself you will have fun later. You think of fun as a reward for getting through another day instead of making fun an intention that you take into your day.

In the "More Fun per Day" exercise I invite my students to consider the following question for themselves: *If I were enjoying my life 10 per cent more than now, what would I be doing differently?* My experience is that everyone can find at least one thing they would do more of, less of, or differently. Most often, the answer is a mental switch. Fun is an attitude, not just an activity. It is an intention, not just something that happens. The decision to have more fun per day immediately improves your chances of having a more enjoyable day.

Happiness research shows a high correlation between happiness and fun. Basically, when you're happy, you want to have fun and you usually do; when you're unhappy, you don't want to have fun and you usually don't. Significantly, psychologists have found that when they get their clients to create a "Pleasant Events Schedule", in which they increase their regular engagement in fun activities, the clients often enjoy benefits like decreased depression, lower anxiety, less stress, more creativity, more confidence and more happiness.[9] The decision to have more fun per day puts you in touch with yourself again and you literally come out to play.

When my students commit to the "More Fun per Day" exercise, they really do come out to play. What I like about this exercise is that everyone has his or her own style of fun and play. It can be extrovert fun or introvert fun. It can be noisy fun or quiet fun. It can be artistic fun or sports fun. It can be running-in-nature fun or reading-a-book fun. It can be dancing fun or singing fun. It can be volunteering fun or time-to-recharge fun. Even just 10 per cent more fun can get you back into your life.

As part of the "More Fun per Day" exercise, I also encourage my students to consider this question: *Who or what is stopping me most from having more fun right now?* Each class comes up with a different range of answers, but the most common answer is the same every time. Can you guess what it is? The answer is, "Myself." The fact is, we often don't do the things that make us happy. We can say, "I forget," but that is not really the answer. Usually, the real answer is some form of self-neglect.

To enjoy your life more, you usually need a special kind of permission. It is permission from yourself. You have to hear yourself say, "It's okay for me to have fun." It also helps to remember that when you make it your intention to have more fun per day, you are not the only person who benefits.

When you come out to play, you are more present, you are more open, you are more attractive, you are more radiant and you give more. Also, by your example, you remind the rest of us to have more fun per day too.

To Travel Lightly

In the course, you spend a lot of time looking at the blocks to happiness. You are encouraged to explore the hurts, the wounds, the defences, the fears and the unworthiness that stop you from enjoying your life more. The idea is that you go into the shadows so that you can come out into the light. To make this journey you will need some essential provisions, like courage, willingness, honesty, forgiveness and your sense of humour.

When I ask my students, "Do you feel like you have had enough pain for one lifetime yet?" the answer is usually "Yes." Some foot soldiers want more, but most of us are ready to be happy. To that end, I encourage my students to enjoy themselves as much as possible. Personal growth is often challenging, but it can also be fun. Personal healing is often excruciating, but it is also liberating. Personal enlightenment can be depressing for the ego at times, but it helps YOU to lighten up, to get the big joke and to travel lightly.

Blessed are they who can laugh at themselves, for they will never cease to be amused. If you can't smile at your ego, you will never let it go. It's your capacity to laugh at yourself that helps you to come through the tough times. Indeed, many of us feel we wouldn't be here today if it weren't for our sense of humour. I find that when we cry and laugh together, we really see ourselves, we connect more deeply, we are more honest and we are more compassionate. To cry well you have to be able to laugh well, and vice versa. Ultimately, it's all about being light and deep.

In each course, students create a community Smile Board in which they share articles, cartoons, jokes, YouTube clips and any other items that spread laughter and cheer. Humour is life's great shock absorber. It gives us resilience and strength. It gives us perspective and hope. It helps us to travel lightly. Here is one of my favourite stories. It is told by a woman who inadvertently found a way to add a bit of sparkle to her life. It reads:

Early one morning, I received a call from the doctor's office to say my appointment with the gynecologist had been brought forward to 9:30 A.M. that day. I had only just packed everyone off to work and school and it was already around 8:45 A.M. The trip to his office took about 35 minutes, so I had no time to spare.

As most women do, I like to take a little extra effort over hygiene when making such visits. But this time there was no time for a shower, so I rushed upstairs, threw off my dressing gown, wet the washcloth that was sitting next to the sink and gave myself a quick wash "down there" to make sure I was at least presentable. I threw the washcloth in the laundry basket, donned some clothes, hopped in the car and raced to my appointment.

I was in the waiting room only a few minutes when I was called in. Knowing the procedure well, I hopped up on the table, gazed up at the ceiling and pretended I was some other place a million miles away from where I was. I was a little surprised when the doctor said, "My, we have made an extra effort this morning, haven't we?" but I didn't respond.

The appointment over, I heaved a sigh of relief, went home and finished my day as usual with the shopping, cleaning, cooking, etc.

After school, my six-year-old daughter, who was playing quietly by herself, went into the bathroom. She called out, "Mum, where's my washcloth?" I told her to get another one from the cupboard. She called back, "No, I need the one that was here by the sink. It had all my glitter and sparkles in it."[10]

One Extra Day

Imagine you receive a letter in the mail. The letter says you have won a prize in a raffle. The prize you have won is an opportunity to enjoy one extra day in your life. To accept your prize, you have to agree to insert your extra day somewhere into the next eight weeks. My question to you is, "How would you enjoy this one extra day of your life?" Take a few moments now to reflect on what you would do with it, where you would go, who you would spend it with and how you would make the most of this precious prize.

The "One Extra Day" exercise is an opportunity to see if you are living your priorities or not. It is a chance to look at your unlived life and to see where you are postponing your joy. One of the biggest blocks to happiness is that we plan to be happier one day. This delay might start out as an honest intention, but it can often end up as an unkept promise. You can only postpone joy for so long. Life *and death* is what happens to you while you are busy making other plans. Look at how you plan to enjoy your life one day and then start enjoying it more now.

In 2002, we did the "One Extra Day" exercise. It was especially poignant because in the class were Barbara and her husband Bill. Bill had been diagnosed with cancer. He had been given six months to live. His six months were already up. Barbara and Bill decided to enrol in the course so as to enjoy every minute of their life together. Barbara and Bill were an inspiration. They participated wholeheartedly in the course. They attended every class. And they reminded us all that every new day really is an extra day.

Bill passed away almost one year to the day after the end of the course. Barbara wrote a long letter to me. Here is a short excerpt from it:

Before Bill was diagnosed with cancer, if someone had asked me, "What would you do if you knew you only had one year left to live?" I imagine I would have said something like, "Take big trips, do extraordinary things, visit the Pyramids and see the wonders of the world." When Bill was told he only had six months to live, we didn't do any of that. Instead, we just loved each other more.

Rather than taking long-haul trips, we decided to appreciate all of the wonders that were already in our life *right here*. Slowing down and being more present helped to open our eyes to the *joy of everything*. A visit to the supermarket was as much fun as a vacation abroad. Breakfast in bed at home was better than a stay at the Ritz. Cooking dinner together, which is something we had never done before, was funny, romantic and wonderful.

Bill did not live for as long as I wanted him to, but I can honestly say that we lived the life we were given. We embraced the "beautiful ordinary". And I continue to embrace it every day.

● ● ● ● ●

CHAPTER 23

the
last
resistance

Living in New York at the age of 21 really was an awesome adventure. My lifestyle was like my morning coffee order at the local deli, which was a high-octane macchiato with double espresso, two extra shots, lots of foam, served extra hot and to go. My friends were beautiful, talented and crazy. The nucleus of our merry gang was me and three New York bankers, Mike Moore, Stevie Rush and Rob Jones. We worked hard and we played hard. Most days were made up of 12 hours of work, 8 hours of partying and 4 hours of sleep. Success for us was having a good time. We even had a drinking motto that was, "Be happy, for tomorrow we die."

One Saturday morning my friends and I set out to see the wonders of the world. We made a visit to the Metropolitan Museum of Art on the Upper East Side of Manhattan. The Met has everything. It houses over two million exhibits of the finest art and treasures of the world. We visited the Renaissance galleries, we did the Greek and Roman tours, we looked in on the Ming Dynasty, we checked out the Pharaohs, we took in some Aboriginal art and we also saw a special exhibition of Buddhist thangka paintings. *And we did the whole thing in under an hour.* As we charged out of the Met and on to our next destination, I remember thinking that something was not quite right with my life.

My New York playmates and I had lots of fun, but the truth was that we weren't particularly happy. Life was a party, but we partied to distraction. Mike Moore was 28 years old, he was high-strung and he took beta-blockers for a heart condition. Stevie, who was 31, had a history of depression and he had taken antidepressants since the age of 18. And Rob, who was 25, would drink, not for fun, but to get wasted. Also, I was the only one in our gang who didn't do illegal drugs. None of the guys was happy about that. Looking back, I see now that this was the first time I consciously thought about the essential difference between having pleasure and being happy.

Two months into my stay in New York, I decided to take a night off from the party scene. The truth was, I was running through my money too fast and I was also absolutely exhausted. I remember thinking "I just can't do this any more." Four hours' sleep a night was four hours too little for me. I felt bad about not going out with the guys, but I knew I had to stay in and do nothing for an evening. That night I got a full eight hours' sleep. The next morning when I got ready to jump out of bed, I experienced something very strange. I literally could not move. I had the thought of getting out of bed, but my body didn't respond to the thought. I felt okay, but it was like my whole system was offline. I couldn't do anything and I couldn't go anywhere, so I just lay there.

As I lay there, I wondered if I had had a stroke. Or maybe I was dreaming. Perhaps I was playing a character in some strange Kafka play. I knew I was okay, though. Nothing bad was happening. It was just that nothing was happening. And there was nothing I could do about it. It was a moment of pure nothingness. It was like I was being pinned to the bed by a big gentle finger of grace that wanted me to stop. Normally by now I would have been out of bed and chasing the next bit of daylight. But there I was, just lying there. And I felt so peaceful and so very happy. I was doing absolutely nothing and I was completely happy. Absolutely nothing was happening to me and I was already happy.

I lay motionless for about one hour. In that time, I saw with startling clarity that nothing has to happen first in order for me to be happy. I realised I didn't need to do anything, go anywhere, have anything, or meet anyone to make happiness happen. I also recognised that while New York is the city that has everything, I'm the one who has my happiness. Lying there, I had the thought *I can just be happy*. I surrendered totally to this thought and it felt wonderfully liberating. *Why not just be happy?* After all, it's cheaper. It's also less exhausting. You don't need to do drugs. And you can catch up on your sleep.

Maybe I really can just be happy.

A few moments later my system came back online, my body started moving again and I got out of bed.

The Be Happy Experiment

In the final week of the happiness course we draw together all of the big themes. In the last workshop we review the journey we have made together over the previous eight weeks. Now we have arrived at the end and the beginning. Now is a time of reckoning. One of the exercises I give my students is called "The Be Happy Experiment". This experiment is so devastatingly simple there really is nothing to it and yet it shows you with complete clarity where you are in your relationship to happiness right now.

To do "The Be Happy Experiment", lie down, do nothing and let yourself be happy. That's it. Very simple, isn't it? When I give my students the instruction for "The Be Happy Experiment", they usually ask me to repeat myself, not just once, but several times. The thing that's so difficult about this exercise is that it's so simple. My students believe that I must have left out a vital instruction, but I haven't. The instruction is to lie down, do nothing and let yourself be happy. That's it.

Because "The Be Happy Experiment" is so simple, I sometimes dress it up a bit to give it a sense of occasion. After my students are lying comfortably, I perform a countdown on each exhalation that goes from 10 down to 1. For example, "Breathing out 10, breathing out 9, breathing out 8 . . . breathing out 3, breathing out 2, breathing out 1." After I get to the number 1, I then say, "Now let yourself be happy." And that's it. I don't do anything else after that. If I did anything more, the experiment wouldn't be simple enough. By the way, the experiment lasts for an hour.

"The Be Happy Experiment" is an exercise in *being*. It is not a meditation or a technique that you *do*. You could describe it as making a choice to be happy, but even the word *choice* sounds a bit too active. This is a *let-it-happen* moment, not a *make-it-happen* method. It is a gentle allowing. You are literally allowing yourself to be happy. All in all, this is a deep relaxation and surrender. You are being invited to enjoy a moment of pure *being-ness*. There should be no effort, no pretence, no faking and no striving. In sum, you will either let yourself do this or not.

Some people find "The Be Happy Experiment" very easy to do. They connect with it right away, they dive deep and they let themselves enjoy the experience of *doing nothing* and *being happy*. Others find the experiment more difficult. Many students report that they experience initial discomfort because they think that they should be doing something more or that something should be happening to them. I tell my students, "If you think you are not doing it right, it's because you aren't supposed to be doing anything at all." The aim is to relax and be happy. If this feels undoable, then relax a bit more.

"The Be Happy Experiment" is so simple that it reveals any last resistance to happiness that you may be holding on to. You find, for instance, that instead of just letting yourself *be happy,* you prefer to work at happiness, to search for happiness, or to become happy later. You find resistance in thoughts like *This is too easy, This is too simple* and *I can't just be happy.* In this experiment, I advise you not to resist the resistance. Rather, I encourage you to greet the resistance openly and to meet the resistance fully. The key is not to feel guilty about it, not to be afraid and not to fight it. The more you accept the resistance, the more it loses its charge and the sooner it fades away.

At some point in your life you will finally let yourself be happy. It might be in this moment, or the next. Either way, you will one day let yourself be happy. *This is true, isn't it?* Or can you find the place in your mind where you have decided never to let yourself be happy? Sometimes people find this place when they do "The Be Happy Experiment". This can be very frightening, but even this thought must not be resisted. As the old saying goes, "What you resist persists." Each time you meet any resistance to happiness with compassion and love, you make it easier to let yourself be happy.

**Being happy is
giving up all resistance to happiness.**

Divine Surrender

"The Be Happy Experiment" exposes *the but of happiness,* so to speak. It brings to light any objection you have to letting yourself be happy now. If you really want to be happy, you will let yourself be happy. If, however, you want to be happy, but you aren't feeling it, it's probably because you have a hidden *but.* In other words, when you say, "I want to be happy," what you really mean is, "I want to be happy, but . . ." Now you face a dilemma. And the dilemma is that *you cannot be happy and hold on to your but.*

To be happy you have to be willing to address *the but of happiness.* Maybe you want to be happy, but you notice that you tense up at the thought of just letting yourself be happy. What is that tension a response to? Search your mind and see if you can find an old belief, a rule, a fear, a judgment, a role you play, or anything else that makes it difficult or impossible for you to just be happy. Maybe you want to be happy, but you prefer to focus on what is missing, to stay judgmental, to be angry, to play the role of martyr, to wave your fist at God, to hold on to your grievances and to maintain your suffering.

How good are you at simply letting yourself be happy? In my experience, many people I meet are too tense, too driven and too hard on themselves to relax and be happy. They are literally working too hard at happiness to just be happy. After Hannah, a young lawyer in her 20s, did "The Be Happy Experiment", she said, "At first, my mind was like a rodeo horse that kept on bucking off the thought that *I could just be happy*. Every time I tried to hold on to the thought, my mind bucked it off. Eventually, I stopped trying to hold and I just relaxed. The more I relaxed, the more my mind settled and the less resistance I felt to letting myself be happy."

Being happy is *giving up all resistance to the present moment*. When you relax and just let yourself be happy, you naturally become more present to each moment. The ego is afraid that no moment is perfect enough for you to let go and be happy and yet the more you relax into each moment, the more perfect each moment feels. As you relax into yourself, you discover something even more amazing, which is that while your ego (a.k.a. your personality) is hard at work trying to make you happy, your being (a.k.a. your Unconditioned Self) is already perfectly happy. The essence of who you are is *perfect joy*.

**Happiness is
giving up all resistance to yourself.**

Doing Nothing

Some people find "The Be Happy Experiment" difficult because they follow a rule that goes, *I will not let myself be happy until everything else is done first.* If you can identify with this rule, then you probably have happiness as the last item on a very long to-do list – a list that is so long you might not get through it before the end of your life. Maybe your to-do list reads a bit like this: Achieve good grades. Get a great job. Find a partner. Get married. Raise children. Be financially better off. Be successful. Make a will. Retire. Die. Be happy.

Happiness is what is left when you stop doing everything else. You don't let yourself be happy, because there is always something else to do first. And when you aren't working on something else, you are working on yourself. You can't just relax and be happy, because you are so focused on becoming your best self first. You have determined that happiness is the prize you earn for becoming your best self. The trouble is, what is *the best self?* And, anyway don't you always feel like you *could do better?* This drive to better yourself first before you will let yourself be happy betrays a sense of unworthiness that blocks happiness now and later.

It is a blessed joy to know that you don't have to do anything first in order to be happy. Indeed, one of the great joys of being happy is that you stop trying to prove yourself, to become a somebody and to win some special acceptance from the world. When you let yourself be happy, you don't have to be perfect first, to be loved first, to be successful first, or to be enlightened first. You can stand outside yourself. You can enjoy the ecstasy of not being anybody. Happiness is not an ego boost; happiness is no ego at all. When you stop all activity, even for just a moment, you realise that it was your effort to be happy that kept you from seeing that your original essence is already happy, radiant and star-like. *Happiness is a lightness of being that you feel when you stop overdoing it.*

When you let yourself be happy, you are less ego-driven and your life works better for you. Happiness is dynamic. It connects you with the natural, effortless talent of your being. Now you experience greater inspiration and success because everything you do issues forth first from your *being* and not from your *ego*. Your ego is not the doer; creation works through you, God makes you an instrument and your *being-ness* works wonders. Being happy is the key to doing well. *Being is the key to doing.*

**Happiness is
giving up all resistance to being.**

Letting Go

"The Be Happy Experiment" brings up resistance to happiness because of any last remaining identification with pain. Suffering is a decision not to let go of the past yet. Happiness is a decision to step into the present now. And being present is what helps you to *let go of what is not happening now.* You may have had an unhappy childhood, but that is not happening now. You may have experienced a romantic heartbreak, but that is not happening now. You may have had a bitter disappointment in your career, but that is not happening now.

Letting yourself be happy is not a denial that suffering ever happened and it is certainly not an attempt to dishonour any old pain. Letting yourself be happy is, however, a signal of intent to be free of more suffering. By choosing happiness, you invite healing. By saying "Yes" to happiness, you invite grace. By being open to happiness, you discover you have a deeper compassion for yourself than even you realised. Letting yourself be happy can be translated as *I have suffered and I want to be free; I feel pain and I choose joy; I feel fear and I ask for help; I feel angry and I am open to forgiveness; I feel sad and I call upon compassion; I feel lost and I welcome grace.*

Until you let yourself be happy, you make an idol of your suffering, which prevents you from seeing the true depth and beauty of your original nature. One of the mantras of my work with The Happiness Project is, "Pain runs deep but joy runs deeper." As you let yourself be happy, you realise that pain and suffering belong to the ego, but true healing and joy belong to your original nature. In other words, you realise that although you have experienced pain, you are not your pain and that although you may continue to experience suffering, you are not your suffering.

**Happiness is
giving up all resistance to letting go.**

Nonattachment

"The Be Happy Experiment" is an invitation to drop the theory of happiness and let yourself have a direct experience. Letting yourself be happy is such a simple task that some people cannot get their heads around it. They will not let themselves be happy because they *suffer from too much psychology.* They want to understand happiness first and *then* be happy. They want to grasp what happiness is, but happiness cannot be summed up or intellectualised because *it* is not an object. The mind is not big enough to wrap itself around happiness. True happiness is not a thought; it is an experience. Not even a genius or an enlightened master can *think happiness.* Happiness can be appreciated by the mind, but it cannot be contained, compressed or squeezed into the mind.

Have you noticed that when you let yourself be happy, you don't think that much? One of the obstacles to happiness is that you are too identified with your thoughts and you literally overthink your life. Yet if you can quiet your mind, even for a few seconds, you discover in that thought gap a natural experience of peace, joy and freedom. In this moment, brief as it may be, you are identified with your *being* and not your mind. The more you connect with your being, the more you realise that happiness does not come and go; what comes and goes is your awareness of happiness. Your true nature is always happy, no matter what your mind may think.

The happier you are, the less you think and the better you think. In other words, when you are happy in yourself, this is reflected in your mind and you think fewer thoughts of anxiety, guilt and fear and more thoughts of courage, faith and love. By letting yourself be happy, you become less attached to your mind and you also become less attached to the world. Operating from the natural ground of your being, you find you can be "in the world but not of it". You are able to wear the world as a loose garment. Your happiness blesses your mind and the world becomes a safe place for you to be in.

Happiness is a natural state of consciousness that already exists in you but is often obscured by all kinds of mental distractions. One such distraction is the search for a reason to be happy. Needing a reason to be happy can cause mental instability, grasping, paranoia and inevitable grief and misery when the reason is no longer here. However, when you simply let yourself be happy, you make a joyous discovery: *Because your natural Self is already happy, you don't really need a reason to be happy.* True happiness is unreasonable. You can be happy for no good reason.

**Happiness is
giving up all resistance to unreasonable joy.**

Being Here

If you believe that you have to get to a certain point in your life first before you can be happy, the chances are you won't ever let yourself be truly happy. Some people spend their whole lives *going to be happy*. For instance, they are *going to be happy* after they find their true purpose. For instance, they are *going to be happy* when they meet their soul mate. For instance, they are *going to be happy* once they get a lucky break or after their next success. This *going after* happiness can end up causing an ongoing delay that means you never really surrender to joy.

Unless you accept the idea that happiness already exists in you, you will not find it anywhere else. Why is this? Psychologically, you only ever see what you identify with. The world you see is made in your image of yourself.

This is why the philosopher Immanuel Kant said, "We see things not as they are, but as we are." If, even for a moment, you would let yourself enjoy the happiness of your true nature, you would start to have a more fulfilling experience of the world around you. When you let yourself be happy, you stop going to somewhere else and you let yourself be more here.

When you let yourself be happy, you begin to see what is always here. Franz Kafka, the philosopher and playwright, explored the theory of perfect happiness. He said that in order to enjoy perfect happiness you have to believe in the "indestructible element within" that is your true nature. He also said that you have to be willing to give up striving toward an external mirage of happiness. Kafka famously wrote, "It is not necessary that you leave the house. Remain at your table and listen. Do not even listen, only wait. Do not even wait, be wholly still and alone. The world will present itself to you for its unmasking, it can do no other, in ecstasy it will writhe at your feet."[1]

The more you let yourself be happy, the more receptive you are to your life as it happens. You are more here now and you discover that there is more here than you previously realised. You notice that the more present you are, the more interesting and rich your life becomes. As you become more spontaneously available to each moment, you experience profound gratitude for what is. "Paradise is where I am," said Voltaire.[2] And eventually, as you give up your resistance to letting yourself just be happy, you make one more joyous discovery, which is that *happiness does not just come to you; it also comes from you. You are it!*

> I welcome happiness,
> and I need do nothing.
> I welcome healing,
> and I need do nothing.
>
> I welcome heaven,
> and I need do nothing.
> I welcome the angels,
> and I need do nothing.
>
> I welcome inspiration,
> and I need do nothing.
> I welcome miracles,
> and I need do nothing.

> I welcome God,
> and I need do nothing.
> I welcome love,
> and I need do nothing.

No Blocks

"The Be Happy Experiment" is an invitation to let yourself be happy now. As such, it gives you an occasion to witness with complete openness and honesty what exactly is stopping you from being happy. In the feedback session that follows the exercise, I often put the following question to my students: "What stopped you, if anything, from being happy?" I get many answers, but two stand out.

The first answer is, "Nothing." This is a revelation for many people because it is the first time in their lives that they actually admit to themselves that *no thing* can really stop them from being happy. *If you want to be happy, the world cannot prevent you from being so.* No one is really stopping you from living your life. Furthermore, many people find that when they let themselves be happy, they discover an astonishing strength of spirit within. By letting yourself be happy, you experience a great freedom of being, which allows you to be the person you most want to be.

The second answer is, "Myself." "The Be Happy Experiment" helps you to see that nothing *out there* is stopping you from *being here*. In truth, there is nothing real in the world that does not want you to be you. *The world is for you, if you are for yourself.* Therefore, it is only you who stops you from being happy, who holds you back, who puts on the brakes and who digs in your heels. This is very sobering, but it is also very liberating. If you will give up your resistance to yourself, you are home free. If you will stop holding yourself back, the world can befriend you and you can be the loving, happy person that you came here to be.

Once in a while, just for a moment, play with the idea that *in truth there are no blocks*. Take five minutes and literally imagine what your life would be like if *there really are no blocks*. Take a few moments to visualise how you would show up in the world, if you really knew *there are no blocks*. Right now, just let yourself be happy and be willing to let go of the idea that there have to be any blocks to happiness.

"Man is unhappy because he doesn't know he's happy.
It's only that. That's all, that's all. If anyone finds
out he'll become happy at once, that minute . . . it's
all good. I discovered it all of a sudden."
– Fyodor Dostoyevsky[3]

CHAPTER 24

the
gift of
happiness

Ionce witnessed a most delightful conversation between a mother and her young daughter. The whole conversation lasted barely a minute and yet I have never forgotten it. It happened while I was sitting in a busy terminal at the New Delhi international airport, in India, waiting for my flight to be announced. The mother and her daughter, who was named Angela, were sitting opposite me. Angela, who was about three years old, was talking and drawing, talking and eating, talking and reading. Meanwhile, her mother was busy sorting out plane tickets and passports.

Although I could hear Angela talking, I wasn't really listening to what she was saying until she suddenly announced, "I am happiness, Mummy." The words caught my ear. And I found myself smiling. *What a great thought,* I thought to myself. After that, Angela leaned over and tugged on her mother's T-shirt so as to get her full attention.

"I am happiness, Mummy," said Angela.

"What, darling?" her mother asked.

"I am happiness, Mummy," repeated Angela.

"No, darling. What you mean to say is, 'I am happy,'" explained her mother.

"No, Mummy," explained Angela. "I am happiness."

By now, I noticed that several other passengers were listening in on the conversation. Angela's mother noticed also. She was a little embarrassed, but we all realised just how sweet and funny the moment was.

"I – am – happy," said Angela's mother in a slow and deliberate voice.

"I – am – happiness," replied Angela in a slow and deliberate voice.

Her mother smiled. "Okay, Angela, you are happiness."

"Yes, Mummy, I am happiness," said Angela, nodding her head.

And that was it. A short and sweet conversation finished as suddenly as it had started. But it really got me thinking.

How would you live your life if you knew you were already happy? Imagine how you would be. Imagine how good you would feel if you knew that your original nature is already happy. Imagine exactly how you would greet each new day knowing that *you are what you seek*. Imagine how much love and healing you would experience if you changed the purpose of your relationships from *finding happiness* to *sharing happiness*. Imagine how fantastic and successful you'd be if you followed your joy and you let your happiness shine through you. Imagine how you would be.

Imagine if, just for one moment, you surrendered completely to the original joy of your true nature. What a baptism that would be! Imagine how freeing it would be if you no longer needed the world to *make you happy*. What a blessing for all! Imagine how rich you would feel knowing your happiness is not separate from you and hidden away inside some external thing. Imagine how your attitude toward money would change. Imagine how much you would let yourself relax and *enjoy each moment* if you knew your joy is always with you and not someplace else. Imagine how your attitude to time would change. Imagine how you would be.

Imagine if every day you were to let the original joy of your *being* bless you and refresh you. Imagine if you made the purpose of your life not to *get happiness* but to *spread happiness*. Imagine how much you would enjoy yourself. Imagine how generous you would be. Imagine how kind you would be. Imagine what a great friend you would be. If you lived your life in the knowledge that your *being* is already happy, you would be free to be the person you "came to be". Being already happy, you would not be afraid to love. In fact, you would probably become the most loving person you could possibly imagine.

Imagine how that would be.

My work with The Happiness Project is based on the radical idea that *you are already happy*.[1] I wish this radical idea of mine weren't so radical. It's radical not because I believe it, but because so few of us do. The idea that *you are already happy* is the starting point for my work both in my private practice and with the happiness course. In essence, my work is about helping people to recover the joy of who they really are. The way I see it, your essence is infused with joy, your *being* is packed with inspiration, and your Unconditioned Self does not require a shrink or a life coach.

When I see the truth of who you are, all I see is love and happiness. I see there is nothing wrong with you. I see that there is nothing missing in you. I see that you were created perfectly. That might not be your story, however. I understand that your personality (a.k.a. your ego) can give you a hard time, and that it can often stand in your way. I respect that your psychology (a.k.a. your mind) might be messing with you. Thoughts and feelings can really mess you up if you identify with them, if you believe in them, and if you keep giving them your power. When you stop doing that, they can't hurt you any more.

Over the eight weeks of the course, we watch each other make many positive changes. Some changes are bold and obvious and others are more subtle and courageous. Each time a person changes on the inside, the changes are mirrored in his or her life. It is a joy to behold. In spite of all these changes, I describe the course not as a change programme, but as a growth programme. Happiness doesn't really change you. What changes is that you become more aware of who and what you really are. The gift of happiness is that it cracks open your personality and your mind and then the cosmic light of your *being* shines through these cracks. And this is how your happiness lights up the world.

Throughout the happiness course, we explore two main paradigms of *human functioning,* the *becoming paradigm* and the *being paradigm.* Both paradigms are essential for personal growth and evolution. They are both necessary for your journey through life. Both paradigms will serve you well at different times. Each has merits and benefits that will help you on your way. That said, only one of these paradigms can help you to have a direct experience of the joy that is your true nature. Eventually, you have to be willing to give up one paradigm for the other if you want to experience true happiness now.

The *becoming paradigm* is a call to awakening. It is an urge inside you that wants to push you forward. It is an itch that wants you to get going. It is a whisper that says, "Grow, grow." The *becoming paradigm* is about aspiration, chasing down the future and becoming the person you want to be *when you really grow up.* The desire to *become* motivates you to keep going each day, it makes you resilient in the tough times and it gives you something to aim for. Wanting to become all that you can be, to become your best self, and to become a truly happy person, for instance, is the hero's journey. And it gives your life both meaning and direction.

The *becoming paradigm* is the paradigm in which you strengthen your intention to be happy, and at the same time you work through your fears of happiness, your erroneous self-concepts, your learned unworthiness, your self-attack, your attachments to old wounds, and any other ego resistance. As you do this, you undoubtedly start to feel better about yourself. In your life you may first experience a corresponding period of undoing. This is when, for instance, unhealthy relationships fall away or unsuitable jobs are suddenly terminated. This may leave you feeling temporarily bereft of old abusive patterns, feeling like you have *lost yourself*, but this doesn't last long. After a period of undoing, you find yourself again and you begin to enjoy a time of flourishing and prosperity.

The *becoming paradigm* can help you to make great gains in your life, and thereby you experience more pleasure (a.k.a. sensory happiness) and more satisfaction (a.k.a. circumstantial happiness). The sense of *becoming* also gets you closer to joy, but not close enough. Here is the moment of choice. The great hope of *becoming* is that it will naturally lead into *being*, but that is not how it works. Ultimately, to *be happy* you must be willing to let go of *becoming*. *Eventually, becoming must give way to being.* You have to stop working at being happier and let yourself *be happy*. Tolstoy said so succinctly, "If you want to be happy, be."[2]

The *becoming paradigm* belongs to your ego (a.k.a. your self-image). It is the paradigm in which the ego betters itself and improves its circumstances. The *being paradigm* is the paradigm in which the ego (a.k.a. your self-image) surrenders to the Unconditioned Self (a.k.a. your true nature). The *becoming paradigm* is ultimately a preparation for surrender, although you may not know that at first. *The being paradigm is surrender.* It is when you give up illusion for truth, pain for joy, personality for *essence*, the past for now, ego for God and fear for love. This is big stuff, but then happiness is not a little thing.

When you step into the *being paradigm,* you choose happiness and you let happiness choose you. *Being is an awareness that the person you "came to be" already exists in potential.* It is a Self that is not made, but realised. It is a Self that is already whole, already okay and already happy. This original Self (a.k.a. the Unconditioned Self) is in essence unchangeable, in reality indestructible and in truth infinite. In the *being paradigm* you experience a consciousness that is outside time and space and you discover the eternal aspect of a fully functioning human. This is what it is to be fully individuated and Self-actualised.

At some point on your journey you will realise the difference between *becoming* and *being*. One paradigm can improve your life but still leave you feeling unsatisfied. It takes you closer to happiness, but never all the way. The other paradigm gets you here now. It is a surrender to *what is*. It reacquaints you with your Unconditioned Self that is happy already. Once again you dance in delight with the great rays of your *being*. And you come to realise something that is so hopeful, so profound and so indelibly true, which is that

> **you can never become happy, but you can always be happy.**

Happiness Symptoms

In the Vision Statement of The Happiness Project there is a line that reads,

> **"It is because the world is so full of suffering that your happiness is a gift."**[3]

I created the course because I believe *your happiness is a gift*. It is a gift both to you and to others. The happier you are, the more we all gain. The benefits are yours and ours. True happiness is always shared. If people try to keep happiness for themselves, it's a sign that a) they are not very happy and b) they have misunderstood the true nature of happiness. You cannot contain the effects of true happiness. If you accept happiness for yourself, then everyone else will prosper – even if only because you are no longer being such a miserable bugger.

Your happiness is a gift because happiness gives you greater access to the natural qualities of your *being* (a.k.a. your Unconditioned Self). The happier you are, the more these natural qualities shine through you. They include, for instance, presence, kindness and love. The relationship between happiness and these *qualities of being* is highly reciprocal. For example, being happy enables you to be present and being present brings greater happiness. *Your happiness is a gift* because it literally brings out the best in you. And the happier you are, the more you become a gift to others.

In the course, we explore the natural qualities of the Unconditioned Self in some detail. These natural qualities are not like physical muscles that need effort and repetition in order to become strong; they are already fully developed within your Unconditioned Self and they flow effortlessly from you when you are relaxed and happy. A good way to think of these natural qualities is as *symptoms of happiness*. When a person is diagnosed as genuinely happy, he or she usually exhibits a few of the following symptoms:

Presence. When you know that your true nature is already happy and that *happiness does not leave its source,* you realise that there is literally *nothing to lose.* Now the world is not such a scary place. Now you show up in a way that is less defended, less self-promoting, less edited, less packaged, less apologetic and less afraid. You participate more fully in your life and you enjoy your life in real time. You understand that the greatest gift you can give another person is your presence and that it costs you nothing to do this. Your presence is like a gentle smile that blesses the people you meet. Your presence is a gift. Who you are is a gift.

Acceptance. Happiness challenges you to make peace with yourself. For as long as you persist in being so self-critical and self-dismissing, you will continue to block out the perfect joy that is your true nature. But if you are willing, even a little, to accept yourself and your feelings, you will find that life becomes less frustrating, that there are fewer flare-ups and that you participate in fewer personal wars. As you accept yourself even more, you relax, you become more present and people feel more loved and accepted by you. Your Self-acceptance is a gift to you and others. People come to you now when they need help with their own Self-acceptance and with remembering the perfect joy of their true nature.

Selflessness. True happiness exists before *the thought of I.* The happier you are, the less preoccupied you are by thoughts of "I am," "I need," "I want," and "I must." True happiness also exists before *the story of Me.* The less caught up you are in your personal stories, the less pride and neediness you feel. The more selfless you are, the less you get in your own way and the more you let people give to you. Also, the more selfless you are, the more you can be there for others, and the more you can give without any *thought of self.* Being truly selfless, it is your joy to receive and to give because you know that they are same.

Authenticity. The happier you are, the more you realise that all you really want is truth. What you are really interested in is true love, true success, true happiness and true freedom. The happier you are, the more you want to live in integrity, which means integrating your values and ethics in your relationships and work. Happiness is never far away if you stay close to your values and ethics. The happier you are, the more you follow your joy and the more you realise your true value. Happiness liberates your natural talents. Happiness yields great success. And your success is your gift to the world.

Equanimity. Being happy helps you to stand outside yourself, to be more objective and to be less identified with either pleasure or pain. The happier you are, the less you let yourself get taken out by emotions like unworthiness, pain, envy and resentment. Your happiness helps you to meet your feelings with compassion and equanimity. Your happiness saves you from much unnecessary drama and suffering. Your happiness brings you more into the present, and you are better able to let go of old wounds. Your happiness and your healing save the world from projections, grievances, resentments and desires for revenge that spew out of unhealed wounds. Your happiness and your healing are gifts to the world.

Wisdom. An honest inquiry into the nature of true happiness helps you to still the mind and to access new levels of clarity and inspiration. Happiness helps you to think more objectively, to listen to your inner wisdom and to put your mind to a creative use. On a basic level, your happiness helps you to think great thoughts, to be funny, to be smart and to get a kick out of consciousness. At the same time, you don't let yourself get lost in thought and you don't just live in your head. On a higher level, your happiness helps you to free yourself from thoughts of misery and death and you can hang out with the perfect joy of your *being*. Now you are no longer confined by the perceptions of your ego. Happiness is thinking the thoughts of God.

Altruism. One of the most delightful side effects of happiness is *altruism*.[4] When people feel good, they naturally want to do good. Many happiness researchers have observed this "feel good, do good" phenomenon.[5] They find that *happiness makes you want to be altruistic and being altruistic increases your happiness.* When you surrender to the joy of your *being*, you realise just how connected you are to life. You know in your heart of hearts that the universe is friendly. This basic trust puts you on solid ground and it helps you to befriend your own shaky ego. *Being a true friend to yourself qualifies you be a true friend to others.* Your happiness makes you want to be a friend to the world.

Enthusiasm. "He who tickles himself laughs when he likes," goes the German proverb. Happiness gives you an attitude and it is an attitude of fun. The happier you are, the more you know how to amuse yourself with every little detail of creation. You feel a natural enthusiasm for each present moment and you give yourself fully to everyone who is before you. Your enthusiasm helps all of the flowers in the garden to bloom. We so enjoy your presence. We love your energy. Your light helps us to grow. Your enthusiasm spreads through us. As you become even happier, you see even more of the Divine in each moment. You feel so grateful because you realie, as Hafiz the poet said,

> **"This place where you are right now**
> **God circled on a map for you."**[6]

Kindness. When you know that you are already happy, it occurs to you that the most fun you can have in life is to be kind. Joy is the realisation that life's true gifts come not from the world but from the heart. And the happier you are, the more you remember to live from your heart. In your busy day, you manage to make time to write a note of appreciation, to speak words of encouragement and to stop and help a stranger. You are generous in a thousand ways and most of your daily acts of kindness go unnoticed by the multitude. This is the way you like it. Kindness is its own reward. If happiness has a heart, it must surely be kindness.

Love. The happier you are, the more loving you are and the more loving you are, the happier you are. When you are happy, it feels like love. When you feel love, it feels like happiness. It occurs to you that you are using two different words to describe the same experience. "Happiness is love and nothing else," wrote Emmet Fox.[7] The greatest happiness of all is to set the world free from your judgments and literally be *the presence of love*. Happiness makes you a lover of life and you so love the world that you send yourself into it each day ready to perform acts of love. It is your joy to let love work through you, and to speak with love, to listen with love and to act with love.

> **To be happy is to love.**
> **To love is to be happy.**

Total Happiness

On the opening day of the course, I introduce you to "The Angel Game". The idea is that over the next eight weeks you will be an angel to someone in the course and someone else will be an angel to you. The process for the assigning of angels may appear rather haphazard, but I like to think a higher plan is at work. First, I give you a piece of paper on which you write your name and also whatever contact details you wish to share with the group.

Next, everyone, including the team and me, puts his or her details in a box. Then, I give the box a great big shake. Finally, the box goes around the room and you pick out a piece of paper. The name on that piece of paper is the person you will be an angel to.

You are now officially an angel to someone and you have two principal tasks to perform. The first task is to help your person *to enjoy the happiness course*. How you do this is up to you. The only rule is that you have to remain anonymous until the last day of the course. For eight weeks you are to be a pair of "unseen hands" helping your person with his or her inquiry into happiness. Being unseen helps you to give freely, with a light touch and in quiet ways. Anything you send through the mail or Internet is signed simply, "From Your Angel". To help you remain unseen, The Happiness Project team sets up Angel Hotmail accounts and at each workshop there is an Angel table on which you can leave messages and gifts.

Now that you are officially an angel, you are encouraged to reflect on what has truly supported you and inspired you in your own life either to heal or to be happy – *and then share it.* Over the next eight weeks you might send your person some words of encouragement, inspirational sayings, a note of appreciation, a much-loved book, a favourite movie, a thought for the day, or anything else that is meaningful to you. The only criterion for giving is *to do what feels good.* Some students already know how to be great angels; for others, this may be their first assignment. Either way, the students who give themselves fully to this game are the ones who gain the most from it.

One of the gifts of playing "The Angel Game" is that it encourages you to reflect on *the happiness of giving.* Specifically, it helps you to identify what you feel most called to give in your life and also to whom you want to give. The calling to give isn't just about giving things; it's also about following your purpose, sharing your talents and giving yourself. Happiness researchers have found that people who serve, who donate money, who volunteer and who engage in pro-social activities experience *the happiness of giving.*[8] People who are happy give more and the more they give, the happier they are.

Your second principal task as an angel is *to wish your person as much happiness as you wish for yourself.* Specifically, the task is to donate one minute a day, for eight weeks, in which you say a prayer or make a wish that your person be given all the help he or she needs today to be happy. In essence, the prayer or wish is, "May YOU be happy today." Many students report profound effects with this exercise. They describe it as being "deeply satisfying", "heart-opening" and "self-healing". Some students say they've never done an exercise like this before, or if they have, it was when they were little children. And some students say they have never wished happiness for themselves, certainly not on a daily basis. I tell them that they have now because

> **when you wish happiness for another,**
> **you wish happiness for all,**
> **and you wish it for yourself.**

My inquiry into happiness has taught me that *when people refuse to wish everyone else total happiness, they subtly (or not so subtly) block and limit their own happiness.* I really do mean *everyone else,* and not *everyone else, with a couple of exceptions.* It must be total. Here's why: The human mind at the deepest level does not understand the difference between personal pronouns like "I" and "you", "me" and "(s)he", "us" and "them" or "it" (as in "the world"). This is significant because what you wish for yourself is interpreted by your mind as a wish for all, and what you wish for others is interpreted as what you wish for yourself. If you can understand this, you have discovered the secret to total happiness.

To explain further, when you say, "I hope *she* is never happy," your mind doesn't understand that you don't mean *you.* How so? When you are angry with "her", it's "you" who feel the effects. Your mind doesn't know how to keep your nerves calm and your heart healthy while you "send angry thoughts" to someone else. *What you send to someone else is what you feel.* This is not theoretical; this is biological. Right now, try to think one thought about someone else and *not* feel the effects yourself and you will see how totally impossible this is. At the deepest level, your mind cannot divide the world up into "me" and "you." What I think about "you" will affect how I think about "me", and *vice versa.*

Understanding how the mind really works, without divisions or separations, reveals a fatal flaw in the reasoning of what happiness researchers call *relative happiness.* The term *relative happiness* describes the satisfaction that rises or falls according to how well off people perceive they are compared to the fortunes of others. The reasoning of *relative happiness* is, "'I' feel happy because 'I' enjoy better fortune than 'they' do." No wonder *relative happiness* is short-lived and manic. It cannot be true that your happiness should depend on others' misfortune or lack of fortune. This is not true happiness; this is fear.

In self-help books, the reader is often admonished to avoid "negative people" and to switch off the "negative news" on TV. Again, this is not true happiness; it is fear. If you are happy, you don't need to run away from these situations. That said, neither do you need to actively seek them out.

Happiness is not made of fear; it is love. Therefore, when you are happy, it means more to you to send a prayer or a good wish to someone who is unhappy or in an unfortunate situation than to avoid or condemn that person. When you pray or wish, "May YOU be happy," you send a blessing into the world that can increase the total happiness of all, including you.

> **"You can no more pray for yourself alone than**
> **you can find joy for yourself alone."**
> – A Course in Miracles[9]

Happiness research proves that people who consistently feel "very happy" are less affected by social comparison and relative status. These people agree with statements like, "The happiness of others adds to my own sense of wellbeing." Like the Buddhists who practise "sympathetic joy", they appreciate that when "I" wish "you" good fortune, it increases both of our chances of enjoying good fortune. Happiness is indivisible. It cannot be divided into a bigger bit for "me" and a smaller bit for "you". Happiness is total and it is equally available to all. When you wish unconditionally for everyone's happiness, it clears your mind of any blocks and your happiness shines out in the world.

Another gift of "The Angel Game" is that every day, for eight weeks, someone in the course is wishing you total happiness. Because your angel is anonymous, it could be anyone. The idea that anyone might be your angel is a powerful thought to take into your day. It's a happy thought that can do nice things to your heart. Every day of the course, you are being an angel for someone and someone is being an angel for you. This generates a feeling of enchantment and wonder that can spread into all of your interactions and relationships. It also encourages you to be more present, more open and more receptive to everyone you meet.

I love to remind my students that, this very moment, people all over the world are praying for your happiness. Even as you read this book, children everywhere are saying their bedtime prayers and they are wishing happiness for everyone (including the birds and the trees). Right now, in at least ten thousand different churches and monasteries, people are praying for your happiness. Right now, in temples, synagogues and mosques, people are reciting prayers of universal peace and joy. Right now, people from the indigenous tribes are wishing happiness to *all relations everywhere*. And in Buddhist ceremonies, also happening right now, a prayer is being said for your benefit. This prayer is a prayer of loving kindness and it goes:

> May all beings be happy and have the
> causes of happiness.
> May all beings be free from suffering
> and the causes of suffering.
> May all beings never be separated
> from the great joy beyond suffering.
> May they always remain in the great
> equanimity beyond attachment
> or aversion.[10]

Happiness Offering

On the final day, the last two sessions are given to the students to present a "happiness offering" to the class. The students have had eight weeks to prepare their offering for us. From what I hear, many students stay up late the night before, busy working on their final draft. The instruction for "The Happiness Offering" is to "share something intimate" and to "speak from the heart" and to "tell the truth about happiness". This is your chance to share your journey, to give your fellow students a gift and to teach us what you know.

For "The Happiness Offering", the whole class sits in the round, just like in traditional theatre. One by one, the students stand in the centre of the room and share their offerings. Many offerings are inspired by personal experiences with exercises and assignments done during the course. A student may share a happiness letter written to a son or daughter, lover or friend. This letter discloses lessons learned, mistakes made, heartfelt wishes and deep personal truths. Some students tell us of conversations about happiness with family members. Perhaps it's the first time they have ever talked about happiness with their mum or dad.

Students often share their definitions of happiness and what true happiness means to them. In the most recent course, Janice presented a collage of paintings, drawings, poetry and photographs that she had created with her husband and children. The theme of *following your joy* is also very popular. Many students use this moment to sing a song for the first time in public and they receive ovations like the ones at Carnegie Hall. Some students show works of art that have never been seen before. Some recite poems that have been shut away in old personal notebooks for a very long time.

Some students share excerpts from their "One Hundred Gratitudes" lists. They tell us about the people and the experiences that have made their entire life worth living. "The Receiving Meditation" gets lots of mentions in the happiness offerings. Students tell us how they feel more present and more alive. They tell us how rich and abundant they feel and how every day feels like a gift. Some students open up their Happiness Journals and read to us about what it has *really* been like being in the course. They share moments of truth, private humor, the hard parts, the turning points and the epiphanies.

"The Happiness Offering" is designed to help you to integrate your experience of being in the course. By teaching us what you have learned, you learn the lessons again, but this time on a whole new level. By sharing with us the gifts you have received, you receive the gifts again. By telling us how the course has touched you and helped you, you feel the effects, I hope, twice as strongly. Your happiness offering is like a gift you give yourself for taking the happiness course. Ideally, you will continue to feel the benefits for a long time to come and everyone in your life – now and in the future – will benefit in some way too.

For some students, "The Happiness Offering" is the biggest stretch by far in the course. It is an invitation to tell us the truth about who you are, what happiness is and what you live for. This may require a level of honesty and courage that you don't normally let yourself feel. Above all, "The Happiness Offering" requires you to be present and to participate. It's a moment when you say, "I'm here." Not just "here" taking a happiness course, but "here" in your life. It's a moment when you realise, "This is it!" This moment now is your life. *Your life is happening now.*

Just like every previous "now" and also every future "now", this present moment "now" is an invitation to know the truth of who you are and *be happy.*

It is never too late to really be here.
It is never too late to enjoy the moment.
It is never too late to love and be loved.
It is never too late to know the truth.
It is never too late to heal an old wound.
It is never too late to feel the oneness.
It is never too late to let yourself be helped.
It is never too late to be wholly grateful.
It is never too late to be innocent again.
It is never too late to be who you
really are.

index

acknowledgments

*B*e Happy has been co-authored with a cast of ten thousand people at least. I am deeply grateful for all the help I have received and continue to receive.

Thank you to the Happiness Project team. In particular, thank you to Ben Renshaw, co-director of The Happiness Project since the beginning. What a wonderful journey we are on. Thank you to Ian Lynch, for your vision and wholehearted enthusiasm. Thank you also to Candy Talbot, Lucy Sydenham, Belinda Beasley, Judy Merrick, Nigel Greswell, Sharon Pryde, Leah Mohammed and Bron Wilton for all your support.

Thank you to Avril Carson for your constant friendship and inspiration. And thank you to everyone who has served on the support team for a happiness course. Thank you to Morag White, Sue Boyd, Robert Norton, Helen Allen, Edwina Neale, Ann Day, Alison Atwell, Charlie Shand, David Bennett, Melanie Watts, Colin and Suzanne McKenna, Ben Bartle, Sue Tait, Linda Benn, Tess Smith, Madeleine Neslaney and many more. Thank you also to Steve Jakab and Rod Steele for creating our websites.

Thank you to all of my teachers. I count myself as blessed to have had so many wonderful teachers of happiness. In particular, I would like to thank Tom and Linda Carpenter, *A Course in Miracles*, Avanti Kumar, Chuck and Lency Spezzano and Don Riso and Russ Hudson. I would also like to acknowledge how I have been inspired by the work of Ramana Maharshi, Erich Fromm, Marianne Williamson, Deepak Chopra, Gangaji and Byron Katie. For happiness research, I am grateful to David Myers, Ed Diener, Barbara Fredrickson and Sonja Lyubomirsky.

Thank you to my family. Thank you to Hollie Holden for all of your love, wisdom and editing. I have loved writing this book with you. Thank you to Bo Holden for the dancing and the Frappuccinos. Thank you to Lizzie Prior, my sister-in-law, for designing the perfect book cover, for your creativity and for taking a stand for happiness. Thank you to David Holden for helping to set up The Happiness Project. Thank you to Miranda Macpherson for your love and inspiration. Thank you to all my family, including Mr Great, for teaching me what it means to love and be happy.

Thank you to the Hay House team. It is a joy to work with a publisher that is so committed to joy and service. Thank you to Louise Hay for your inspiration and for writing a beautiful foreword. Thank you to Reid Tracy for giving me such a rich canvas to paint on. Thank you to Patty Gift for your editorial vision and allegiance. Thank you also to Anne Barthel, Laura Koch, Richelle Zizian, Christy Salinas, Summer McStravick, Donna Abate and Nancy Levin.

Thank you to the William Morris Agency and especially to my agent Jennifer Rudolph Walsh. You are heaven-sent.

Thank you to Oprah Winfrey. Your interest in my work and in The Happiness Project has been the catalyst for a whole new level of service across the world.

Finally, thank you to everyone who has participated on one of my happiness courses. I am deeply grateful to you for helping me to learn how to be happy.

Amen.

endnotes

PROLOGUE

1. Read QED *How to be Happy* by Brian Edwards and Wendy Sturgess, page 6, BBC Education (1996). To find out more about the work of True Vision, visit the website: www.truevisiontv.com

2. Both the OHI and Affectometer are featured in the book QED *How to be Happy* (as above). For further reading on Michael Argyle's work, I recommend *The Psychology of Happiness*, Routledge, 2nd Edition (2001).

3. Read QED *How to be Happy* by Brian Edwards and Wendy Sturgess, page 23, BBC Education (1996).

4. Read QED *How to be Happy* by Brian Edwards and Wendy Sturgess, page 24, BBC Education (1996).

5. QED *How to be Happy* by Brian Edwards and Wendy Sturgess, page 26, BBC Education (1996).

6. *Learning to be happy:* A good overview article is "Achieving Sustainable New Happiness: Prospects, Practices, and Prescriptions," by K.M. Sheldon & S. Lyubomirsky, in Positive psychology in practice, edited by A. Linley & S. Joseph, pp 127–145, John Wiley & Sons (2004). And "A Program to Increase Happiness: Further Studies," by M.W. Fordyce, in *Journal of Counseling Psychology,* Vol. 30, pp 483–498 (1983).

7. Copies of BBC QED *How to be Happy* television documentary are available from The Happiness Project. Visit the website: www.behappy.net

PART I: HELLO HAPPINESS

chapter 1: the happiness genie

1. *Happiness, attractiveness, and likability:* Read "Physical Attractiveness and Subjective Well-being," by E. Diener, B. Wolsie, & F. Fujita, in *Journal of*

Personality and Social Psychology, Vol. 69, pp 120–129 (1995). There is also a good summary of research in "The Benefits of Frequent Positive Effect," by S. Lyubomirsky, L. King, & E. Diener in *Psychological Bulletin,* Vol. 131, page 827 (2005).

2. *Happiness and health:* Henri Frederic Amiel: "In health there is freedom. Health is the first of all liberties." Mahatma Gandhi: "It is health that is real wealth and not pieces of gold and silver." Publilius Syrus: "Good health and good sense are two of life's greatest blessings."

3. *Happiness and heaven:* Read "Are Scandinavians Happier than Asians? Issues in Comparing Nations on Subjective Well-being," by E. Diener and S. Oishi, in *Asian Economic and Political Issues:* Vol. 10, pp 1–25, Nova Science (2004). Also, for further information on Ed Diener's work, visit the website: www.psych.uiuc.edu/~ediener

4. *Benefits of happiness:* An excerpt from the webpage of Sonja Lyubomirsky, Ph.D., at www.faculty.ucr.edu/~sonja/index.html. For more information on benefits of happiness read, "The Benefits of Frequent Positive Effect," by S. Lyubomirsky, L. King, & E. Diener in *Psychological Bulletin,* Vol. 131, page 827 (2005). I also recommend Sonja's book: *The How of Happiness: A Scientific Approach to Getting the Life You Want,* by S. Lyubomirsky, Penguin Press (2008).

5. *Happiness attracts success:* For further information on Barbara Fredrickson's work on the benefits of positive emotions visit the website: http://fredrickson.socialpsychology.org

6. Read "The Value of Positive Emotions," by Barbara Fredrickson, in *American Scientist,* Vol. 91, page 335 (2003).

chapter 2: talking about happiness

1. *The Happiness Project:* For a brief history of The Happiness Project visit "Our Story" at the website: www.behappy.net

2. *Ben Renshaw's work:* Ben is the co-director of The Happiness Project and Success Intelligence. He has written several books including *Successful but Something Missing,* Rider (2000) and *Together but Something Missing,* Rider (2001) and *Balancing Work & Life,* with Robert Holden, Dorling Kindersley (2002) and *Super Coaching,* with Graham Alexander, Random House (2005).

3. *Stress Busters Clinic:* I ran the Stress Busters Clinic in Birmingham, England, from 1989 to 1994. It offered free weekly classes to local residents who were either referred by their doctor or self-referred. My clinic was financed by the National Health Service in the West Birmingham Health Authority area. For further information on my work at this time read *Stress Busters,* by Robert Holden, HarperCollins (1992).

4. Read *The Prelude: Or Growth of a Poet's Mind* (Text of 1805), by William Wordsworth, Prelude II: 428–431, Oxford Paperback (1970).

chapter 3: defining true happiness

1. *Embracing the Moment* by Robert Norton is available for purchase at the website: www.robertnortonmusic.com. Also see Reference 1 for Chapter 8: *Follow Your Joy.*

2. *Synaesthesia:* Read *The Hidden Sense: Synaesthesia in Art and Science* by Cretien van Campen, MIT Press (2007). I met Cretien van Campen at a conference on happiness hosted by the brand *Snuggle.* His work on synaesthesia is most interesting.

3. *Desire theories:* I recommend the following online article entitled *Well-Being* at: http://plato.stanford.edu/entries/well-being/#4.2. For further reading, read *Well-being* by J. Griffin, Oxford: Clarendon Press (1986).

4. *Subjective Well-Being:* Read *Culture and Subjective Well-being* edited by E. Diener & E. Suh, MIT Press (2003).

5. *A short half-life:* "Satisfaction has a short half-life; it's very fleeting," says Richard Ryan, quoted in an article entitled "In Pursuit of Affluence, at a High Price," *New York Times,* Feb 2nd, 1999.

6. *Describing joy:* I highly recommend *Ecstasy: Understanding the Psychology of Joy* by Robert A. Johnson, HarperSanFrancisco (1987).

7. *Mundaka Upanishad:* Read *The Upanishads* by Eknath Easwaran, Nilgiri Press (1987).

chapter 4: a new learning curve

1. *Subjective Well-Being:* Read *The Science of Subjective Well-Being,* edited by M. Eid & R. J. Larsen, The Guilford Press (2008).

2. *Positive Psychology:* Read *Handbook of Positive Psychology,* edited by C. R. Snyder & Shane J. Lopez, Oxford University Press, USA (2005) And *Flourishing: Positive Psychology and the Life Well-Lived,* edited by Corey L. M. Keyes & Jonathan Haidt, American Psychological Association (2002).

3. *Enneagram:* I highly recommend, *The Wisdom of the Enneagram,* by Don Richard Riso & Russ Hudson, Bantam (1999). The Enneagram Institute, run by Riso and Hudson, offers excellent workshops, trainings and other resources. Visit the website: www.enneagraminstitute.com

4. *BBC The Happiness Formula:* A comprehensive summary of the findings of this BBC documentary series is available at the website: http://news.bbc.co.uk/1/hi/programmes/happiness_formula/

5. *Decline in happiness levels:* Visit *The Happiness Formula* BBC website: http://news.bbc.co.uk/1/hi/programmes/happiness_formula/4771908.stm

6. *Happiness and money:* Read *Authentic Happiness: Using the New Positive Psychology to Realise Your Potential for Lasting Fulfilment,* by Martin E.P. Seligman, page 53, Free Press (2004). Also, visit the website: www.authentichappiness.com

7. Ibid.

8. *Happiness and circumstances:* Read "Objective Circumstances, Life Satisfactions, and Sense of Well-being: Consistencies Across Time and Place," by Richard Kammann, in *New Zealand Journal of Psychology*, Vol. 12, pp 14–22, (1983).

9. *Happiness and education:* Read "The New Science of Happiness," by Claudia Wallis, online at the TIME magazine website: http://www.time.com/time/magazine/article/0,9171,1015902,00.html

10. *Happiness and future:* Read *Happiness NOW!*, by Robert Holden, page 48, Hay House (2007).

11. *Happiness and you:* Read "Who is happy?" by D. G. Myers & E. Diener, for *Psychological Science*, Vol. 6, pp 10–19 (1995).

12. *Happiness and human progress:* Mark Easton's summary in Episode 6: "Future Happiness" of the BBC television documentary *The Happiness Formula* (See Reference 4).

PART II: YOUR SPIRITUAL DNA

chapter 5: a spiritual path

1. *Coaching Happiness:* This training programme is open to anyone who wants to learn the principles and practices that are the heart of the work with The Happiness Project. Many people who attend this happiness school often use it to set up their own happiness course. For further information visit the website: www.behappy.net

2. *Avril Carson's profile:* A full profile of Avril Carson and her wonderful work is available on the websites: www.behappy.net and www.successintelligence.com

3. Read "A Proposal to Classify Happiness as a Psychiatric Disorder," by Richard Bentall, in *The Journal of Medical Ethics*, Vol. 18, pp 94–98 (1992).

4. *A Course in Miracles:* This remarkable course combines perennial wisdom and spiritual psychology. It teaches you how to replace a mindset of guilt, fear and lack with a mindset of unconditional love. For more information about courses contact: Foundation for A Course in Miracles, 1275 Tennanah Lake Road, Roscoe, New York, 12776-5905, Tel: (607) 498-4116. Their website is: www.facim.org. And The Miracle Network, 12a Barness Court, 6/8 Westbourne Terrace, London W2 3UW. Their website is: www.miracles.org.uk. Book reference: *A Course in Miracles,* Foundation for Inner Peace, Combined Volume (2007).

5. Read *A Course in Miracles,* Foundation for Inner Peace, in Workbook Lesson 139, page 267 Combined Volume (2007).

6. Ibid, Text, Chapter 21 Verse 1: "The Forgotten Song," pp 445–447.

chapter 6: a tale of two selves

1. *The #1 Happiness Principle:* Read *Happiness NOW!*, by Robert Holden, pp 67–74, Hay House (2007).

2. *Self-Acceptance Formula:* Read *Happiness NOW!*, by Robert Holden, pp 89–118, Hay House (2007).

3. *Happiness and self-acceptance:* For further reading on the science of happiness and self-esteem I recommend the paper, "What are the Differences Between Happiness and Self-esteem?," by S. Lyubomirsky, C. Tkach, & M. R. DiMatteo, in *Social Indicators Research*, Vol. 78, pp 363–404 (2006).

4. *DSM:* The Diagnostic and Statistical Manual of Mental Disorders (DSM) is the standard classification of mental disorders used by mental health professionals in the United States. Book reference: The Diagnostic and Statistical Manual of Mental Disorders, Fourth Edition (DSM-IV), American Psychiatric Press Inc.; 4th Ed edition (1994).

5. *Keira Knightley article:* Read "The Secret of How Flat-Chested Keira Became a Buxom Pirate Girl," by James Tapper, in *The Daily* Mail, February 2008. Available online at www.dailymail.co.uk

6. *Emma Watson article:* Read "Harry Potter and the mystery of Hermione's curves," by James Tapper, in *The Daily* Mail, May 2007. Available online at www.dailymail.co.uk

7. See Reference 3.

chapter 7: fear of unhappiness

1. *"Happy People":* "We (Diener & Seligman, 2002) found that even the happiest people, the top 10 per cent in happiness, have moods that go up and down – they are not stuck in euphoria. It is functional to have a mood system that reacts to events, including negative events. In some circumstances unpleasant emotions such as anxiety or sadness can facilitate effective functioning, and the happiest people occasionally feel such emotions – it is just that they do not do so very often." Quoted in: "Are Scandinavians happier than Asians? Issues in Comparing Nations on Subjective Well-being," by E. Diener and S. Oishi, in *Asian Economic and Political Issues:* Vol. 10, page 14, Hauppauge, NY: Nova Science (2004).

2. *Happy Pill Survey:* Read "Scientists' Short-cut to Happiness," by Mark Easton, on the BBC website for *The Happiness Formula*.

3. Copies of BBC *How to be Happy* television documentary are available at The Happiness Project. Visit the website: www.behappy.net

4. *Anti-Bullying Campaign:* For more information about Dawn Willis's work visit the website: www.quinonostante.com

5. See Reference 1, Chapter 5: *A Spiritual Path*.

6. *The Guest House:* Read *Essential Rumi* by Jalal al-Din Rumi and Coleman Barks, HarperOne (1997).

7. Read *Letters to a Young Poet*, by Rainer Maria Rilke, Dover Publications (2002).
8. Read *Shift Happens!*, by Robert Holden, Chapter 47: *If You Are Alive, You Need Help!* pp 216–219, Jeffers Press (2006).

chapter 8: follow your joy

1. *Robert Norton's work:* For more information about Robert Norton's music visit the website: www.robertnortonmusic.com. And for information on Robert's Creative Journeys workshops, co-created with Helen Allen, visit the website: www.creative-journeys.co.uk
2. *"Follow Your Joy":* You can purchase this album online at: www.robertnortonmusic.com
3. *Van Morrison:* The song "I Forgot That Love Existed" is from the album *Poetic Champions Compose,* by Van Morrison, Polygram (1994).
4. *Dr Matthew Anderson:* For further information on Dr Matthew Anderson's work visit the website: www.mattcoyote.com
5. *Dropping the Knife:* Read *The Subject Tonight is Love: 60 Wild and Sweet Poems of Hafiz,* translated by Daniel Ladinsky, page vii, Pumpkin House Press (1996).
6. See Reference 4, Ch 5: *A Spiritual Path.*
7. Read *Love All the People: The Essential Bill Hicks,* by Bill Hicks, Soft Skull Press; Revised edition (2008).

PART III: THE UNHOLY TRINITY

chapter 9: choosing happiness

1. *Happiness and life circumstances:* Read "Why Are Some People Happier Than Others?: The Role of Cognitive and Motivational Processes in Well-Being," by S. Lyubomirsky, in *American Psychologist*, Vol. 56, page 240 (2001).
2. Ibid. page 244.
3. *Happiness set point:* Read "Hedonic Relativism and Planning the Good Society," by P. Brickman & D. T. Campbell, in *Adaptation Level Theory: A Symposium,* edited by M.H. Appley, Academic Press, pp 287–305 (1971). And "Hedonic Adaptation," by Shane Frederick and George Loewenstein, in *Well-Being: The Foundations of Hedonic Psychology,* edited by Daniel Kaheman, Ed Diener & Norbert Schwarz, pp 302–329, Russell Sage Foundation (1999).
4. *Lottery Winners Research:* Read "Lottery winners and accident victims: Is happiness relative?," by P. Brickman, D. Coates, & R. Janoff-Bulman, in *Journal of Personality and Social Psychology,* Vol 36, pp 917–927 (1978). And "Re-examining adaptation and the set point model of happiness. Reactions

to changes in marital status," by R. E. Lucas, A. E. Clark, Y. Georgellis and E. Diener, in *Journal of Personality and Social Psychology*, Vol. 84, pp 527–539 (2003).

5. *Genes and happiness:* Read "Pursuing Happiness: The Architecture of Sustainable Change," by S. Lyubomirsky, K. M. Sheldon, & D Schkade, in *Review of General Psychology*, Vol. 9, pp 111–131 (2005). And "Achieving Sustainable New Happiness: Prospects, Practices, and Prescriptions," by K. M. Sheldon & S. Lyubomirsky, in *Positive psychology in Practice*, edited by A. Linley & S. Joseph, pp 127–145, John Wiley & Sons (2004).

6. *Changing your genes:* Read *The Biology of Belief: Unleashing the Power of Consciousness, Matter & Miracles*, by Bruce Lipton, Hay House (2008). And visit the website: www.brucelipton.com

7. *Pre-conscious choice: The Private Life of the Brain: Emotions, Consciousness, and the Secret of the Self*, by Susan A. Greenfield, Wiley (2001). Also, watch a short film on preconscious choice online at: http://www.youtube.com/watch?v=fl1624SwYnI

chapter 10: the happiness contract

1. *Happiness workshops:* I still occasionally run the workshop *How to be So Happy You Almost Feel Guilty, but not Quite*. For details of forthcoming events visit the website: www.behappy.net

2. *The Success Contract:* Read *Success Intelligence*, by Robert Holden, pp 71–80, Hay House (2008).

chapter 11: fear of happiness

1. *Fear of good things:* I highly recommend *Escape from Freedom*, by Erich Fromm, Holt Paperbacks (1994).

2. *Fear of success:* Read my Fear of Success Indicator (FOSI) in *Success Intelligence,* by Robert Holden, Ch: "The Big Fear," pp 319–333, Hay House (2008).

3. *Happiness and unselfishness:* Read "The Altruism Paradox" by Bernard Rimland, *Psychological Reports*, Vol. 51, pp 521–522 (1982).

4. *Happiness doctorate research:* An Executive Summary of my doctoral thesis is available on request at The Happiness Project.

5. *Happiness and sociability:* Read: "The Happy Personality: A Meta-Analysis of 137 Personality Traits and Subjective Well-Being" by K. DeNeve and H. Cooper, *Psychological Bulletin*, Vol. 124. pp 197–229 (1998). And, "An Alternative Description of Personality: The big-five factor structure," by L.R. Goldberg, in *Journal of Personality and Social Psychology,* Vol. 59, pp 1216–1229 (1990).

chapter 12: one hundred gratitudes

1. *Barry Neil Kaufman's work:* Read *Happiness Is a Choice* by Barry Neil Kaufman, Ballantine Books (1994). And visit the website: www.option.org
2. *Robert Emmon's work:* Read *Thanks!: How the New Science of Gratitude Can Make You Happier,* by Robert Emmons, Houghton Mifflin (2007). And visit the website: http://psychology.ucdavis.edu/faculty/Emmons
3. *Happiness and gratitude:* Read "Counting Blessings versus Burdens: Experimental Studies of Gratitude and Subjective Well-being in Daily Life," by R.A. Emmons & M.E. McCullough, in *Journal of Personality and Social Psychology*, Vol. 84, pp 377–389 (2003).
4. *Gratitude and personality:* Read "The Grateful Disposition: A Conceptual and Empirical Topography," by M.E. McCullough, R.A. Emmons, & J. Tsang in *Journal of Personality and Social Psychology,* Vol. 82, pp 112–127 (2002).
5. *"THANK U" song:* Appears on the album *Supposed Former Infatuation Junkie,* by Alanis Morissette, Maverick (1998).
6. *Gratitude and spirituality:* Read "Is gratitude a moral affect?" by M.E. McCullough, S. Kirkpatrick, R.A. Emmons, & D. Larson, in *Psychological Bulletin*, Vol. 127, pp 249–266 (2001).

PART IV: EVERYDAY ABUNDANCE

chapter 13: the daily unconscious

1. *William Wordsworth's work:* Read "Ode: Imitations of Immortality," in *Complete Poetical Works,* edited by Thomas Hutchinson, University Press (1996).
2. *Rabindranath Tagore's work:* Read *Stray Birds* by Rabindranath Tagore, Forgotten Books (2008).
3. Read *Herb Gardner: The Collected Plays*, Applause Books (2001).
4. Read *A Course in Miracles,* Foundation for Inner Peace, in Workbook Lesson 71, page 122, Combined Volume (2007).
5. *Inner Smile Cards:* These cards are available for purchase at the Happiness Project website: www.behappy.net
6. *Navajo prayer:* Read *The Native American Oral Tradition: Voices of the Spirit and Soul,* by Lois J. Einhorn, Praeger Publishers (2000).
7. Read *A Course in Miracles,* Foundation for Inner Peace, in Workbook Lesson 106, page 190, Combined Volume (2007).
8. Ibid, Workbook Lesson 315, page 458.

chapter 14: ready, steady, NOW

1. *Declaration of Independence:* Visit the website: www.wikipedia.org for a comprehensive overview essay on the US Declaration of Independence.
2. *Blaise Pascal's work:* Read *Pensées and Other Writings*, written by Blaise Pascal, edited by Anthony Levi, Oxford University Press (2008).
3. *Optimistic futures:* Read "Anxiety, Depression, and the Anticipation of Future Positive and Negative Experiences," by A.K. Macleod & A. Byrne, in *Journal of Abnormal Psychology,* Vol. 105: pp 286–289 (1996).
4. *16 year longitudinal study:* Read "Explaining Happiness," By Richard A. Easterlin in *Proceedings of the National Academy of Sciences*, Vol. 100, pp 11176–83 (2003). And *Roper Reports 79-1*, Roper-Starch Organization, University of Connecticut (1979). And *Roper Reports 95-1*, Roper-Starch Organization, University of Connecticut, (1995). And for further information on Professor Richard Easterlin's work visit the website: www. rcf.usc.edu/~easterl
5. Read *Happiness: The Science Behind Your Smile*, by Daniel Nettle, pp 76–77, Oxford University Press (2006).
6. Read *St. Augustine Confessions*, edited by Henry Chadwick. Oxford University Press (1998).
7. Read *I Try to Take One Day at a Time, but Sometimes Several Days Attack Me at Once*, by Ashleigh Brilliant, Woodbridge Press (1987).
8. *Gangaji's work:* Read *The Diamond in Your Pocket: Discovering Your True Radiance*, by Gangaji, page 20, Sounds True (2007). Also visit the website: www.gangaji.org
9. Read *A Course in Miracles,* Foundation for Inner Peace, in Workbook Lesson 188, page 357, Combined Volume (2007).
10. See Reference 5, pp 110–111.

chapter 15: the real more

1. *Magazine Poll:* These magazines were published between November 2007 and January 2008.
2. Read *A Course in Miracles,* Foundation for Inner Peace, in Text, page 85, Combined Volume (2007).
3. *Steven Wright's work:* Listen to *I Have a Pony*, by Steven Wright, Rhino (2005 Edition). Visit the website: www.stevenwright.com
4. *Gallup poll:* Read "Americans Widely Disagree On What Constitutes Rich," by G.G. Gallup & F. Newport, for *Gallup Poll Monthly*, July 28–36 (1990).
5. *Lord Richard Layard's work:* Visit the website: http://cep.lse.ac.uk/layard
6. Read *Happiness: Lessons from a New Science*, by Richard Layard, page 42, Penguin (2006). Also, read General Social Survey Data, quoted in *The Loss of Happiness in Market Democracies*, by Robert E. Lane, page 25, Yale University Press (2001).

7. *Happiness and money:* "People who value money more than other goals are less satisfied with their income and with their lives as a whole," writes Martin Seligman, author of *Authentic Happiness*, page 55. Also, read "A Consumer Values Orientation for Materialism and its Measurements: Scale Development and Validation," by M.L. Richins and S. Dawson, in *Journal of Consumer Research*, Vol 19, pp 303–316 (1992). And "Materialism and Quality of Life," by M.J. Sirgy, in *Social Indicators Research*, Vol 43, pp 227–260 (1998).

8. *Werner Erhard's work:* Visit the website: www.wernererhard.com

9. *Eric Hoffer's quote:* Visit http://www.quotes.net/quote/6341

10. See Reference 2, Text, Page 368.

11. Read *Shift Happens!*, by Robert Holden, Chapter 18: *There are no Shortages, Only a Lack of Willingness to Receive*, pp 87–90, Jeffers Press (2006).

chapter 16: the receiving meditation

1. See Chapter 14, Reference 9.

2. *Benefits of Journaling*: Read "The Health Benefits of Writing About Intensely Positive Experiences," by C.M. Burton and L.A. King, in *Journal of Research in Personality,* Vol. 38, pp 150–163 (2004).

3. Read *The Artist's Way: A Spiritual Path to Higher Creativity* (10th Anniversary Edition), by Julia Cameron, Tarcher/Putnum (2002).

4. Read "Health-related Effects of Creative and Expressive Writing," by Geoff Lowe, in *Health Education Journal*, Vol 106, pp 60–70 (2006).

5. *Nancy Spiegelberg's work*: To read a collection of Nancy's articles visit the website: www.godthoughts.com

PART V: LOVE AND HAPPINESS

chapter 17: the family story

1. *Happiness and culture:* For more information on happiness, families and culture, visit the website: http://worlddatabaseofhappiness.eur.nl. And read the article: "Culture and Subjective Well-being," by E. Diener & W. Tov, in *Handbook of Cultural Psychology*. New York: Guilford (2007).

chapter 18: the relationship questionnaire

1. Read "Correlates of Avowed Happiness," by Warner Wilson, in *Psychological Bulletin*, Vol. 67, page 304 (1967).

2. *Rich and Satisfying Relationships*: Read "Very Happy People," by E. Diener & M. Seligman, in *Psychological Science*, Vol. 13, pp 80–83 (2002).

3.   Read "The Effect of Marriage on the Well-being of Adults: A Theoretical Analysis," W. Cove, C. Style & M. Hughes, in *Journal of Family Issues*, Vol. 11, pp 4–35 (1990).

4.   *Marrying Later:* The average male isn't marrying until 26.7 years old (up from 22.8 in 1960) and the average woman until 25 years old (up from 20.3 in 1960). Reference: US Bureau Census: "Marital Status and Living Arrangements" (1998). website: www.census.gov

5.   *Divorce Rates:* For the United States see the National Center for Health Statistics website: www.cdc.gov/nchs/Default.htm. For the UK see *Social Trends*, edited by A. Self and L. Zealey, Office of National Statistics (2007). website: www.statistics.gov.uk

6.   *Happiness and Relationships:* Read "Close Relationships and Quality of Life," by D. G. Myers, in *Well-Being: The Foundations of Hedonic Psychology*, edited D. Kahneman, E. Diener, & N. Schwarz, Russell Sage Foundation (1999).

7.   *German study of marriage and life-satisfaction:* Read "Re-examining Adaptation and the Set Point Model of Happiness: Reactions to Changes in Marital Status," by R.E. Lucas, A.E. Clark, Y. Georgellis, & E. Diener, in *Journal of Personality and Social Psychology*, Vol. 84, pp 527–539 (2003).

8.   Read *The Best Kept Secret: Men and Women's Stories of Lasting Love*, Janet Reibstein, Bloomsbury (2006).

chapter 19: making the connection

1.   *The Self Principle:* Read *Success Intelligence*, by Robert Holden, pp 59–69, Hay House (2008).

2.   *The Communication Age:* Read *Winners and Losers in Globalization*, by Guillermo de la Dehesa, Wiley-Blackwell (2006)

3.   *Diseases of isolation*: Read *Love and Survival*, by Dean Ornish, HarperPerennial, New York (1998).

4.   *WHO Report:* Read "The World Health Report 2001 – Mental Health: New Understanding, New Hope," available online at the website: www.who.int

5.   *Happiness and relationships:* Read "Happiness and the Invisible Threads of Social Connection: The Chicago Health, Aging, and Social Relations Study," by J.T. Cacioppo *et al*, in *The Science of Subjective Well-Being*, edited by M. Eid and R. Larsen, pp 195–219, The Guilford Press (2008).

6.   *Relationships and money:* Read *How to Be Happy*, Liz Hoggard, page 50, BBC Books 2005.

7.   *TV households:* "The average American home now has more television sets than people. That threshold was crossed within the past two years, according to Nielsen Media Research. There are 2.73 TV sets in the typical home and 2.55 people, the researchers said," quoted in article entitled "Average Home Has More TVs than People," *USA Today*, 9/21/2006. Read this article online at the website: www.usatoday.com

8. *Robert Putnam's work:* Read *Bowling Alone: The Collapse and Revival of American Community,* by Robert D. Putnam, Simon & Schuster (2001). And, *Better Together: Restoring the American Community* by Robert D. Putnam *et al,* Simon & Schuster (2004).
9. See Chapter 4: Reference 4.
10. *Happiness and Friendship:* Read The Secret to Happiness? Having at Least 10 Good Friends, by Fiona Macrae, available at the website: www.dailymail. co.uk
11. Read *Tao Te Ching,* written by Lao Tzu, translated by Stephen Mitchell, Harper Perennial (2006).
12. *Nature-Deficit Disorder:* Read *Last Child in the Woods: Saving Our Children From Nature-Deficit Disorder,* by Richard Louv, Algonquin Books: Expanded edition (2008).
13. *Happiness and faith:* Read "The Funds, Friends, and Faith of Happy People," By D.G. Myers, in *American Psychologist,* Vol. 55, pp 56–67 (2000).
14. *Church attendance decline:* Read "Religious demographics: The Greying of Churchgoers," by Peter Brierley, June 2008, available online at the website: www.religiousintelligence.co.uk
15. *Gallup research:* Read "Commentary on the State of Religion in the U.S. Today," in *Religion in America: The Gallup Report,* pp 1–20, March 1984.
16. *Happiness, prayer, and meditation:* "Religious Involvement and Subjective Well-being," by C. Ellison, in *Journal of Health and Social Behaviour,* Vol. 32, pp 80–99 (1991). Also, "Religious Involvement, Stress & Mental Health," by C. Ellison, *et al,* in *Social Forces,* Vol. 80, pp 215–249 (2001).
17. *Happiness and spirituality:* Read "Remarkable Surge of Interest in Spiritual Growth Noted as Next Century Approaches," by George H. Gallup, Jr, in *Emerging Trends,* page 1, December 1998.
18. *Sri Anandamayi's work:* Visit the website: www.anandamayi.org
19. *Erich Fromm's work:* Read, *To Have or To Be,* by Erich Fromm, Page 50, Abacus Books 1979. Also *The Art of Loving,* by Erich Fromm, Harper Perennial (2006). And *On Being Human,* by Erich Fromm, Continuum (1997).

chapter 20: the joy of forgiveness

1. *The Forgiveness Network:* Tom and Linda Carpenter are the Founders of a global initiative called The Forgiveness Network, which supports people who wish to experience the power of forgiveness. Visit the website: www. tomandlindacarpenter/forgiveness.html
2. Read *Shift Happens!,* by Robert Holden, Chapter 28: *Forgiveness Gives You Wings,* pp 129–132, Jeffers Press (2006).
3. Read *A Course in Miracles,* Foundation for Inner Peace, in Workbook Lesson 198, page 380, Combined Volume (2007).

4. Read *Strength to Love*, by Martin Luther King Jr., Augsburg Fortress Publishers (1981).
5. *George Gurdjieff's work:* Read *In Search of the Miraculous: Fragments of an Unknown Teaching*, by P. D. Ouspensky, Harvest Book (2001). Visit the website: www.gurdjieff.org
6. *Eckhart Tolle's work:* Visit the website: www.eckharttolle.com

PART VI: FINDING THE PRESENT

chapter 21: the open road

1. *U Shaped happiness:* Read "Is Well-Being U-shaped Over the Life Cycle?" by David G. Blanchflower & Andrew J. Oswald, in *Social Science & Medicine*, Vol. 66, pp 1733–1749 April (2008).
2. Read *Leaves of Grass: The Original 1855 Edition* by Walt Whitman, Dover Publications (2007).
3. *Above average:* Read "The Better-Than-Average Effect," by M.D. Alicke & O. Govorun, in *The Self in Social Judgment,* edited by M. D. Alicke, D. A. Dunning, & J. I. Krueger, New York: Psychology Press (2005). And "The Inflated Self," by D. G. Myers, *Christian Century*, pp 1226–1230 (1982).
4. Read *A Course in Miracles,* Foundation for Inner Peace, in Workbook Lesson 47, page 76, Combined Volume (2007).

chapter 22: the beautiful ordinary

1. Read *Letters to a Young Poet*, written by Rainer Maria Rilke, translated by Stephen Mitchell, pp 7–8, Random House (2001).
2. Read *The Dhammapada*, translated by Juan Mascaro, Penguin (1973).
3. *Georgia O'Keefe's work:* Visit the website: www.okeeffemuseum.org
4. *The Happiness Prayer:* The prayer that begins "Dear God, so far today . . . " is unsourced. If you know the name of the author I would be most grateful if you would let me know.
5. *Meister Eckhart's work:* Visit the website: www.ellopos.net/theology/eckhart. htm
6. *Prayer of St. Francis:* For translations and commentary of this famous prayer visit the website: www.wikipedia.org
7. *Mary Jean Iron:* unsourced.
8. *Woody Allen's work:* Visit the website: www.woodyallen.com
9. Read "Cultivating positive emotions to optimize health and well-being," by B. L. Fredrickson, for *Prevention and Treatment*, Vol. 3, (2000).

10. *Adding Sparkle story:* This story is unsourced. If you know the name of the author I would be most grateful if you would let me know.

chapter 23: the last resistance

1. *Franz Kafka's work:* Visit the website: www.kafka.org
2. *Voltaire:* "Le paradis terrestre est où je suis." In *Le Mondain* (1736). Visit the website: http://en.wikiquote.org/wiki/Voltaire
3. Read *The Possessed,* written by Fyodor Dostoevsky, translated by Constance Garnett, Barnes & Noble (2004).

chapter 24: the gift of happiness

1. Read *Shift Happens!,* by Robert Holden, Chapter 1: *Happiness is an Inner Light with No Off Switch,* pp 15–18, Jeffers Press (2006).
2. *Leo Tolstoy quotation:* Sourced from the website: www.thinkexist.com
3. *Happiness Project Vision Statement:* Read *Happiness NOW!,* by Robert Holden, page 118, Hay House (2007).
4. *Happiness and altruism:* Read "Altruism, Happiness, and Health: It's Good to Be Good," by Stephen G. Post, in *International Journal of Behavioral Medicine,* Vol. 12, No. 2, pp 66–77 (2005).
5. *Feel-Good Do-Good:* "In experiment after experiment, happy people are more willing to help those in need. It's the feel-good, do-good phenomenon," writes David Myers, in *Pursuit of Happiness,* page 20, Avon Books (1993).
6. Read "This Place Where You Are Right NOW," in *The Subject Tonight is Love: 60 Wild and Sweet Poems of Hafiz,* translated by Daniel Ladinsky, page 12, Pumpkin House Press (1996).
7. Read *The Yoga of Love,* by Emmet Fox, Harper & Row (1961).
8. *Happiness of giving:* Read "Spending Money on Others Promotes Happiness," by Elizabeth Dunn and Lara Aknin, *Science,* Vol. 319. pp 1687–1688 (2008).
9. Read *A Course in Miracles,* Foundation for Inner Peace, in Text, page 162, Combined Volume (2007).
10. *Loving Kindness prayer: Read Loving kindness: The Revolutionary Art of Happiness,* by Sharon Salzberg, Shambhala Press (2008).

· · · · ·

APPENDIX A

the
happiness
interview

Welcome to your happiness course. Over the next eight weeks you will explore one of life's most cherished and yet elusive goals – *happiness*. To help you prepare for your course you are invited to set aside one hour this week to reflect on the following questions. Please bring a copy of your answers to give to Robert and the team. We look forward to seeing you soon.

1. *What is your definition of happiness? And how well are you living it?*

2. *Who is the happiest person you know? What specifically have they taught you about happiness?*

3. *What are the three wisest lessons you have learned about happiness in your life so far?*

4. *Make a list of the possessions, achievements, people and events you hoped would bring happiness but didn't. What did you learn?*

5. *What is the main block to happiness in your life right now? And what do you think is the solution?*

6. *How are you currently limiting your own happiness? What beliefs, ideas, habits, defences, old wounds or fears are holding you back?*

7.   *What are your fears of happiness? For instance, what are you afraid might happen if you were too happy?*

8.   *What would you say is the real secret to happiness?*

9.   *If you were to follow your joy more than ever befor,e what would you do differently?*

10. *What is the main gift you hope to receive from taking the happiness course?*

APPENDIX B

the happiness genie

Imagine that you find an old bottle in your back garden that you haven't seen before. You are curious about the bottle. You rub some of the dirt off and read the old label. All of a sudden, a genie appears. Just like in the fairy tales. You and the genie introduce yourselves to each other. The conversation is quite pleasant. The genie then asks you if you would like to make a wish. You were wondering if he might ask. "Okay," says the genie, "I have ten options for you. Ready?" "Yes," you say.

"If you could have just one thing, wealth or happiness, what would you choose?" _____

"If you could have just one thing, success or happiness, what would you choose?" _____

"If you could have just one thing, fame or happiness, what would you choose?" _____

"If you could have just one thing, status or happiness, what would you choose?" _____

"If you could have just one thing, attractiveness or happiness, what would you choose?" _____

"If you could have just one thing, sex or happiness, what would you choose?" _____

"If you could have just one thing, health or happiness,
what would you choose?" _____

"If you could have just one thing, enlightenment or happiness,
what would you choose?" _____

"If you could have just one thing, authenticity or happiness,
what would you choose?" _____

"If you could have just one thing, love or happiness,
what would you choose?" _____

APPENDIX C

happiness
timelines

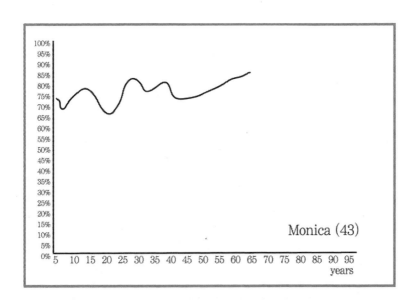

Monica (43)

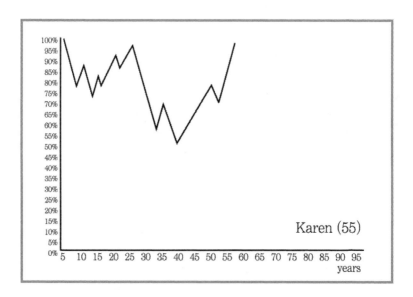

Karen (55)

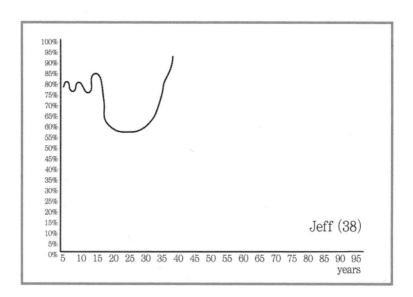

Jeff (38)

about
the
author

Robert Holden, PhD, is the director of The Happiness Project and Success Intelligence. His innovative work on happiness and success has been featured on *Oprah* and in two major BBC-TV documentaries, *The Happiness Formula* and *How to Be Happy,* shown in 16 countries to more than 30 million television viewers. He is the author of the best-selling books, *Happiness NOW!, Success Intelligence* and *Shift Happens!* He lives in London with his wife and daughter.

websites: **www.behappy.net**
                 www.successintelligence.com
                 www.robertholden.org

Courses – Trainings – Masterclasses – Products

Are you interested in attending a live event with Dr Robert Holden and The Happiness Project?

The Happiness Course. The eight-week happiness course is run in the UK every year. The first eight-week course in the United States is soon to be announced. For news of new course dates, Dr Robert Holden's speaking tour and also the launch of a new E-happy course online, visit either the Happiness Project website or Hay House website.

Happiness Training Programme. Dr Robert Holden and his team run a certificated training programme, called Coaching Happiness, that teaches the essential principles and practices of the eight-week happiness course. This programme is of interest to you if you want to deepen your understanding of happiness, integrate it into your own work or run your own happiness course.

Happiness Talks and Masterclasses. The Happiness Project team of presenters works closely with leading brands and organizations like Dove, Virgin, The Body Shop and Unilever. If you want to book a presenter for a conference or event, contact either the William Morris Agency in New York (www.wma.com) or The Happiness Project office in London.

Happiness Project UK Office: +44 (0)845 4309236
www.behappy.net
www.successintelligence.com
www.robertholden.org
www.hayhouse.com

Hay House Titles of Related Interest

YOU CAN HEAL YOUR LIFE, the movie, starring Louise L. Hay & Friends
(available as a 1-DVD programme and an expanded 2-DVD set)
Watch the trailer at: w ww.LouiseHayMovie.com

AMBITION TO MEANING: Finding Your Life's Purpose, the movie,
starring Dr Wayne W. Dyer
(available as a 1-DVD programme and an expanded 2-DVD set)
Watch the trailer at: **www.DyerMovie.com**

● ● ● ● ●

**THE BREAKTHROUGH EXPERIENCE, A Revolutionary New Approach
to Personal Transformation,** by Dr John F. Demartini

**CHANGE YOUR THOUGHTS – CHANGE YOUR LIFE:
Living the Wisdom of the Tao,**
by Dr Wayne W. Dyer

FEEL HAPPY NOW!, by Michael Neill

**7 PERSONALITY TYPES, Discover Your True Role for Success and
Happiness,** by Elizabeth Puttick PhD

**VIRUS OF THE MIND, The Revolutionary New Science of the Meme
and How It Affects You,** by Richard Brodie

YOU CAN HEAL YOUR LIFE, by Louise L Hay

● ● ● ● ●

All of the above are available at your local bookshop,
or may be ordered by contacting Hay House (see final page).

Notes

Notes

Notes

Notes

Notes

Notes

Notes

Notes

Notes

Notes